MW00484367

THE BLACK BIBLICAL HERITAGE

FOUR THOUSAND YEARS OF BLACK BIBLICAL HISTORY

Dr. John L. Johnson

Published and Distributed By:

Johnson Books, Inc.

P.O. Box 5822

St. Louis, MO. 63134

New and revised edition 2003

First printing 1975
Second printing 1975
Third printing 1976
Fourth printing 1979
Fifth printing 1981
Sixth printing 1982
Seventh printing 1987
Eighth printing 1988
Ninth printing 1992
Tenth printing 1993
Eleventh printing 1994
Twelfth printing 1999
Thirteenth printing 2001
Fourteenth printing 2002
Fifteenth printing 2003

For Consistancy, use the King James Bible, not the New King James Bible, Published in 1979.

Now available-Student/Teacher Study Guide: Volume I
                                             Volume II

Library of Congress Catalog Card Number: 99-073776

Johnson, John L., 1945
        The Black Biblical Heritage: four millenniums of Black History
        By John L. Johnson; [foreword and introduction by author]

        Reprint. Previously published: Houston: Black Biblical Heritage Pub. Co., 1987.

        Includes bibliographical references and index.

        ISBN 0-9709715-0-8
        1. Blacks in the Bible.   2. Bible-Biography.

        Printed, Johnson Books Inc. St. Louis, MO. 63134 October, 2003.

PUBLISHED BY:
Johnson Books, Inc.
P.O. Box 5822
St. Louis, MO. 63134

Printed in the United States of America

To my grandmother, Sarah Whimper
whose patience and understanding
helped inspire me in writing
this book.

ACKNOWLEDGMENTS

Special Thanks

I would like to express my gratitude to one of God's jewels, a "grandlady" of distinction and a great authority on Black history. I refer to none other than Mrs. Julia Davis of St. Louis, Missouri. Without God's help and the encouragement and dynamic constructive criticisms of Mrs. Davis, I could not have acheived so much so fast.

I would also like to thank William H. Bailey, Sr., Spencer T. Banks, Denise Beck, Dr. James A. Carey, Roger Harlan, Artimese Johnson, Julian Johnson, Vincent P. Love, Jerome Miller, Bill Murphy, Jr., Kattie Turner, and Dr. Andrew Wall for their encouragement toward this publication.

THE INSPIRING LIGHT

About 6,000 years ago mankind's brightest light of knowledge was developed on the continent of Africa, the center set of civilization for some 2,000 years before its rays of light streamed out from its shores into the remote nations of darkness. A pearl of knowledge including medicine, science, astronomy, art, architecture, military technique, agriculture, and religion—which would bring forth writing, the alphabet and the Bible—for centuries gave birth to new civilizations such as ancient Israel, Persia, China, Greece, Rome, Scandinavia, and the British Isles. This ancient light has risen throughout the history of man from the Stone Age to Modern Civilization.

Ex Africa Semper Aliquid Novi
(Out of Africa comes something always new.)
The Roman historian Pliny (23–79 A.D.)

"A people will never look forward to posterity
who never look backward to their Ancestors"
Edmund Burke

TABLE OF CONTENTS

FOREWORD

The *Black Biblical Heritage* is designed to be used in conjunction with Bible study for those who wish to learn more about the true development of Judaism and Christianity as recorded in the Bible. It is a reference tool to teach and familiarize students of the Bible with African Biblical Ancestry. This book is not a conglomerate of sources to propagandize Black Biblical Heritage, rather it is a work whose objective is to reveal and restore the rightful lineage of Jesus of Nazareth with his original peoples of Africa.

Over the centuries, great pains have been taken to conceal and destroy the physical evidence of the Biblical Jesus, replacing him with the one taught by western missionaries. Now those who once used the Bible and Christianity as instruments to exploit, enslave, and oppress nations must consider a new course.

Today, the independent churches of Africa and the African diaspora are moving away from the fanatical western religious concepts of early Catholic and Protestant assemblies and are accepting the fact that *God truly did call him son out of Africa (Egypt)*.

AUTHOR.

Studying the past divines the future.

Know thyself.

INTRODUCTION

Prior to the black political and cultural revolution of the 1960's, the word Africa was offensive to most African Americans. The very thought of Africa conjured images of barbarism and illiteracy. But since the cultural "transformation," black people's thirst for knowledge and insight into themselves and Africa has been exuberant. Scholars of Europe and Africa began to research and write about truths of Africa to the development of modern civilization. Imports from Africa to other parts of the world have escalated. African literature, art, and sculpture are sought after by individuals, and for academic, social, and religious institutions. African dress, customs of marriage, generousness, and research have taken a renewed priority in the global community. Archaeological and anthropological discoveries have given evidence to contradict western myths concerning the "darkness" of Africa.

The archaeological dig in Ebla, Syria, a prominent ancient district that attracted Israel and other nations of that epoch, uncovered a tablet written forty-five centuries ago that is said to have contained the most complete record of ancient civilization. This discovery initiated revisions to theories of the origin of Judaism, Christianity, and Islam, even making some comments in modern Bible translations obsolete and compelling modern Biblicists to honor the Bible with greater historical accuracy.

Not only did the discovery of the tablet give light to Biblical names such as Adam, Eve, David, and Jonah, it also reflected evidence of a flood story. How does this acquaint with the African Continent? It sheds light on Ham, a son of Noah who declared to be the patriarchal-ancestral father of Africa and parts of Asia, thus dictating that their complexion was black. This was the beginning of Africa's contribution to Judaism and Christianity, and all religions of antiquity that are said to have their own origins in Africa.

In fact, as knowledge began to spread of Christianity following the crucifixion of Jesus, Madonnas, icons, crucifixes, and all related Christian relics were portrayed as Africans. The African Saint Maurice, became the guardian saint of Rome, and there were several African popes. But it was not long after the first slaves were transported from Africa by Europeans that Pope Julius II, in 1505 ordained the painting of certain religious works by Michelangelo, and in so doing endowed the concept of a white God. The paintings also included the portrait of Mary, mother of Christ, whose traditional black features were altered to resemble a Florentine Roman woman. Michelangelo also applied this same misrepresentation to the Child Jesus, the three wise men, and Christ in the Last Judgment and Resurrection; eliminating all traces of their original skin color! Not only were the images changed (like the ancient Egyptians, the Hebrews, Babylonians, Persians, and Chinese, but facial features came to resemble that of white ancestry. Today Spain and Poland still honor a black Madonna as their protecting saint The black Polish Madonna, Our Lady of Czestochowa, is believed to have been painted by Jesus' disciple Luke, and is one of a few remaining paintings that depict the true features of a ancient Hebrews-black People.

To this day American and European clergy are still promoting the fable, that Ham's black skin was the result of being cursed by his father Noah. They have preached this tale with such vigor and consistency that it would appear they have convinced even themselves of it. No such thing is recorded in the Bible. To the Contrary, every curse spoken of in the Bible dealing with skin color states that the cursed ones were turned white.

In fact, Miriam, Naaman, Gehazi, Uzziah and the hand of Moses were all turned white as a result of a curse. Therefore, it could not be more obvious that they were originally black.

AUTHOR.

St. Louis, Missouri
June, 1999

I

THE BEGINNING

THE CREATION AND THE GARDEN OF EDEN

It has been recorded that in the beginning God created the heaven and the earth, and that it took the Lord God six days to complete His creation, where upon the seventh day He rested, but it was on the sixth day during the creation that God said: "Let us make man in our image, after our likeness: and let them have dominion over the fish of the sea, over the fowl of the air, and over cattle, and over all the earth, and over every creeping thing that creepeth upon the earth."

So the Lord God formed man out of the dust of the ground and breathed into his nostrils the breath of life, and man became a living soul.

God then planted a garden eastward in Eden, and there He put the man whom He had formed. And out of the ground made the Lord to grow every tree that is pleasant to the sight and good for food, and the tree of knowledge of good and evil.

A river went out of Eden to water the garden, and from there it divided and became four heads. The first river was called Pishon (Blue Nile), which compasseth the whole land of Havilah ("Havilah," located in Africa, son of "Ethiopia" Gen. 10: 6–7).* The region is modernly called Djibouti or Somaliland. The name of the second river was Gihon (Nile-River, the same as it that compasseth the whole land of "Ethiopia" Gen. 2:13); the third was Hiddekel (called Tigris, same as Nigris since in the Hebrew Athbash the T and N were interchangeable); and the fourth was Euphrates.

The Lord God then took the man and placed him in the Garden of Eden to attend it. And the Lord God commanded the man, saying: "of every tree of the garden thou mayest eat: but of the tree of knowledge of good and evil, thou shalt not eat of it: for in the day that thou eatest thereof thou shalt surely die."

Africa is definitely the birthplace of man (does that include Adam and Eve?). In Genesis 2:13, the Garden of Eden is associated with Ethiopia. The black Jewish historian Josephus and the 11th Century Bible commentator Rashi both agreed that the Gihon River which departed from Eden was the "Nile" in Africa. The Jewish Rashi is usually called Rabbi Solomon ben Isaac. His commentary on the Bible is so comprehensive that scholars still use it today).

Even though the Bible, in Genesis 2: 7–14, associates the Gihon (Nile River) and Pishon (Blue Nile), that circled "Havilah" (Son of Ethiopia." The land of Havilah was occupied by the Negro Children of "Ham") to the Garden of Eden (Adam's vicinity), these rivers are seldom mentioned and often omitted by many European and American Bible storybooks.

The Garden of Eden was like an earthly utopia or a parklike heaven that grew every tree being pleasant to the sight, with various kinds of vegetation. The paradise Eden contained every living animal and fowl of the air–a kingdom that required a unique steward like Adam (before yielding to sin) to live in it. The sanctuary Eden was also a dwelling area for Jehovah's administration over Adam's affairs.

*Havilah was also spelled Hamilah, since the Hamitic-Semitic V was interchangeable with M (Assyrian Grammar, Delitzsch, 1889: 112; 115–116).

The beautiful Garden of Eden probably lost its perfect glamour following Adam's departure, since Adam was no longer present to attend it, and during the Great Flood became obliterated!

The only Biblical territories that have been compared with the Garden of Eden are the Negro-Land of Canaan and Egypt. Lot and Moses described both lands as Eden-like (Gen. 13: 10; Deut. 11: 10-12)!

Some Biblicists and scientists will advocate Asia instead of Africa as man's first home. There is overwhelming reports that at the dawn of Asia's history, existed a black-skinned, woolly-haired, snubnosed and puffy-lipped race dwelling therein. The Greek Herodotus and Homer spoke of a huge Negro civilization living in the far East.

World researchers are aware that Africa exhibits astounding evidence authenticating man's birthplace; that the oldest bones, weapons, tools, utensils, and civilizations are found in Africa, not Asia.

R. Davidson, Genesis I-II; (Gihon and Pishon, which departed from Eden, were associated with Ethiopia and Upper Egypt), p. 33. 1973.

Ezekiel 29: 10 mentions more than one river between Egypt and Ethiopia; this substantiates the Pishon as an upper branch of the Nile. Professor Aharoni and Avi-Yonah, the Macmillan Bible Atlas (identify the Pishon with an upper branch of the Nile),p. 21. 1977; Y.M. Grintz, Mozaei Dorot, pp. 35-50. 1969; Peloulbet's Bible Dictionary, p. 241. 1973; The Roman historian Pliny (Pliny EP. vi. 28), spoke of a Havilah in East Africa; and The Hastings' Dictionary of the Bible (the Cushite Havilah journeyed from Africa to Arabia), Vol. II, p. 311.

Moses, Job and Ezekiel spoke of the precious stones of Eden. In Genesis 2: 11-12, Moses spoke of Havilah (today's Djibouti or Somaliland), which was positioned in East Africa, of having gold, bdellium and the onyx stone.

In Job 28:19, Job mentioned the topaz stone of Ethiopia, whereas Ezekiel listed the topaz as a stone of Eden (Ezek. 28: 13)!

The Encyclopedia Judaica says that the topaz was imported from Ethiopia, Vol. 13, p. 1009. 1971.

The ancient Greeks, including Alexander the Great, were convinced that the Garden of Eden was located in Africa (Houston's Wonderful Ethiopians of the Ancient Cushite Empire, chapter 2, also the Babylon Talmud (Yamid, 32-b).

The Egyptians pronounced the word garden, "Kam," the same as Ham (Egypt and Israel, W. Brewer, p. 255. 1910; and Comparative Grammar of the Semitic Languages, O'Leary, p. 42. 1923).

Gen. 1: 1- 13; 2:17; 19:7; Ezek. 29: 10.

ADAM AND HIS COMPANION

The God said: "It is not good that the man should be alone; I will make him an help meet (woman) for him." So the Lord God put Adam into a deep sleep, and while he slept God took one of his ribs and made woman.

This pleased Adam and he said: "This is now bones of my bones and flesh of my flesh; she shalt be called Woman because she was taken out of Man."

Adam and the woman were naked; but had no knowledge of their nakedness; therefore they were not ashamed.

The word Negro (Blacks) in reference to race was nonexistent during the Adamic age. Nevertheless, the Negro's feature and physical structure was in existence during the Antediluvian period. The earliest earthlings of ancient Africa and Asia (The oldest artifacts and human remains are found in Africa, not Asia) possessed a Negroid description.

The name Adam was anciently spelled Adham, Adhamah, Adamu and Adamatu, meaning black or black blood, and dark red earth, by the Hebrews and the Ethiopian-Babylonians. The Ad- of Adam means God or Elohim (Eloham), whereas Am- of Adam means Ham. Eve can also acquire the spelling Eme (Heme or Ham), since the Hebrew "V" was exchanged for "M." The Hebrews also called Eve, "Havvah (Hava)" meaning Hammah. She was also called Heva or Hava in Hindi.

Adam and Eve were the world's first Hammelech-King and Hammoleketh-Queen.

The above information is found in the following sources: Encyclopedia of Religion and Ethics (Adam was called Adham), Hastings, Vol. 1, p. 84. 1908; A Dictionary of First Names (see Adam; In Gaelic Adam is called adhamh), Hanks, 1990; A Dictionary of English Surnames (Adhams means Adam), Reaney, p. 2. 1991; The Beginning of History (Adamu means black), Lenormant, pp. 310-314. 1889; A New System (Adham means Ham and Lord Ham. Ham or Cham was called Ad and Adon), Bryant, Vol. 1, pp. 2, 30, 69; Vol. 4, p. 267. 1807; A Comprehensive Persian-English Dictionary (Adam means Brown and mulatto), Steingass, p. 29. 1975; Jones' Dictionary of Old Testament Proper Names (Adam means Lord Ham), p. 91. 1990; Hebrew English Lexicon (Adam was reddish brown): The Hebrew and Chaldee Words in the Old Testament Scriptures with their Meaning in English, p. 4, Bagster & Sons; Assyrian Dictionary (Adamatu means black blood), pt. 1, p. 95. 1964; Encyclopedia Judaica (Adamatu means black blood and dark red earth. Eve was called Havvah), Vol. 1, p. 235; Vol. 6, p. 979. 1971. Hebrew Union College Annual (Ham was Lord Hammon. Ad means Father), Vol. 18, p. 474. 1994; Vol. 48, p. 20. 1977; The Negro is a Man (Adam and Eve were colored people), Armistead, p. 3. 1903; Oxford English Dictionary (Ham means Am; see Od (Ad), 20 Vols., 1989; Dr. William Smith's Dictionary of the Bible (Ham means Am or Ammon), Vol. 4, p. 3648, 1890; A Complete Pocket Hebrew-English Dictionary of the Old Testament, Feyerabend, pp. 78, 250. 1931; Sacred Books and Early Literature of the East (Am or Amma was the Old Testament Ham), Horne, Vol. 1, p. 226. 1917; Strong's Exhaustive Concordance (Ad): No. 5703; and A Book of the Beginnings (Have was Hav), Massey, Vol. 1, p. 456. 1995.

Gen. 2:18-25.

THE SERPENT DECEIVES EVE

The serpent was the most deceitful creature that God made, for it was the serpent that said unto the woman: "Yea, hath God said, Ye shall not eat of every tree of the garden?" The woman said: "We may eat of the fruit of the trees of the garden: But of the fruit of the tree which is in the midst of the garden, God hath said, Ye shall not eat of it, neither shall ye touch it, lest ye die."

Then the serpent said: "Ye shall not surely die: for God doth know that in the day ye eat thereof, then your eyes shall be opened, and ye shall be as gods, knowing good and evil." So the woman being desirous to become wise, and took of the tree and ate it, and also gave Adam the fruit, and he ate it. Then their eyes became open to the knowledge of their nudity and with fig leaves they hid themselves.

When God walked in the garden in the cool of the day to fetch Adam, the man Adam heard Him and said: "I heard Thy voice in the garden, and I was afraid, because I was naked; and I hid myself." Then the Lord God said: "Who told thee that thou was naked? Hast thou eaten of the tree?" Adam said: "The woman whom thou gavest to be with me, she gave me of the tree (fruit), and I did eat." Then God said unto the woman: "What is this that thou hast done?" And the woman said: "The serpent beguiled me, and I did eat."

Many contemporary biblicists are in error by titling Adam and the Antediluvians as Semites, Hebrews or Jews. Such name classification, prior to the flood, was absolutely unheard of! The term Semite came into focus following the flood through Noah's second son, Shem. The names Hebrew and Jew derived centuries later through a descent of Shem called Abram (Gen. 11:10-27; 14:13; II Kings 16:6). The Antediluvians were styled as Adamites, which was previously spelled Adhamites, meaning black or black blood, and dark red earth, by the Hebrews and the Ethiopian-Babylonians.

The biblicists also erred by claiming the first spoken language to be Hebrew. The African-Antediluvians spoke a pure language called Adhamism, since the original name of Adam was spelled Adham. This same language following the flood became known as Khamism or Hamism, which millenniums later produced the impure multi-languages throughout the world. Christian Karl Josias Bunsen states that the original language was called Khamism, which survived the Antediluvian, settling in Asia and the Nile valley, later producing the corrupted Semitic, Arian and European languages (Egypt's Place, Books 4 & 5, 1854).

The above information is found in the following sources: Encyclopedia of Religion and Ethics (Adam was called Adham), Hastings, Vol. 1, p. 84. 1908; The Beginning of History (Adamu means black), Lenormant, pp. 310-314. 1899; A Comprehensive Persian-English Dictionary (Adam means Brown and mulatto), Steingass, p. 29. 1975; Hebrew English Lexicon (Adam as reddish brown): The Hebrew and Chaldee Words in the Old Testament Scriptures with their Meaning in English, p. 4, Bagster & Sons; Assyrian Dictionary (Adamatu means black blood), pt. 1, p. 95. 1964; and Encyclopedia Judaica (Adamatu means black blood and dark red earth), Vol. 1, p. 235. 1971.

GOD'S DISCONTENT WITH MAN

The Lord God said to the serpent: "Because thou has done this, thou art cursed above all cattle, and above every beast of the field; upon thy belly shalt thou go, and dust shalt thou eat all the days of thy life: and I will put enmity between thee and the woman, and between thy seed and her seed; he shall bruise thy head, and thou shalt bruise his heel."

And the Lord God said to the woman: "I will greatly multiply thy sorrow and thy conception; in sorrow thou shalt bring forth children; and thy desire shall be to thy husband, and he shall rule over thee."

To the man He said: "Because thou has hearkened unto the voice of thy wife, and hast eaten of the tree, of which I commanded thee, saying, Thou shalt not eat of it: cursed is the ground for thy sake; in sorrow shalt thou eat of it all the days of thy life; thorns also and thistles shall it bring forth to thee; and thou shall eat the herbs of the field; in the sweat of thy face shalt thou eat bread, till thou return unto the ground; for out of it wast thou taken: for dust thou art, and unto dust shalt thou return."

The Lord God made coats of skin for Adam and Eve, and dressed them. Then God said: "Behold, the man is become as one of us, to know good and evil: and now, lest he put forth his hands, and take also of the tree of life, and eat, and live forever."

Therefore, the Lord God sent Adam out of the Garden of Eden to attend the ground from which he was taken. He drove out the man and placed Cherubim at the east of the Garden of Eden, with a flaming sword which turned every way to safeguard the entrance to the tree of life.

Adam lived to be nine-hundred thirty years old, and during that span he had sons and daughters who multiplied the earth until the days of Noah. It was not long after his death that God became even more displeased with man, as the Lord God said: "Behold, I will destroy the earth with a flood, and all flesh of the breath of life, under the heaven and in the earth shall die." But Noah found favor with God; therefore, he, his wife, and his three sons, Shem, Ham, and Japheth with their wives, were saved! Many creatures were also saved with them.

There is overwhelming evidence designating Africa as man's first home and continent to which Noah's Ark was built. The Bible and natural history have produced a wealth of information toward this acknowledgment. The Bible and Africa have shed more light on an African-Eden and Antediluvian, than any other book and continent.

During the Great Flood the Ark uplifted from the Continent of Africa to Asia, which became man's second home. The Postdiluvians remained in Asia until the breakup of Babel (Gen. 11:7-9), before returning to their ancestral land, Africa, originally called Ham (Gen. 10:6; Ps. 78: 58; 105:23-27; 106:19-23).

Gen. 3:14-24; 6:7-14, 17-22.

THE ARK RESTED ON MT. ARARAT

Eastward the ark rested on Mt. Ararat with Noah and his three sons, Shem, Ham and Japheth. All human life after the flood is credited to Noah's family. His three sons are responsible for the fathers of all nations, the producers of all races (Gen. 9:18-19).

In Genesis 11:7, God confounded their language, which compelled them to separate according to Noah's sons Shem, Ham and Japheth. By this act, new nations were formed. Japheth and his family traveled north, settling north of the Mediterranean Sea. He became the father of the Caucasian race in Europe.

The families of Shem and Ham moved southeast and southwest (few of them remained in the Babel area). Shem occupied lower Syria, Assyria, the Persian Gulf, and a large part of Arabia. He was also the father of the Hebrews.

Ham had four sons, which only three journeyed south, settling "East Africa," below the 30th parallel. His youngest son Canaan settled an area, called "Canaan," which was also known as "Northeast Africa,"since ancient Canaan was inhabited by the Negro children of Ham (also ruled by Cush, Egypt and Phut) Before the construction of the Suez Canal, the entire eastern coast of the Mediterranean was a single land mass, adjoining Africa. It was for these reasons that Canaan was called "Northeast Africa," before acquiring the names, Palestine and Israel. Mesopotamia (Iraq), Persia (Iran and Afghanistan), the Arabian peninsula, Asia Minor (Turkey) and Ararat (Armenia) were also called "Northeast Africa."

The Canaanites were a Black race of people who ruled Canaan for nearly one thousand years before losing it to the children of Shem. In Genesis 9:18, God calls Ham, who was Noah's third son, the father of Canaan before his children entered the Land of Canaan. Ham's descendants also settled Asia, India, the Islands of the Pacific, Australia, Central and South America, etc.*

The sons of Noah shared the same blood (through Noah from Adam), but differed only in physical appearance.† Following the desertion of the Tower of Babel, the children of Ham, Shem and Japheth, only then, were classified into races according to their physiques (anatomy) and facial characteristics.

*Ham's settlement was called the Land of Ham for thousand of years, and is the same as what is known as Egypt and Africa to this day (Ps. 78:51; 105:23-27, 106:19-23; Gen. 14:5; Deut. 2:10; I Chron. 4:40).

†The ancient Hamitic-Semitic name for Noah was Naham, Niham, Nacham, Haim and Chaim. The word Naham was altered to the spelling Noah, since the word Na (Ni) is identical to No, and Ham to Ah. The term Ah is a reversal of Ha (Ka) the same as Ham or Kam. Noah's wife was called Amzara, the equivalence of Ham, since the term Am- of Amzara means Ham.

The above information is found in the following sources: The New Schaff-Herzog Encyclopedia of Religious Knowledge (Noah was called Naham), Vol. 8, p. 183. 1910; Encyclopedia Judaica (Noah was Niham), Vol. 12, p. 1193. 1971; Jewish Family Names and their Origins (Noah was called Haim and Chaim), Guggenheimer, pp. 315, 552. 1992; The Legends of the Jews (Amzara was Noah's wife), Vol. 5, p. 179; Strong's Exhaustive Concordance of the Bible (Ah means Ha), No: 5162-5163; Egypt's Place (Ha means Home; same as Hame and Ham), Vol. 6, p. 712. 1854; and Sacred Books and Early Literature of the East (Am was the Old Testament Ham), Horne, Vol. 1, p. 226. 1917.

THE SONS OF NOAH

"These are the three sons of Noah: and of them was the whole earth overspread." Gen. 9:19, 10: 1-32.

JAPHETH
("Caucasian")
The father of the Gentile nations.
Gen. 10:1-5 (In most revised Bibles the word Gentile, in relation to Japheth, has been removed).

Gomer	Cimmerians
Magog	(Europeans)
Madai	Medians
Javan	Grecians
Tubal and Meschech	Russians
Tiras	Thracians
Ashkenaz	Germans
Tarshish	Spaniards

HAM
("Hamitic")

Cush	Ethiopians
Mizraim	Egyptians
Phut	Libyans
Canaan	Canaanites

SHEM
("Semitic")

Elam	Persians
Asshur	Assyrians
Lud	Lydians
Aram	Syrians

According to Sir Arthur Keith, M. Fishberg, G. Massey, the Greek Herodotus, and the Roman Tacitus, because of centuries of miscegenation, the Semites (including the Hebrews) and Hamites (Blacks or Negroes) were largely a blend of one race.

HAM'S DESCENDANTS

Cush	**Mizraim**	**Phut**	**Canaan**
Ethiopia	Egypt	Libya or Cyrenacia	Canaanites and Phoenicians

KEY WORDS

Name	*Definition*	*Origin*
Amorite	Highlanders	Descendants of Canaan
Canaan	Humble	Fourth son of Ham
Cush	Black	First son of Ham
Cushan	Blackness	Derived from Cush
Cushi	Ethiopia	Derived from Cush
Cushite	Ethiopia	Derived from Cush
Heth	Hittite	Second son of Canaan
Hittite		Descendants of Heth
Hivite	Villagers	Descendants of Canaan
Jebus	Jerusalem	Third son of Canaan
Mizraim	Egypt	Second son of Ham
Phut	Libya	Third son of Ham
Sidon or Zidon	Fishing	First son of Canaan

The black sons of Ham and their offspring are characterized throughout the Bible and their nations are the first to be mentioned therein (Gen. 2: 10-13). Within the past 150 years, archaeological and anthropological research in the ruins of Ethiopia, Egypt, and Canaan (Palestine), has produced overwhelming evidence that the children of Ham had developed nations and civilizations as old as Man's history.

Professor C. Seignobos in his book, *History of Ancient Civilization*, states that religion and government, as well as the skills of sculpture, writing, painting, weaving cloths, working metals, and cultivating the soil were developed by the Negroes while the Jews, Persians, Greeks, Romans and Hindus were still in a savage state.

The world's culture is deeply indebted to the children of Ham for their Biblical involvement (Ethiopia worshipped Israel's God during the Queen of Sheba's reign and remains a Christian nation to this day) and contributions to medicine, science, astronomy, art, architecture, military technique and agriculture.

The Black man's contributions to the Bible and natural history furthered the growth of modern civilization.

RASAKA (ROOTS)

The name Ham has been Scripturally used to describe people, places and things; besides its original meaning (black), the name has also adopted other definitions, such as dark, ebony, sunburned, chocolate and brown.

Scholars throughout the ages have agreed that Ham and his offspring belong to the Negro family of nations. Ham and his children are recorded in Genesis 10:6-20.

"A forgotten people, while others were uncivilized, discovered science and art. A race which is modernly rejected because of their wooly hair and dark skin, are the founders of the laws of nature, religious and civil systems which still control the universe"... Count C.F. Volney, *Ruins of Empires*, pp. 16-17. 1890; *Oeuvres*, Vol. 2, pp. 65-68. 1803.

"Back in the ages which are barely historic, where history renders only faint hintings, are evidence of a broad ancient civilization, raw, unripe, flashy, barbaric, yet all at the same period, controlled the world from its headquarters of power in the Euphrates, the Valley of the Ganges, and the Nile, and it was of the Negro race! The Babylonians and Egyptians seem to have been Negroes, who built eminent empires long before the Semites, Mongols or Aryans. Deep-down in the mud and mire of the beginnings..., rest the contributions of the Negroes to the superstructure of modern civilization." J.P. Widney, *Race Life of the Aryans*, Vol. 2, pp. 238-39, 241. N.Y. 1907.

"It seems likely that at a time when the European was still satisfied with rude stone tools, the African had invented and adopted the art of smelting iron. Consider for a moment what this has meant for the advance of the human race. As long as the hammer, Knife, the saw, drill, spade, and hoe had to be chipped out of stone or had to be made of shell or hard wood, effective industry and work was not impossible, but difficult. A great progress was made when copper found in large nuggets was hammered out into tools and later on shaped by smelting, and when bronze was introduced; but the true advancement of industrial life did not begin until the hard iron was discovered. It seems not unlikely that the people who made the marvelous discovery of reducing iron ore by smelting were the African Negroes. Neither ancient Europe nor western Asia nor Ancient China knew iron, and everything points to its introduction from ancient Africa." Dr. Franz Boas, also Elizabeth Lawson's "Study Outline" of Africa's Accomplishments.

"The Hamitic family as Rawlinson proves must be given the credit for being the fountain head of civilization. This family comprised the ancient Ethiopians, the Egyptians, the original Canaanites and the old Chaldeans. The inscriptions of the Chaldean monuments prove their race affinity. The Bible proves their relationship. It names the sons of Ham as Cush, Mizraim, Phut and the race of Canaan. Mizraim peopled Egypt and Canaan the land later possessed by the Hebrews. Phut located in Africa and Cush extended his colonies over a wide domain." Philosophy of Ancient History, Bunsen, p. 52.

"...that this race of blacks who nowaday are slaves and the objects of our scorn is the very one to which we owe our arts, our sciences and even the use of spoken word: and finally recollect that it is in the midst of the people claiming to be the greatest friends of liberty and humanity that the most barbarous of enslavement has been sanctioned and the question raised whether black men have brains of the same quality as those of white men." Voyage to Syria and Egypt, Volney, Vol. 1, pp. 74-77, Paris. 1787.

"The African continent is no recent discovery; it is not a new world like America or Australia.... While yet Europe was the home of wandering barbarians one of the most wonderful civilizations on record had begun to work out its destiny on the banks of the Nile...." History of Nations, Vol. 18, p. 1. 1906.

"Artists, architects, merchants, merchanic operatives, sailors, agriculturists and shepherds of ancient Egypt were undoubtedly of Negro stock." Gurowski, Slavery in History, p. 5. 1860.

"Modern canons, flying missiles, ship propellers, automatic hammers, gas motors, meat cleavers, and even the upholstery tack hammers... were developed in Africa's early use of power." John W. Weatherwax, *The African Contribution.*

II

HAM AND HIS SONS

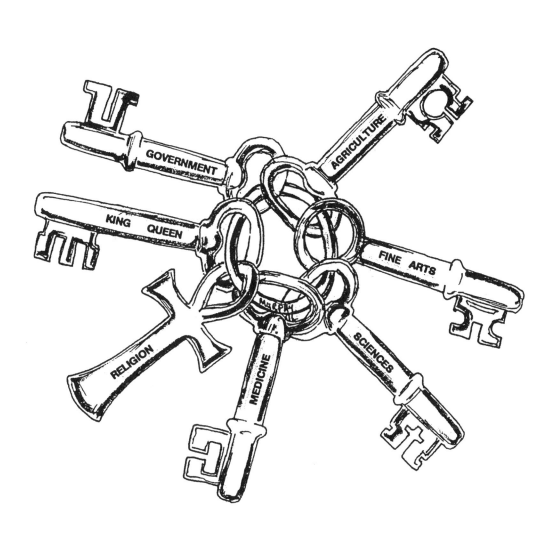

HAM: "BLACK" OR "DARK"

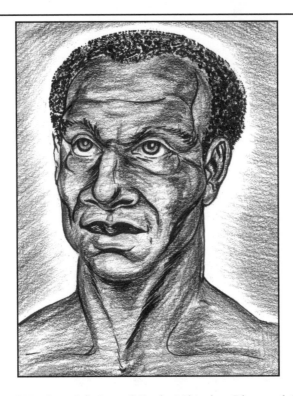

Ham was the youngest son of Noah and father of Cush, Mizraim, Phut and Canaan. Much controversy arose over Ham's judgement, as many felt he was changed dark because of a curse pronounced on him by his father Noah; however, Genesis 9:25 mentions nothing about his skin changing. The curse only specified that his offspring through his youngest son Canaan (who were Black Canaanites) become "temporary" servants under Japheth and Shem. This curse did not include the African descendants of Cush, Mizraim and Phut.

Ham the Patriarch was not cursed dark but created (born) dark. He is considered the paternal ancestor of Ethiopia, Egypt, Libya, Canaan, Carthage, and many African tribes, Northern and Southern Arabia, Crete, Cyprus, Asia Minor (Hittite or Turkey), a portion of Israel, and the Black Americans. These progenies are called Hamites, and for centuries many ruled with imperial power.

The Patriarch Ham was extremely loved by God (Gen. 9:1), who showered him with compassion, mercy and blessings, by disallowing his father Noah to place a curse upon him. It is proven by Scripture that Ham was beloved, esteemed and redeemed by God and Noah, and that Noah's retribution for Ham was gracefully switched to his grandson Canaan (Gen. 9:19-27), indicating that Ham the Patriarch was liberated; a forgiveness that some of the world's most well known clergymen find difficult to acknowledge. The life of Ham and Jesus in many ways are similar, since both are universally hated, victimized and falsely accused (Isa. 53:3; Matt. 5:10-11; John 15:25). Ham and Jesus (Amen, Rev. 3:14), the instruments of God, are the least loved by those who know not God (I John 4:20-21).

The Israelites, before possessing sovereignty over the Black Canaanites, experienced an earlier slavery themselves in "Negro-Egypt," an occurrence which fulfilled the prophecy "servant of servants" (Ex. 1:8-14; 3:7-22; Gen. 9:25).* The children of the Hebrew race (Afro-Israelites) were born on the Continent of Africa, and much of their philosophy, mathematical sciences, custom, etc., were borrowed from the African Negroes through Moses (Acts 7:22).

Ham the father of a multitude of nations, was a symbol of courage, determination, will, action, wisdom and works; generated by individuality and spiritual empowerment. The Patriarch and his offspring were the most energetic of all the descendants of Noah in the times of the post-diluvian.

Rawlinson says, "The descendants of Ham acted as pioneers and led the world in various new fields of art, science and literature including alphabetic writings, astronomy, architecture, historical chronology, plastic art, sculpture, agriculture, navigation and textile industry.... The first inventors of any art are among the greatest benefactors of their race." Rawlinson went on to emphasize that the human race at present, are heavily indebted to the genius and industry of early ages. Rawlinson's comments can be found in the following source: "Seven Great Monarchies," Vol. 1, pp. 40-41. 1884.

The name Ham was praised in ancient times, and was viewed as Divine! The Ethiopians and Egyptians called their father Ham, "Amen," or "Amen-Ra." The Hebrews postured the name Ham as a suffix of Elohim, the same as Eloham, since the Hebrew letter I, was interchangeable with A. The ancients also called Elohim, "I Am (Ex. 3:14; John 8:58)," the same as Ham (Amen), since the Semitic letter I was exchanged for C (C), the C (Ch) for K (Kh), and the K (Kh) for H, therefore altering I Am to "Cam" (French for Ham), "Cham" (Hebrew and Latin for Ham), "Kam" (Dutch for Ham) and "Ham" (English). The Hebrews also called Yahweh, "Ham-A-Kom." The name Ham was later used as a suffix to the word Abraham: an infix to Has-Ham-Ma-Im, which is another Hebrew word for God, and a prefix of the Hebrew word "Ham-Melech," "Ham-Ellkh," "Ham-Ashiah" or "Ham-Mashiah," meaning Amen (Rev. 3:14), Jesus, Messiah, Anointed or King, long before the physical presence of Abraham and Jesus! The Arabs called Ham, "Yam," the same as I Am, since the ancient Y was exchanged for I; the I for C, the C for K, and the K for H. The transliteration of the name Ham, Kam, Cam, I Am or Yam, was universally linked to all ancient Deities.

The above information is found in the following sources: The Universal Jewish Encyclopedia, Vol. 5, p. 191. 1969; The Jewish Encyclopedia, Vol. 8, p. 505. 1912; Anacalypsis, Higgins, Vol. 1, pp. 315-316, 328, 673. 1836; The Hebrew Union College Annual, Lewy, Vol. 18, pp. 473-480. 1944; The Zohar, I Copy, Vol. 1, p. 65, Soncino Press, 1933; Fausset's Bible Dictionary, pp. 34, 269, 513. 1961; A Comprehensive Persian-English Dictionary, Steingass, p. 1527. 1975; Oxford English Dictionary (Y = I; I = Ch, and the Ch = C, K, I Am, Aham or Cham), 20 Vols.; A Comparative Grammar of the Semitic Languages (T = K, C and D), O'Leary, pp. 52, 54-55, 89, 242. 1923; Development of the Canaanite Dialects (T = H), Harris, p. 25. 1939; and Eloham (www.Yahoo.com).

*The art of slavery originated with the children of Ham through Nimrod who first enslaved the children of Japheth (Book of Jasher 7:34-37; Josh. 10:13; II Sam. 1:18).

Gen. 10:6, 9:22-25; Deut. 7:1; 11:23; Nahum 3:9; Hab. 3:7.

NIMROD: "BRAVE"

Nimrod, the "mighty hunter before God" (Gen. 10:9) and grandson of Ham, was the first man to attempt to build his way to heaven. With his fertility of invention, he managed to draw and start a gigantic tower, so that he and his fellow servants could see heaven as well as earth. This tower was built in a city called Babel, which was the beginning of his empire. Nimrod sought help from Japheth and Shem's family, as they made and hauled baked bricks under his supervision.

God was not pleased with their eagerness to reach His heaven, so He paid them a visit that caused confusion in their speech. This chaos of tongues caused them to scatter abroad leaving Nimrod's dream unfinished. In Micah 5:5-6, Babylon is noted as being the region of Nimrod; and for centuries, prior to and after "Micah," Babylon was constructed, inhabited and governed by the seed of Ham.*

Nimrod was the world's first Hammelech-King following flood. The Greeks venerated Nimrod, they called him Hercules.†

The original Babylonians were Negroes, through Nimrod (Gen. 10:8-10). Rawlinson says, "The Babylonians were Ethiopians by blood, and the Chaldeans should be viewed as Negroes, not Semites or Aramaeans ...." Rawlinson's remarks are found in the following source: "Seven Great Monarchies," Vol. 1, pp. 29, 34. 1884.

The Encyclopedia Britannica, Vol. 8, p. 118, 1959, and The New Funk and Wagnalls Encyclopedia, Vol. XII, pp. 4199-4200, 1950-51, mentions the earliest Sumerians of Babylonia, to have been a non-Semitic Negritic people. The earliest sculptural remains found in Elam, which bordered Babylonia, presented indisputable evidence of an early Negro regional dominance.

The Chaldean city of Ur, which was located south of Mesopotamia and southeast of Babylon, was inhabited by the dark-skinned Semites. The Negro-Babylonians and Chaldeans for centuries intermixed, and because of this, became one in race, language and civilization. Being the father of the Hebrews, Abram's ancestral roots are traced from the city of "Ur" (Gen. 11:28; 15:7; Neh. 9:7; I Chron. 11:35). Ancient records found in Mesopotamia reveal that the religion and science of Babylonia and Ur are of one language having much in common with the language of Ethiopia.

The World's first government was called Adamacracy or Adhamacracy, which following the African-Antediluvian became known as Khamacracy or Hamacracy, that later produced Democracy which the Greek, Roman and Hebrew scholars learned from the Negro-Egyptians (Acts 7:22). The Post-diluvian rulers Nimrod and Hammurabi made major contributions toward government, so that Khamism could become a model for all future bureaucrats. The judicial systems of England and the United States are the embryos from Hamacracy. The word Dem- of Democracy is synonymous to Dom (Dome) which means House, Home, Hame, Ham or Kham. The ancient letter D was exchanged for T; the T for Ch and Kh, thereby transliterating Democracy to the spelling "Khamacracy," "Khemocracy," or "Hamacracy!"

†Great Britain built an aircraft fighter, and other planes called Nimrod, whereas the United States built a transport plane called Hercules.

Gen. 10:8-10; 11:3-9.

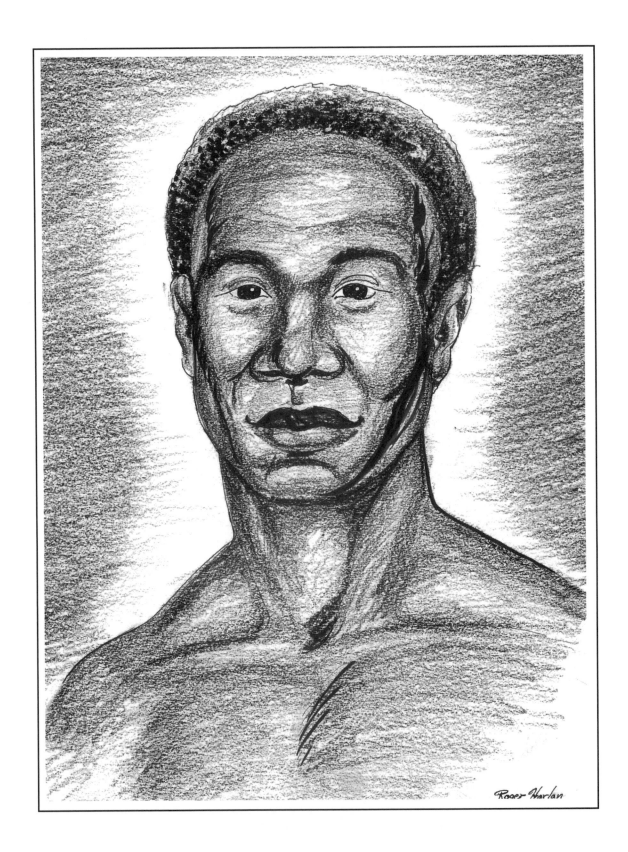

CUSH: "ETHIOPIA"

Cush was the firstborn of Ham; his sons were Havilah, Seba, Sabtah, Raamah, Sabtechah and Nimrod. When Jehovah confounded their language at Babylon, Cush gathered his family and moved south into Africa. He settled northeast Africa, near his brother Mizraim (Egypt).

Cush is called the father of Cushi, meaning Ethiopia. This ancient land was ruled by many kings and queens such as King Ra Nahesi, Piankhy, Thothmes III, Queen Amentere (reigned in Ethiopia during the birth of Christ), and Candace (Acts 8:27). There were two types of Ethiopians, who differed physically only in hair texture. The northern Ethiopians had wooly hair while those dwelling south had straight hair. There is no genetic reason for the difference in their hair within that period; however, it can be assumed geographically that those who settled closer to the equator obtained hair differentiation due to the heat of the sun. The Bible also speaks of the Arabian Ethiopians, who were Cush's offspring living in Midian (II Chron. 21:16; Hab. 3:7; Jasher 25:5).

Cush established an empire extending through China, India, Afghanistan, etc.* The Ethiopians controlled those regions for ages, and to this very day the dwellers of those lands retain the old Ethiopian religious symbols, fine art, and concepts of science, medicine, and engineering. The original architectural structures and municipalities were modified and sometimes mutilated but never destroyed.

The ancient Ethiopians fought continuous wars with the Egyptians, Persians, Hebrews, Assyrians, Arabians and Greeks. The military conqueror Alexander the Great felt Cush's might in 332 B.C. After conquering Egypt easily, the Greeks decided to devastate the Ethiopians. During that adventure, Alexander suffered grief and aggravation, as Cush forced his once unconquerable army to retreat to Egypt. Even Rome, in all her glory, was incapable of conquering the mighty Cush (Jer. 46:9). Augustus Caesar was defeated by Cush around 25 B.C. He, like Alexander, realized Ethiopia's military might, withdrew his forces and made no other effort to venture south of Egypt's border. Thus, Rome's empire was contained at the northern border of Ethiopia.

The Greeks worshiped Cush, they called him Apollo.†

Ancient Greece, Rome and the rest of the world were well aware that Cush was no push-over (playboy), that he was fully capable of obliterating the most advanced militaries. Imperial Ethiopia was the world's first super power, who crossed continents with huge armies, and the first to cross the great oceans in ships. The Greek Herodotus described Ethiopia as having an enormous wide empire where the sun never set. Ancient Cush administered the same global authority as today's super powers, having over 60 nations throughout Asia and Europe under its rule.

In many Catholic and The New Jerusalem Bibles, Ethiopia is described as a strong masterful conquering race (Isa. 18:1-7); a tall smooth bronzed skin people, who were always feared from their beginning onward. This description is not found in the KJV and other texts, largely due to the conspiracy to erase any evidence of an early Negro rule.

*The word India means black, the Hindu Kush (Cush) Mountains were anciently named by the Black Children of "Cush."

†The United States launched a cone shaped spacecraft called Apollo that took astronauts to the moon.

However, most Bibles describe Ham, and his descendants as a mighty race, who served God-Elohim or Elo-Ham (Gen. 10:6, 9; Ex. 18:17-20; Ps. 68:31; Isa. 18:1-7; Jer. 13:23; 38:7-8, 10-12; 39:16; 46:9; Acts 8:27)!

The Ethiopians were Atlanteans who built the world's first skyscrapers (the Tower of Babel, Gen. 10:9-10; 11:1-4), an architectural achievement which took the rest of the world over 4,000 years to rival. France and the United States copied the old African engineering and architecture to build the Eiffel Tower and the Empire State Building. The crafty Ethiopians and Egyptians, long before Da Vinci and the Wright Brothers, conquered the law of gravitation by drawing and constructing airships, that could fly a few hundred feet above ground. In 1922, Professor Howard Carter found a model of a sailplane in the tomb of King Tut. Dr. Khalil Missiha, who studies birds, while looking through a box of bird models in a Cairo museum storeroom, was stunned to have rediscovered a 2,000 year old model of an airplane, made of sycamore wood. Messiha's brother, a flight engineer, reproduced it in balsa wood and launched it and it flew a considerable distance with only a slight jerk of the hand! The hieroglyphs on the airplane read "the Gift of Amon," indicating that it was built in honor of "Amen," whom today's Christians unknowingly call "God-Jesus," or "I Am (Ex. 3:14; Rev. 3:14)!" The name Amon (Amen) is an ancient translation of Hamen or Ham, a title which the Hebrews incorporated into the Divine names of God (Hamma-Kom, Elo-Him or Elo-Ham), Jesus (Ham-Ashiah) and the Holy Spirit (Na-Ham)!

The prophet Ezekiel, who lived about 2,500 years ago, witnessed a flying airship (Ezek. 1-3, Chapters). There is nothing new under the Sun (Eccl. 1:9).

Lost Atlantis, Bramwell, p. 197. 1973; Journal of Africa Civilization 1, no. 2 (Nov. 1979); and Ethiopia and the Missing Link in African History, Reverend Means, pp. 19-20; The Hamitic Bible Dictionary, Dr. Johnson; and www.catchpenny.org/model.html.

During the early nineteen hundreds only Ethiopia and Liberia, out of 47 African nations, were free of white (Japhite) colonialism. However, Liberia was virtually a subsidiary of the Firestone Company. Therefore, Ethiopia was left as the last African independent nation.

In the 20th Century, Ethiopia, under the rule of Menelik II and Haile Selassie, both of whom boasted direct descendancy from the Ethiopian Queen of Sheba, electrified the world by twice defeating Italy's large fleet of fighter planes, bombers and cannons, with only mind, muscle and obsolete weapons. This Biblical land of Cush, developed long before Rome was drawn on a map, had once again passed the test of battle.

Ethiopia is the world's oldest Christian country and Africa's oldest free nation. It is the oldest monarchy known to the history of man, having maintained a monarch for some 3,000 years. For Cush (Ethiopia) was a great nation before the first book of the Bible was written, as it has been during and after the Biblical recordation period.

The offspring of Cush led civilizations for millenniums, that claimed development in arts, sciences and public works, while Asia, especially China, were barbaric, London and Paris were swamplands, and Athens and Rome were vacant sites.

Gen. 10: 6-8; I Chron. 1: 8-10; Jer. 13: 23.

MIZRAIM: "EGYPT"

Mizraim was the second son of Ham (an African by blood) and the father of Ludim, Anamim, Lehabim, Naphtuhim, Pathrusim and Caphtorim (from whom came the Philistines).

During the desertion of Babel, Mizraim followed his two brothers Cush and Phut to Africa. There he dwelt, populating an area known as Lower Egypt which was once named Mizraim. The term Mizraim is still the alternative name for Egypt and is revealed several times as the Land of Ham in Ps. 78:51; 105:23-27; 106:19-23.

The Egyptians were ruled by great Pharaohs such as Menes, Ahmose I (Amos or Hamose), Zoser, Khufu, Amenophis or Amenhotep III (an Ethiopian), and Ramesses II. Several of these Pharaohs reigned in Egypt during Israel's oppression.

Egypt had a vast army that protected its borders, and its high culture marked it as a superior nation.

The Egyptians, like the Ethiopians, were masters of architecture, astronomy, medicine, science, art, agriculture, and military technique; knowledge they primarily borrowed while under the Ethiopian Dynasty.

Reclus says Egypt was a great civilized power during the period in which Europe was being overrun by savage tribes. Arithmetic, architecture, geometry, astrology, all the arts, and nearly all of today's industries and sciences were known while the Greeks lived in caves. The pattern of our thinking originated in Africa..... Reclus' comments can be found in the following source: The Earth and its Inhabitants. Vol. 1, p. 207. 1893.

God called the Negro-Egyptians in Isaiah 19:25 "My people." Egypt during Isaiah's era was ruled by the Negro-Ethiopians.

Gen. 10:13-14; Jer. 47:4; Amos 9:7.

PHUT: "LIBYA"

Phut was Ham's third son; the Scriptures do not mention any of his sons by name, but it is certain that he had sons from whom the Libyans or Cyrenians are descended. These people were located on the upper northern part of Africa and their principal city was Cyrene. They played a vital and fatal role during and after the Crucifixion. As we remember, it was Simon the Cyrenian who helped Christ carry his cross to Golgotha (Mark 15: 21-22). We even find the Cyrenians during the Pentecostal period listening to Peter's instructions.

When Stephen attempted to preach salvation in Jerusalem, a few Cyrenians and other groups had him stoned. There were, however, some Cyrenians who did not approve of his execution and continued to preach Christ's word. These Cyrenians (Phutites) were black people of the Jewish faith, and it was they who spread Christianity to the Greeks (Acts 11: 20).

The Great Jewish historian, Flavius Josephus, states that Phut was the founder of Libya, and that he called the inhabitants Phutites after himself. The Greek Septuagint and the Latin Vulgate on four occasions identify Phut as "Libyans" or "Libya."

Gen. 10: 6; Ezek. 27: 10; 30: 5; Nahum 3: 9; Acts 2: 10; 6: 9.

CANAAN: "HUMBLE"

Canaan was Ham's youngest son who fathered eleven nations, seven of which fell under the hands of Israel. During their dispersion from Babel, Canaan did not follow his three brothers Cush (Ethiopia), Mizraim (Egypt) and Phut (Libya) to Africa below the 30th parallel. Instead, he journeyed southwest, settling a region, which took on his name, "Canaan," which was also called "Northeast Africa," since ancient Canaan was dominated by the Negro children of Ham (also ruled by Cush, Egypt and Phut). The entire eastern coast of the Mediterranean, before the construction of the Suez Canal, was territorially adjoined to Africa. It was for these reasons that Canaan was called "Northeast Africa," before acquiring the names, Palestine and Israel.*

When Canaan entered the land, it was uninhabited. But as time passed, smaller groups entered who were not of Canaan (Philistines). During Israel's invasions, the smaller groups showed minor resistance, nevertheless, the chief strength existed among Canaan's descendants, since they were greater in number and more established culturally. Some of the largest fortresses were controlled by them, such as Ai and Jericho. The Bible refers to this land, and its adjacent territories as Ham's (Gen. 9:22; 14:5; Deut. 2:10; I Chron. 4:40).

Canaan is the most talked-about black character in the Bible. The Sidonians, Hittites, Jebusites, Amorites, Girgasites, Hivites, Arkites, Sinites, Arvadites, Zemarites and Hamathites, who also occupied and commanded the principal city of upper Syria (Gen. 10:18) were all black nations living in the land during Israel's invasion. These blacks dwelt in Canaan Land with the Israelites for centuries, where it has been revealed in the Scriptures that the Hebrews were the blacks' closest relatives through genealogy (Judg. 1:21; 3:5-6; Ezra 9:1-2; 10:14, 16-19, 44; Ezek. 16:1-3).

World War II correspondents altered the name "Northeast Africa" to "Middle East." This scheme was adopted for two purposes; to wipe out the belief that Africa is the mother of civilization, and to reduce Africa's geographic size from the largest to second largest Continent.

The Canaanites were an ingenious race and were the early developers of arts and sciences. The construction of their cities was superior to later Hebrew edifices; they were talented in ceramic arts, music, musical instruments, architecture, and military warfare.

One of Jesus' twelve disciples was a Negro called Simon the Canaanite. He was called a Canaanite because of his descent from the black man Canaan (Matt. 10:1-4, Luke 6:12-16; Acts 1:1-14; Mark 3:18-19).

Rabbi Dr. I. Epstein says, "The nations of Africa strongly disfavored the Jewish occupation of Canaan, by declaring to Alexander the Great that the Land of Canaan was originally African soil:" as it is written, the Land of Canaan with the coasts thereof, Canaan (the Negro son of Ham) was the father of the people (therein). This information is found in the following source: "Babylonian Talmud," section called "Sanhedrin," Vol. 2, London: The Soncino Press, pp. 608-609. 1935.

In ancient times, Canaan and all territories below the 45th parallel, west of China and east of Africa, were not called the "Middle East," but "East Africa" or "Ham (as Hawaii and Alaska are called the United States or North America)," by the Negro children of Ham, who settled those regions. They named the land after their God, "I Am (Cham)" or "Elohim (Eloham)," which is the same as saying "Ham!" Mr. Roux says: "Damascus and Palestine were called the region of Homs (Homs, the old Eastern way of saying Hams or Ham). Mr. Baird and Dillon says: "All of Kanaan was a part of Ethiopia, which in its time (Ethiopia) appear to have reached from Indian to the Atlantic." (Gen. 14:5; I Chron. 4:40; Ancient Iraq, Roux, p. 29. 1976; and The Family Bible: see Pre-History Nations, Baird and Dillon, 1884.

A part of Canaan's name, if not all, means "Ham," if considering that Can- of Canaan is also spelled Kan and Khan, meaning Cham or Ham. The name Genghis Khan (a Chinese conqueror) was also spelled Genghis Kham (Ham), since the ancient letter N was exchanged for M; all of Genghis Khan's descents were called "Cham."

The name Canaan is also defined "Humble." The term Hum- of Humble is also spelled Ham, since the Hamitic and Semitic vowels U and A are interchangeable. The word "ble" of Humble means "Color."

The above information is found in the following sources: Oxford English Dictionary (see I, Ch, C, Cham, Khan, Kan and Ble), 20 Vols., 1989; The Concise Scots Dictionary (see Ham and Hum), pp. 63, 303. 1985; A Comparative Grammar of the Semitic Languages (N = M; the A = 0 and the 0 = U), O'Leary, pp. 64, 77, 99, 106, 110-111. 1923; and Funk & Wagnalls New Practical Standard Dictionary (Khan), Vol. 1, pp. 228, 735. 1955.

Gen. 10:15-19; 12:5-6; 34:2, 9, 16, 21; Deut. 7:1; Josh. 9:7-16; 15:63.

III

THE GRANDSONS OF HAM

Roger Harlan

SIDON OR ZIDON: "FISHING"

Sidon was the first son of Canaan. During the evacuation of Babylon he accompanied his father and two brothers Heth and Jebus to the Land of Canaan (The Land of Canaan is known today as Palestine). When Israel advanced in Canaan, Sidon and his offspring somehow avoided major conflict with Joshua. Their good behavior with Israel endured until the fall of Solomon's empire.

Sidon's offspring were called Zidonians or Phoenicians. They were peaceful people who were craftsmen, merchants and navigators. In 961 B.C., many Zidonians were hired by Solomon to build a costly temple (I Kings 5: 1-8). The Zidonians were also known for their wealthy colony (Carthage) in northern Africa which for a period controlled every seaport along the Mediterranean Sea.

The prophet Isaiah spoke of five cities in Egypt that would speak the language of Canaan (Isa. 19: 18, territorially, Egypt is the same as Ham-Africa, Ps. 78: 51; 105: 23-27; 106: 19-23).

The Hebrew invasion of Canaan touched off much bitterness, causing hundreds of thousands of black Canaanites to flee to Africa.*

*Shabat 18.

Gen. 10: 6, 15; I Kings 5: 1-8.

HETH: "HITTITE"

Heth was Canaan's second son. During the scattering of Babel, the family of Heth divided itself into two groups. One of the groups followed its grandfather "Canaan" to the Land of Canaan, while the other journeyed northwest into a region known today as Asia Minor or Turkey. It is uncertain with which of these groups Heth journeyed.

Many centuries later when Israel entered Canaan, there were four million Hittites living in the land. They were mighty, with huge armies and high walls to protect their cities. During their engagement with Joshua, the Hittites were pushed out of residential areas but were never destroyed (Ex. 3: 17; 23: 28; Josh. 3: 10; Judg. 2: 3). They managed to keep their strength as a nation (I Kings 10: 29; II Kings 7: 6) from Israel's invasion of Canaan to the last king of Judah (Zedekiah).

The most popular black Hittites in the Bible are Uriah, his wife Bathsheba, and Ahimelech.

Gen. 10: 6, 15; I Chron. 1: 8, 13; I Sam. 26: 6-7; II Sam. 11: 14-27.

JEBUS: "JERUSALEM"

Jebus was the third son of Canaan and father of the Jebusite race. During the breakup at Babylon, Jebus followed his father and two brothers, Sidon and Heth, to the Land of Canaan (Later called Israel). While living in the land, he founded a city west of Jordan and named it Jerusalem (Josh. 18: 28; Judg. 1: 21; 19: 10; I Chron. 11: 4-5). His offspring had occupied that city long before the Hebrews left Egypt as slaves (Ex. 3:17; 23:23; 33:1-2; 34:11; Josh. 3:10). But forty years after the Exodus, many Jebusites were driven out of Jerusalem by Joshua (Gen. 15:18-20; Neh. 9:8. When Joshua invaded Jerusalem, the city was very old). Their territory was assigned to the children of Benjamin; however, they were permitted to remain in Jerusalem where there occurred much false worshiping and intermarrying between the two races (Judg. 1: 21; 3: 5-6).

In 1190 B.C., the Jebusites rebelled against Israel to retain strategic grounds; their stronghold was "Zion" which remained hostile to Israel for two hundred years (Josh. 15:63). Thereafter, the Jebusites were constantly harassed by David until their fall in 988 B.C. Their defensive city Zion became the capital of Israel's empire and is often called the city of David following its captivity (II Sam. 5:7; I Chron. 11:5-8).

During Solomon's era, the Jebusites were used as bond servants and keepers of the "great Temple" which was built in Zion. Finally, Jebus' offspring as a race lost their identity through mix breeding among the Hebrews.*

*Dr. M. Hirschfeld, *Racism* (There is Negro strain among Jews . . .), p. 61. 1938.

Gen. 10:6, 15-16; I Kings 9:20-21; II Chron. 8:7.

CAPHTOR: "CRETE"

Caphtor was the seventh son of Mizraim ("Egypt"), grandson of Ham, and father of the black Philistines (Jer. 47: 4; Amos 9: 7).

During the break up at Babel, Caphtor and his offspring journeyed to the island of Crete, but were later forced off the island by a ruinous change in the earth (earthquakes). They migrated from Crete to Canaan (their great "uncle") and settled southwest of Canaan's land. They built the cities of Gaza, Ashod, Ashkelon, Ekron, Gittite and Avite. For many years each of those cities was governed by an axis lord (Josh. 13: 3; I Sam. 29: 7).

When Israel entered Canaan, three of the Philistines' strongholds were seized by the tribe of Judah. However, the Philistines were never destroyed by Israel, because of their great warriors and wide advancement in war equipment, for they had war chariots with iron scythes (Judg. 1: 18-19).

The Philistines remained prominent and powerful throughout the Davidic-Solomonic empire. Many of them even married into the Hebrew race (Neh. 13: 23).

The most popular black Philistines in the Bible are Delilah and Goliath.

Gen. 10: 6, 13-14; Judg. 16: 1-31; I Sam. 17: 23-24.

RAAMAH

Raamah was a son of Cush, grandson of Ham, and father of the Cushite Dedan and Sheba. Raamah and his children were famous for their outstanding trading. The Old Greek Septuagent and the early Latin Vulgate Bibles, identified the word Raamah with "Ragmus" or "Rema."

The Jewish historian Josephus called Raamah, "Ragmus," whom had two sons, Dedan and Sheba, of whom Dedan, known as Judadas (Judah), settled the Judadaens (Judeans), a nation of Western Ethiopians, and left them his name. Josephus" remarks are found in the following source: "The Life and Works of Flavius Josephus," by W. Whiston. 1981.

The 4th Century Palestinian historian and Bishop Eusebius, reminds us of a tribe called Juda before Abraham.

There were Ethiopians who used the name Eber or Heber, meaning Hebrew. Heber the Kenite, the husband of Jael was an Ethiopian (Judg. 4:11, 17). The name Kenite means Kemite, Kamite or Hamite, since the Hebrew N and M were interchangeable. Heb- of Hebrew means Hem or Ham, since the ancient letter B- of Hebrew, was exchanged for M.

The above information is found in the following sources: Strong's Exhaustive Concordance: No. 5677 (also Greek Dictionary: No. 1443-1446); A Comparative Grammar of the Semitic Languages (N = M; K = Kh and H), O'Leary, pp. 52, 61-62, 64, 77, 106. 1923; The Bible Dictionary (Ken means Ham), Smith; A Dictionary of Jewish Surnames From The Kingdom of Poland (Kin means Kam and Cham), Beider, No. 560000: p. 526. 1996; Canaanite Myths and Legends (Km means Ken; see glossary), Gibson, 1978; Anacalypsis (Juda), Higgins, Vol. 2, p. 352. 1936; The Assyrian Grammar (B = M), Delitzsch, pp. 35, 104, 112, 115-116. 1889; A Book Of The Beginnings (B = M), Massey, Vol. 1, p. 456. 1995; and The Ancient Egyptians (B = M), Wilkinson, Vol. 1, p. 43. 1878.

Gen. 10:7; Ezek. 27:22; 38:13.

`

DEDAN AND SHEBA

Dedan and Sheba were the great grandsons of Ham and grandparents of northern and southern Arabia.* Following three centuries of settlement in the Arabian peninsula, the children of Dedan and Sheba were accompanied by the family of Joktan (Shem's grandson). There occurred extensive miscegenation (interbreeding) between the two races. The offspring of Sheba settled farther south in a spicy land, a land that made the Queen of Sheba famous during Solomon's empire.

Josephus called Dedan, the son of Raamah (Ragmus) , "Judadas (Judah)" whom settled the Judeans, a nation of Western Ethiopians, by which he left the inhabitants his name. Josephus' remarks are found in the following source: "The Life and Works of Flavius Josephus," by W. Whiston. 1981.

The historian Eusebius reminds us of a tribe called Juda before Abraham.

Ancient Arabia was inhabited by two races, the Cushites (Dedan, Sheba and Raamah, who were offspring of Ham's son "Cush," Gen. 10:6), and the Semites, who for ages intermarried, and developed what we recognize as the modern day Arabs.

The Cushites were the first race to settle the country and were joined by the Semites three centuries later. The name Semite is termed in the Arabic lore, "moustaribes," or foreigners, because of their late arrival.

Arabia was undoubtedly a part of the African-Ethiopic dominion, whose traces abound in every district of the peninsula, especially in the area of astronomy, mathematics, navigation, philosophy and theology. The great Ethiopian empire had declined and was disunited within centuries, before the Semites held any recognized place in Arabia.

Gen. 10:7; I Kings 10:10; II Chron. 21:16; Isa. 21:13; Ezek. 27:20-22.

IV

BLACKS' INTERACTION WITH ABRAHAM AND JACOB

ANER: "SONG"

Aner, an Amorite chief of Hebron, with his brothers, Eschol and Manre, joined Abraham in a pursuit to rescue Lot, who had been abducted by a group of kings. After a clear-cut victory, he and his brothers divided the spoils seized during the slaughter.

Aner and his brothers were blacks, great descendants of Canaan, who was Ham's fourth son (Gen. 10:6, 15-16).

The black Amorites at one time dominated Jerusalem (Josh. 10: 5); however, Jerusalem is shown elsewhere to be inhabited by the Negro Jebusites, who were the earlier inhabitants and builders about five hundred fifty years before the Hebrew's presence. The ancient Jerusalem acquired its name from the Negro man Jebus, the third son of Canaan (Gen. 10: 6, 15-16, Joshua 10: 5; 15: 8; 63; 18: 28; Judg. 1 :21; 19 :10).

The area of Jerusalem was a lucrative region, often conceptualized by the Israelites, prior to their release from Negro-Egypt, as the "land flowing with milk and honey (Ex. 3: 8, 17; 13 :5; 32: 3)." Jerusalem's major importance began about 988 B.C. when David seized it from the Hamitic Jebusites, making it the capital city of Israel's empire. His son Solomon, in honor of Jehovah, built a marvelous temple in Jerusalem, as well as palaces for himself and his numerous black wives. By 888 B.C., after the death of Solomon, Israel's empire divided, leaving Jerusalem as the capital of the southern kingdom Judah. By 575 B.C., the Babylonians defeated Judah and devastated the temple in Jerusalem. The temple was rebuilt around 526 B.C. during the Persian empire. By 400 B.C., Jerusalem was controlled by the priests of the temple. They modified the city into a flourishing religious center, which sparked Jerusalem to become a religious paradise.

The Negro Jebus, being the founding father of Jerusalem (Gen. 10: 6, 15-16; Josh. 10: 5, 15: 8, 63; 18: 28; Judg. 1: 21; 19:10), has been remembered in that sacred light for some four thousand years. It is nearly impossible to discuss Judaism or Christianity without mentioning the name of Jebus (Josh. 15: 8; 18: 28). That is why many clergymen and theologians throughout the ages have preached that Canaanites were the children of Shem (Semites) instead of Ham (Negroes), (Gen. 10: 6).

Gen. 14: 12-13, 24.

MELCHIZEDEC: "JUST"

A Hamitic king of Salem (Jerusalem, named after Canaan's third son of Jebus) and high priest of Jehovah, Melchizedec traveled out to salute Abraham for a triumph over the Hamitic King Chedorlaomer. He gave the conqueror bread and water, including blessings, and in return was given one-tenth of the spoils captured from Chedorlaomer (Gen. 10:6, 15-16; Josh. 18:28; 19:10).

Melchizedec's life in many ways resembled that of Christ: both were high priests and faithful to the most high God. He and Christ seem to have characterized bread and water as a means of restoration for the soul (John 3:5; 6:35, 48, 58). Melchizedec's and the Savior's names were not written on the Aaronic priesthood, nor were they from a Levitical family.

This perpetual "Hamitic Amorite-priest" arose and lived among Ham's descendants, where it is certain that he used the Hamitic identity in the same manner as Christ, who was after the order of Melchizedec, displayed Himself as a Jew to the Jews (Ps. 110:4; John 8:58; Heb. 5:7).*

According to Dr. William Smith, Melchizedec was of one blood with the children of Ham, among whom he lived, chief of a settled Canaanitish tribe. The word Mel-of Melchizedec means Black or Melas (Negro). In the book of Jasher, Melchizedec is called Adonizedek, which is certainly a Negro-Canaanite name (II Sam. 1:18). Modernists have concealed this information to farther their effort to cover-up his Negro origin through Canaan. Some texts refer to Melchizedec as Shem, but fail to explain that Shem is synonymous to Hham or Ham, since the Hebrew S was exchanged for H.

The above information is found in the following sources: "The Jewish Family Names & Their Origins," Guggenheimer, p. 505. 1992; "Smith's Bible Dictionary," Vol. 3, p. 1876. 1890; Jasher 16:11-12; "Jones Dictionary of Old Testament Proper Names (Ham, the same as Hham)," p. 138. 1990; "A New System (Sham and Shem means Ham)," Bryant, Vol. 1, pp. 81, 106, 296. 1807; and "An Introduction to the Comparative Grammar of the Semitic Language (S=H)," Moscati, pp. 104, 153. 1964.

*The first Biblical priests mentioned in the Bible were of Ham's posterity; the Canaanite Melchizedec, the Egyptian Potipherah, and the Ethiopian Jethro. The royal king Melchizedec was the first to hold the office of priesthood, a godly position which was later administered by the Afro-Semitic Aaronic priest line. The priest Phinehas, whose name means Negro, was half Semitic and Hamitic. (Gen. 14:18; 41:45; 46:20; Ex. 2:16; 3:1; 6:25; 3:1:10; Ezra 9:1-2; Ezek. 16:1-3; Gal. 3:16; Heb. 7:1-5, 11-24; I Peter 2:9, 12). The moral fabric of the Americans and Europe's Priestly office, originated from the Hamitic priesthood.

For centuries, the clergy and theologians have blundered by promoting secular beliefs above Biblical evidence! They have falsely preached that the Canaanite Melchizedec, the Egyptian Potipherah, and the Ethiopian Jethro, who were offshoots of Ham, to be descendants of Shem and Japheth. Such misrepresentations are aimed to eliminate or erase any Biblical evidence of any early African presence, contradicting the very declaration of Genesis 10:1-6, I Chronicles 1:1-8; Pro. 30:5-6 and Revelation 22:18-19.

Gen. 14:18-20; Ps. 110: 4; Heb. 7:1-4, 11, 15-17, 21.

ISHMAEL: "ALLAH–GOD HEARS"

Ishmael was a son of Abraham and Hagar, a black handmaid from Egypt. Allah-God had made a covenant with this lad's father, and for a time it seemed he might become an hair. His father had loved and prepared him for years to guide his people, but when Isaac was born, his chances were greatly lessened. After waiting over thirteen years to see a younger brother exult him, caused Ishmael to bewail his fate! He then became angry and quarrelsome with Sarah, only to find himself being disbarred. Ishmael and his mother were reluctantly asked by Abraham to depart. They were given bread and water as they journeyed toward Beersheba. It was there that Hagar said, "Let me not see the death of the lad." And she sat over against him and lifted up her voice and wept. Then Allah-God appeared unto her, saying He would make Ishmael a great nation, afterward opening Hagar's eyes to see a well of water with which to revive her son's strength.

Ishmael grew in a land named Paran (Sinai, located on the Arabian peninsula) and became an archer. There he married a Hamitic Egyptian woman who bored him twelve princes and one princess. Two of his sons, Kedemah and Tema, journeyed north of Arabia and founded cities. Mahalath, his daughter married Esau the brother of Israel (Gen. 28:9).

Israel was a wild man as foretold by an angel: "A man whose hand would be against every man and every man's against his." This half-breed, with other Negro tribes, became one of the fathers of the Arab race.

The Negro Ethiopians settled in Arabia soon after the desertion of the Tower of Babel. They inhabited the peninsula some three and a half centuries before Ishmael was born. When Ishmael's descendants entered Arabia Deserta, they were not of a pure breed, since Ishmael was bi-racial, through his black mother, Hagar. These Ishmaelites mixed among the ancient people of the land, and developed what we recognize as the modern day Arabs.*

*Strong's Exhaustive Concordance define the name Arab as a mongrel mixed people; to darken; to grow dusky; night or evening: No. 6150-6154.

In ancient times, Arabia and all territories below the 45th parallel, west of China and east of Africa, were not called the "Middle East," but "Northeast Africa" or "Ham (as Hawaii and Alaska are called the United States or North America)," by the Negro children of Ham, who settled those regions. They named the land after their God, I Am "(Cham)" or "Elohim (Eloham)," which is the same as saying "Ham!" Volney says: "The Ethiopians had colonies all over Iraq-Arabia, as far as Persia." Mr. Baird and Dillon says: "Arabia was first called "Cush," and was often translated "Ethiopia" (Gen. 14:5; I Chron. 4:40; II Chron. 21:16; Hab 3:7; Volney's New Researches on Ancient History, Volney, p. 179. 1856; and The Family Bible, Baird and Dillon, pp. 7-11. 1884).

Gen. 10:6; 16:3-4; 21:10, 16-18.

ABIMELECH OF GERAR: "FATHER OF KINGS"

Abimelech was a Philistine king of Gerar during the time of Abraham. He was moved by Sarah's beauty and took her from Abraham,* not knowing she was Abraham's spouse. But God appeared to him in a dream, threatening his life, for the woman he took was married (Gen. 20:1-3). The king feared God! Knowing he had not touched her, he begged God for mercy, promising to set her free, giving her cattle, servants, land to dwell on, and plenty of silver. She was given silver to buy a face veil to conceal her beauty. This was a custom in Gerar for married women. His plea was granted, and the king's life was spared.

Philistines were great black descendents of Mizraim and Caphtor, who were descendents of the black man Ham (Gen. 10:6, 13-14).

There was a similar incident with Sarah and a Negro-Ethiopian Pharaoh during the Twelfth Egyptian Dynasty (Gen. 12:10-20). H.R. Hall, in his book called "The Ancient History of the Near East," and D.D. Houstan's "Wonderful Ethiopians of the Ancient Cushite Empire," clearly states that the Twelfth Egyptian Dynasty was ruled by the Negro-Ethiopians. According to the 1957 "Unger's Bible Dictionary," Abraham and Sarah entered Egypt during the Twelfth Dynasty (2000-1775).

The Bible tells us that Abraham's wife Sarah was fair (Gen. 12:11, 14). Many clergymen, theologians and scholars have assumed the word fair, in this particular usage, to mean light or not dark. This bears little relevance, since the word fair has other meanings, such as pretty, desirable, beautiful, favorable, elegant, pure, just, honest, etc. When the Bible mentions Sarah, Rebekah, Tamar, Abishag, Moses and others as being fair (Gen. 24:16; 26:7; I Kings 1:4; Acts 7:20), the terminology merely signifies good stewardship, clean-heartedness, spiritual dedication and faithfulness to God. The word "fair" in relation to God had nothing to do with man's physical shapes, heights or colors. One should keep in mind that in those early centuries there were no bright-skinned Semites (Hebrews) dwelling on the earth. It was some 982 years following the death of Abraham that the first white Semites appeared on earth (II Kings 5:27). They were small in number, compared to the black Hebrews (Jews), a contrast that still exists to this day.

The Arabians, in their account "El Makreezee, Khitat," claimed Abraham's second wife Keturah (Gen. 25:1-6) to have been Hamitic, "Canaanite." The Revered Armistead in his book, "The Negro is a Man," pp. 8, 123. 1903, corroborated, by calling Keturah, a Negro Canaanitish! The book of Jasher calls Keturah a Canaanitish (Josh. 10:18; II Sam. 1:18; Jasher 25:5).

The third syllable of the name Abra-ham (Ham) means black, a suffix that Jehovah originated Himself (Gen. 17:5-7).

Gen. 20:1-18; 34:1-31.

EPHRON: "DUST"

Ephron, a descendant of Ham's fourth-born through Canaan, made preparation to sell Abraham a plot of land for burial purposes. This landowner was a Hittite and dwelt among the children of Heth.

Abraham the patriarch paid him four hundred skekels of silver (one hundred ninety dollars) and the name of his purchase was Machpelah. There he buried his wife "Sarah" in a cave, and was later united with her, while Ishmael and Isaac were mourners.

Abraham was a native of the Chaldean city, Ur, and left it within the period of the Hamitic king Guti (Gen. 11 :28-31). The 1884 edition of "The Family Bible," by Baird and Dillon, contains the identical books of the King James Version, with additional texts (Apocrypha), as Judith, Tobit, Esdras I and II, The Wisdom of Solomon, Baruch, The Prayer of the Manasses King of Judah, the first and second book of Maccabees, etc. It states in the book of Judith 5: 1-24, that Abraham was a descendant of the Chaldeans.* The builders of Chaldea were Hamitic in race, language and civilization. Archaeological discoveries of rock-written annals and ancient cuneiform records have conclusively demonstrated that the Hamitic Negroes were the earlier settlers of Ur. The African-Ethiopian empire had for ages dominated Ur!

*The Bible only mentions Abraham's Semitic father. His mother may have been Ethiopian, for Abraham was called a Chaldean; whereby convincing some scholars that Abraham was Hamitic, since Chaldeans during his birth, were a mixed race of Semitic and Hamitic, with strong Negro features. The early Semites and Hamites possessed deep black skins and woolly hair. Yellow and white hair found among the ancient Semites (Hebrews) were feared and socially shunned (Lev. 13: 1-6; 30, 32).

Gen. 10: 15; 23: 7-20; 25: 8-10; 49: 31-33; 50: 13.

HAMOR: "CLAY"

Hamor was a Hivite prince of Shechem, which was named after his son. He dealt fairly with Jacob as he sold him a plot of land. But their relationship crumbled when his son Shechem seduced Dinah, Jacob's daughter (Gen. 34: 1–2, 9, 16).

This immoral act caused much grief among Jacob's sons Simeon and Levi. They advanced upon the city of Shechem and slew every male, including Hamor and his son.

Hivites were great black descendants of Ham through his fourth son, Canaan (Gen. 10: 6, 15–17).

The Hebrews' miscegenation amongst Blacks was so immense that God sold them into bondage to a king of Mesopotamia for eight years (Judges 3: 5–8). The taking of Negro Amorite wives still constituted a thorny problem among the returned Jews following the Babylonian exile (Ezra 9 :1, 2). Canaan and Isaac's descendants, by crossbreeding, produced today's black and white Hebrews. The ancient Jews were so black that many Romans mistook them for Ethiopians. The most rigid codes among Jews to prevent miscegenation failed. Even the Jewish father Abraham opposed such restrictions by sexually indulging a non-Jewish woman of Africa, the Negro Hagar.

Gen. 12: 6; 33: 19; 34: 1–31.

SHUAH: "PIT"

Shuah was a Canaanite and father of Judah's wife (Judah was Jacob's fourth son, Gen. 29: 35).* Shuah's daughter bore the Hebrew three sons: Er, Onan and Shelah; Er and Onan at later ages were put to death by God for wrong doings.

The crossbreeding between Hebrews and blacks went on, in spite of all laws (Deut. 7: 3; Neh. 31: 17-18; Ezra 9: 1-15; 10: 1-44). Such law restrictions existed for the purity of religion, not race, because Jews were already a mixed people before departing Negro-Egypt. This is why some historians wrote of Hebrews to be of Negro origin. The Greek historian and geographer Strabo said that during his lifetime, it was not unusual for historians to think of Jews to be of Negro ancestry. Strabo went on to say that Jews living in western Judea were partly African (Egyptian). The Roman Tacitus supported Strabo by saying, "Jews were of the Ethiopian race."

The modern white Jews receive much of their praise, culture and popularity from the history of the early ancient black Jews, who were the original Hebrews. The bright complected Jews contributed nothing to the early Hebrew development, nor were they present during the Exodus from Egypt under Moses or the invasion of Canaan. The white Jews appeared about one hundred years after the death of Solomon (II Kings 5: 27). Abraham, Isaac, Jacob and their descendants until the book of the second Kings, were black-skinned people, largely mixed with the African (Hamitic) element.

*Following the death of Judah's wife, he fathered twin sons, Perez and Zerah, by his black daughter-in-law Tamar. The first born Perez became an ancestor of the Messianic King (Ruth 4: 12, 18–22; I Chron. 2: 4; Matt. 1:3; Luke 3: 33).

Gen. 38: 1-11; I Chron. 2: 3.

TAMAR

Tamar was a Canaanite wife of the two sons of Judah, Er and Onan. Her prime concern was to preserve the lineage of Judah, feeling that since Er and Onan had successively perished suddenly, and Judah's wife Bathshuah had also died, was a clear indication of the family's extinction. Judah, as it appeared with Tamar, was reluctant to allow the younger Shelah to marry her, lest he should meet of the same fate as his brothers. Tamar through desperation ensnared the father himself by pretending to be one of the common women.

Following this union she became the mother of twins, Pharez and Zarah, and through the Negro Pharez the holy line was continued.

The name Tamar is also spelled Camar, Kamar or Hamar, since the ancient letter T was interchangeable with C; the C with K, and the K with H.

The above information is found in the following sources: A Comparative Grammar of the Semitic Languages (T = K, C and D), O'Leary, pp. 52, 54-55, 89, 242. 1923; and Development of the Canaanite Dialects (T = H), Harris, p. 25. 1939.

The Reverend Armistead says, "Tamar was a black Canaanitish," Armistead's remarks are found in the following source: "The Negro is a Man," pp. 129-130, 149-150. 1903.

Gen. 38: 6-30.

V

PRIOR TO AND DURING THE OPPRESSION

ASENATH

Asenath was the charming daughter of the Egyptian Patipherah, priest of On. She was given in marriage by the Pharoah to Joseph (Gen. 41: 45).

Beyond this, nothing more is said about her except for the mention of her two sons, Manasseh and Ephraim.

The beautiful Asenath was a member of a pure black African race which intermixed its seed among the free and enslaved Hebrews. The Israelites, prior to and after the Exodus, were definitely black-skinned and biracial. The Greek historian and geographer Strabo (63 B.C.–24 A.D.) said that during his lifetime, it was not unusual for historians to think that Jews were of Negro ancestry. Strabo went on to say that Jews living in western Judea were mixed with African blood.

The modern day Egyptians, who are largely composed of European blood (fifty percent), are descendants from an ancient Black-Negro race.[1] Their forefather (ancestor) was a Negro called Mizraim, meaning Egypt (Gen. 10: 6).[2]

Gen. 41: 45, 50–52; 46:20.

MANASSEH AND EPHRAIM

Manasseh and Ephraim were born on the African continent, and were the sons of the Egyptian Negress Asenath and her Hebrew husband Joseph. They were both adopted by their grandfather Jacob upon hid deathbed, who for some unknown reason gave the first place birthright blessing to the younger Ephraim (Gen. 48:1:13-20), thereby indicating that Ephraim was to become greater than his older brother.

Little is known concerning their personal lives; however, it is recorded in Chronicles 7:20-27 that Joshua Ben Nun,* who led the Black-skinned Hebrews into the Promised Land, was a distant descendant of the Colored man Ephraim.

The tribes of Manasseh and Ephraim were not taken captive during Shalmanezer's conquest of Israel, but remained in the land with a new arrival called Cuthah (Ethiopians). It was through this encounter that the two tribes intermingled their seed with the Ethiopians, which sprung forth a mongrel people called the Samaritans who claimed to be the bloodline of the Jewish Joseph, Jacob and Rachel (II Kings 17:3, 24, 30). In John 8:48, Jesus was asked if He was a Samaritan with a demon, He denied having a demon, but wouldn't deny Himself as a Samaritan.

*The term Nun is an Egyptian word deriving from the primeval Deity Ni, which before the existence of vowels was original pronounced N, indicating Supreme Creator and water. The name Ni (N) is found in the world's oldest known written Bible called "The Egyptian Book Coming Forth by Day," which the Europeans renamed "The Egyptian Book of the Dead." The term Ni is acknowledged as an infix in the word Om-Ni-Potent, which means "God Almighty." Ni is also a translation of Na, No or Nu, since all vowels in the Hebrew alphabet were interchangeable. In the African nation of Benin the Egyptian word Nun is pronounced Ni and Niger!

The Jewish Josephus in his essay called "Against Apion," spoke of the exiled Hebrews being of Egyptian origin. The classical writers Plutarch, Tacitus, Eusebius, Celsus Diodorus and Strabo, supported the tradition that the original Hebrews were a group of Ethiopians and Egyptians, who journeyed from Egypt to Canaan. The English poet and lecturer Gerald Massey stated that after residing 430 years in Egypt, the children of Jacob became fully Egyptianized by race, language and culture.

The above information is found in the following sources: Dictionary of the Bible (The Cuthean-Ethiopians intermixed with the Israelites. Their descendants were Samaritans, described by the Hebrews as Cutheans), Hastings pp. 195, 880. 1973. The One Primeval Language, "The Fall," Forster (Black Jews; the tanned or sun-blacked Manasseh), p. 330. 1854; From Babylon to Timbuktu (Black Israelites), Windsor, 1899; Encyclopedia Judaica (see Black Jews). 1971; Against Apion, Josephus, Book 2. 2; and A Book of the Beginnings (Jews mixed with Africans; Nun, Ni and Niger), Massey, Vol. I, pp. ix, x; Vol. 2, pp. 23, 610. 1995.

Gen. 41:50-52; 48:; Num. 2:18-21; Josh. 16:17; Ezra 4:2; Neh. 13:27-28; Isa. 11:13; Jer. 31:6; 50:19; Luke 10:30; 17:11-19.

AHMOSE: "MOON CHILD"

Ahmose was the first Pharaoh of the Eighteenth Egyptian Dynasty (according to J. A. Rogers),[1] which was ruled by Negroes, prior to and during Israel's oppression. He was an African by blood, of the lineage of Ham's second son Mizraim, whose name is translated "Egypt." He and his beautiful black Ethiopian Queen, Nefertari (grandmother of Queen Hatshepsut), ruled Egypt stringently.[2]

We first recognize Ahmose in Ex. 1: 8 (Pharaoh who knew not Joseph), at a period Israel was growing economically and in number. Ahmose, after realizing their continuous growth, feared them, feeling they would soon become mightier than the Egyptians. He constantly cautioned his people of their fate, if Israel wasn't brought under heavy burden: "Come on, let us deal wisely with them, lest they multiply, and it come to pass that, when war occurs, they join also unto our enemies, and fight against us, and so get them up out of the land." The Egyptians yielded to his plea, which lead the once-freed Israelites into a massive labor force.

Egypt under Ahmose made the lives of the Israelites unpleasant with harsh afflictions, in all affairs.

Egypt's provocation with the Israelites arose during the Hyksos rule, a period known as the "Great Humiliation." When the Israelites entered Egypt, the Hyksos welcomed and supplied them with land and freedom (privileges the indigenous Egyptians were denied). This close association among the Israelites and Hyksos provoked the Egyptians to expel the Hyksos, under Ahmose. The Egyptians and Ahmose viewed the Hebrew cohesion with the Hyksos as an unforgivable treacherous act, whereupon the Hebrews should undergo humiliation, as the Egyptians experienced under the Hyksos. *

Lucian, Galen and Block who journeyed to Egypt at different periods, all agreed that the Egyptians' large flat nose and puffy lips were proof of their Negro origin. Lucian, Galen and Block's comments can be found in the following source: Bulletins et Memoirs Society de Paris, pp. 393, 403. 1901; Specimens of Ancient Sculpture Society of Dilettanti, Vol. 1.

*The Negro Hyksos was a branch of the Cushite family who lived in Arabia prior to invading Egypt. The Hyksos' quick triumph in Egypt was due to superior archery and the horse-drawn chariot, a military technique that was previously unknown to the Egyptians.

The warlike Hyksos were a people of enormous strength, for they were giants in stature.

Ex. 1: 8.

PHARAOH'S DAUGHTER

A Black princess (According to the Jewish historian Josephus, her name was "Thermuthis") and daughter of Pharaoh Seti I, while Israel underwent slavery, saved the life of a Hebrew infant while bathing in a river, accompanied by maids. The princess insisted her servants to bring the child to her, and as she heard him crying, became compassionate toward the child saying: "this is one of the Hebrews' children." She named the tiddler Moses and reared him in the Pharaoh's palace. It was this Moses who led the Exodus of the slaves from Egypt under Ramesses II.

The Egyptians called themselves Kmt, meaning coal black, which is equivalent to Kamit, or the Biblical Kam (Ham), meaning Negro or sooty. The above information is found in the following sources: Worterbuch der Aegyptischen Sprache, Vol. 5, pp. 122, 127. 1971; and The African Origin of Civilization, Diop, pp. 7-8. 1974.

H.M. Stanley commented that the ancient sculptures of Egypt's monuments, most mummies, the Sphinx, wooden and stone statues, bear a strong resemblance to the Afro-Asians (Keep in mind that the early Asians were Negroes through Cush and Canaan). Stanley went on to say that the Egyptians had wooly hair and dark-dusky skins. Stanley's remarks can be found in the following source: "North American Review," Vol. 170, p. 656. 1900.

The Greeks historian Herodotus (484-425 B.C.), who is styled as the father of history, clearly stated that the Egyptians of his day possessed black skins and wool hair.

Ex. 2:5; 3:7, 11-12.

RAMESSES II: "SUN-BORN"

Ramesses II, a Pharaoh of Egypt during the closure of Israel's oppression, was a Black man from Ham's second son Mizraim, whose name is translated "Egypt" (According to R. R. Windsor, Ramesses II was a pure black African with heavy lips and a wide nose.... Rawlinson and Sergi agreed by claiming Ramesses and his father Seti I, as having Negro features).

Egypt's greatest building period flourished under the flamboyant Ramesses. He spent most of his life erecting buildings and statues of himself. Ramesses even went as far as stripping past Pharaohs of their building credits to ensure his own. His ambition to build caused heavy burdens upon his three million Hebrew slaves. It was these people who built special cities and temples for him throughout Egypt.* They were set free around 1230 B.C., following a pestilence upon Egypt which was prophesied by Moses. It was recorded that this Pharaoh's entire army drowned as they pursued the Hebrews across the Red Sea.

Ramesses compelled his Hebrew slaves, under the directorship of Egyptian stonemasons, artisans and craftsmen, to build two huge temples carved out of the rock, in honor of the "Sun-God Amen (Mal. 4:2; Rev. 3:14; 5:14)," who was none other than "Ham." The country's largest Temple was built at Karnak in deference of Ham. It had more than thirty columns that rose about eighty feet. In their temples, the Egyptians worshiped God-Jehovah-Yahweh-Elohim (Ps. 78:51; 84:11; Isa. 19:21-25).

The Egyptian historian Manetho, and also a priest under Ptolemy I, said that the son of Amenophis was Ramesses, that Ramesses was a Black king and father of Seti (Seti I was the father of Ramesses II).

D.D. Houston, in her book, "Wonderful Ethiopians of the Ancient Cushite Empire," stated that Seti I married the granddaughter of Amenhotep III, known as Princess Tai, and that Ramesses II became the legitimate king from this matrimony. Houston also stressed that Amenhotep III was an Ethiopian, and was often called the Black Prince.

Gen. 10:13-14; Num. 33:3-5; I Chron. 1:11-12; II Chron. 35:20-26; Isa. 19:19-25.

THE GREAT PYRAMID

The Great Pyramid of Giza, the surviving member of the Seven Wonders of the Ancient World, was built during the 4th Dynasty by the Hamitic-Negro King Khufu, whom the Greeks called Cheops.* The Great Pyramid was originally 481 feet and 5 inches, which has a base covering 13 acres, and built from 2.5 million limestone and granite blocks, each weighing between 2.6 and 80 tons. Khufu's Pyramid, which was built at the center of the earth's land mass, and in the midst of Egypt (Isa. 19:19-25), having a foundation which is astonishingly leveled, was geometrically constructed (Pi and the triangle) thousands of years before the Greek Pythagoras, the so called father of geometry. The African pyramids including the Great Pyramid were built in honor of the Patriarch Ham, whom the Ethiopians and Egyptians revered as God-Ham, El-Ham, Eli-Ham (Eli-Am, II Sam. 11:3; 23:34), Elo-Ham, Elo-Him, Amen-Ra (Hamen-Ra), Amen (Hamen), etc. The Pharaonic pyramids were an architectural marvel designed from the Ethiopian Nimrod's Ziggurat Pyramid (Tower of Babel, Gen. 10:9-10; 11:4), and remained for the next 4000 years the world's tallest historical skyscraper until the construction of the French "Eiffel Tower;" and the American "Chrysler" and "Empire State Building."

*The Harvard Professor Reisner who directed the Harvard Camp at the pyramids, called the portraits of Cheops' family, builder of the Great Pyramid, "Negroes."

The majestic pyramids, proceeding the break-up of Babel, were first built in Ethiopia, and were later perfected in Egypt (Ham, Ps. 78:51; 105:23-27; 106:20-22) while Egypt was a colony of Ethiopia. The Ethiopian Pyramids, which reached a height of 30 to 90 feet, were employed as tombs for a long line of queens called Candaces, who ruled Ethiopia from (350 B.C. to 350 A.D.). There are over 80 pyramids discovered in Ethiopia which were buried under the sand, whereas 60 pyramids in Egypt.

The giant pyramids were also called Ra's (Re's) Pyramids. Remember, the ancient Ethiopians and Egyptians referred to Ham as Ra, Amen (Hamen) and the Sun, whereas the Babylonians, "Sham-Ash," or "Shem-Esh," which became the Hebrew poetic form for Hammah, Chammah, Hammanim *or Chammanim, indicating Sun, Hot, Heat, Fire, Flame, Blaze, Scorch, Burnt, Fervent, Warm, Ra, Amen (Hamen)** Ham, etc. The word pyr- of pyramid means Ham or Fire, whereas -Am, "Ham," and Id (also Od, Ad, Ed, Yd or Ud, since all vowels in the Semitic Alphabet are interchangeable), "God."*

The Great Pyramid, like no other geometric structure, was divinely designed to a blueprint inspired by the Hamitic God "Amen (Hamen)" or "I Am," whom the Hebrews following their enslavement in Egypt, called Yahwe, Jesus or God; an identity which is still used by today's Judaeo-Christians (Ex. 3:14; 6:3; Num. 5:22; Ps. 87:1-7; John 8:58; II Cor. I:20; Rev. 3:14).

Any cone-shaped object is called Ham, Hamat, Hamate, Hamiform or Hemi-pyramid. The Divine name Ham, the correlative form of pyramid, was frequently altered to represent world Deities. The Greeks called Ham, "Zeus," the Romans "Jupiter-Hammon," and the Hebrews "Elohim," the same as Eloham, meaning God-Ham.

**Jesus Christ is called Amen (Hamen) while God-Elohim called Himself, "the Sun (Ps. 84:11; Mal. 4:2; Rev. 3:14; 5:14)." The Ethiopian word Amen is a duplicate of Amon, and was anciently spelled Hamen as for Amon,"Hamon." Before there were vowels in the alphabet, the name Haman, Hamen or Hamon was spelled Hmn. Most Pharaohs inherited the sacred name Ham, Hamen or Amen, as the Boy Pharaoh, Tutank-hamen, whose father was called Amen-hotep or Hamen-hotep.

The above information is found in the following sources: Roget's International Thesaurus (see Hamiform and cone); The Origin of Races and Color (pyramid designed for Ham), Delany, p. 46. 1879; Oxford English Dictionary (Hemi-Pyramid and Hamate), 20 Vols., 1989; Hebrew Union College Annual (Ham means Hamat), Lewy, Vol. 18, p. 473. 1944; Wonderful Ethiopians of the Ancient Cushite Empire (pyramids in Ethiopia), Houston, pp. 32, 39, 50, 62. 1985; Anglo Egyptian Sudan (Candaces buried in pyramids), Reisner; The Negro in Greek and Roman Civilization (Reisner's comments of Cheops), p. 12. 1929; The African Origin of Civilization (80 pyramids), Diop, p. 150. 1974; Fausset's Bible Dictionary (Ham was called Aman, Amen, Amon, Amon-Re the Sun, Hamon and Zeus), pp. 269, 513. 1961; Jones' Dictionary of Old Testament Names (Ham was called the Sun), pp. 89, 138-139, 296. 1990; A Commentary, Critical and Explanatory of the Old and New Testaments (Ham was called "Amon the Sun" or "Amon-Re"), Fausset, Vol. 1, pp. 551, 700. 1870; Religions of the World (Re was Osiris; Sun-God of the Nile), Berry, pp. 8-9. 1968; The Jewish Encyclopedia (Amon was pronounced Amen, Amen-Re, Amanu, Amun or Sun. He was also called Zeus.), Vol. 1, p. 526. 1912; Calmet's Dictionary of the Holy Bible (Ham was called Hamon and Jupiter-Hammon), Taylor, p. 55. 1849; A Dictionary of the Bible (Hammah), Hastings, p. 628. 1902; Cyclopaedia of Biblical Theological and Ecclesiastical Literature (Chammah and Chammanism), Strong, Vol. 10, pp. 16-17. 1969; A New System (Sham and Shem means Ham, Ham was called Ad), Bryant, Vol. 1, pp. 2, 81, 106, 296. 1807; Dr. William Smith's Dictionary of the Bible (Ham means Am or Ammon), Vol. 4, p. 3648, 1890; Sacred Books and Early Literature of the East (Am or Amma was the Old Testament Ham), Horne, 1, p. 226. 1917; Oxford English Dictionary (Ud, the same as Ad and Od, means God), 20 Vols., 1989; Eloham (Askjeeves.com); and Middle English Dictionary (Hamen means Amen, Ham and Hom), Kurath, Vol. 4, pp. 466, 883. 1963.

I Maccabees 13:28-29; Isa. 19:19-25.

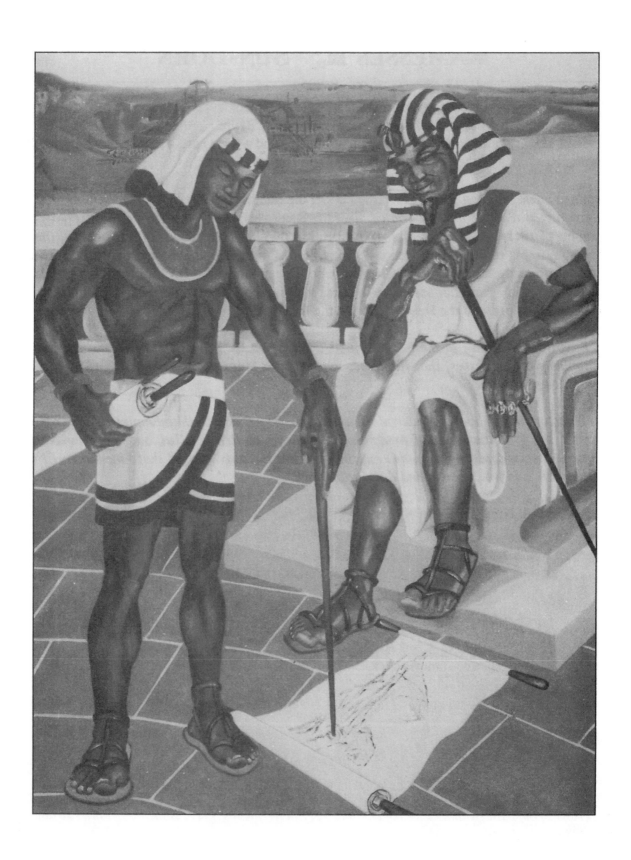

MOSES: "SAVED OUT OF THE WATER"

Moses was a black-skinned Hebrew living in the Negro-Land of Egypt during the period of the Israelite's enslavement. Following his miraculous rescue from the Nile River, the energetic Moses, for the next forty years, would enjoy a lucrative lifestyle within Egypt's finest years of prosperity. As a member of the Pharaoh's household, young Moses received the best institutional training the ancient world could offer. The black Pharaoh Seti I, whom Moses believed to be his earthly father, surrounded Moses with the wisest men in Egypt, a maneuver which enabled Moses to learn Egypt's political, social and natural sciences. He excelled in subjects such as politics, religion, mathematics, engineering, chemistry, geometry, botany, zoology, anatomy, law, linguistics, and military techniques, knowledge which he passed on to the freed Israelites (Ex. 2:1-10; Acts 7:22). Moses undoubtedly was in a favored position among his colleagues. His mind and spirit merited him the highest honors, unlimited opportunities, years of admiration, and a promising future in the Egyptian bureaucracy.

However, Moses' popularity suffered a heavy blow following the tragic death of an Egyptian whom he had murdered (Ex. 2:12). When Pharaoh Seti learned of this slaying, Moses out of fear fled Africa to the Land of Midian, which the book of Jasher calls the Land of Cush (Ex. 2:11-15; II Sam. 1:18; Acts 7:23-29; Jasher 25:5).* It was forty years later when an angel appeared to him in the form of a burning bush, and during this wondrous moment, God-Elohim (Elo-Ham) called to Moses from out the midst of the burning bush and instructed him to return to Africa for the release of His people.

*While living in Midian, Moses found his Ethiopian wife Zipporah, whom Guggenheimer, The Reverend Armistead, Josiah Priest and ancient Biblicists, called a Negro-Colored woman. Moses himself, according to these same scholars was a black skinned man. This information is found in the following sources: "The Jewish Family Names & Their Origins (husband of a black woman. The name Moses is linked to the terms black and Neger)," p. 529. 1992: "The Negro Is A Man (Moses was a Colored man)," p. 8. 1903; "Al Koran (Moses was black skinned)," Sale, pp. 128, 257. 1784; "The Preaching of Islam (Moses was Black)," p. 106. 1896; "A Dictionary of Nick Names (Moss and Mose, the same as Moses are names for Negroes)," p. 71. 1963; and "The Bible Defense of Slavery," 1853.

Seti I, according to Rawlinson, had a strong "complete" African face with thick lips and a depressed nose. Rawlinson's comments are found in the following source: "The Story of Egypt," p. 252. London, 1887.

Moses experienced a startling event when God ordered him to put his hand into his bosom then withdraw it. Moses obeyed and after withdrawing his hand, discovered it to be "Leprous white." Then God instructed him to repeat the process, as he obeyed the white hand changed back to its original color (Ex. 4:6-7).

The Jewish Rabbi Silver commented: "Grannies, Sunday school teachers and movie producers can be forgiven if they view Moses to have been white complected. But world's scholars should know better, because Moses' culture and linage suggested him to be dark (black)." Rabbi Silver comments are found in the following source: "The Images of Moses," pp. 5-6. 1982.

The name Moses is pure Egyptian, and was not used in the Hebrew vocabulary until the birth of Moses ("The Ancient History of the Near East, Hall," p. 408. 1920; and "Moses and Monotheism," Freud).

Ex. Chap. 2-4; Num. 12:1.

ZIPPORAH: "BEAUTY"

Zipporah was an Ethiopian who married the prophet Moses, and was daughter of a Midian priest called Jethro or Raguel.

She happened to meet Moses during his exile from Egypt. As she and her six sisters went to draw water for their father's flock, they were harassed by herdsmen. Moses, being near, counteracted the men's ruthlessness and assisted the women with further chores.

Zipporah was given to Moses for the sake of good manners, Jethro's means of showing his appreciation. She bore the prophet two sons, Gershom and Eliezer. Their marriage endured, but there were some harsh disagreements between them; one can be attributed to circumcision, to which Zipporah was not accustomed, but managed to accept.

The Reverend Armistead called Zipporah, a "colored woman," Armistead's remarks are found in the following source: "The Negro is a Man," p.8. 1903.

The great Jewish historian Flavius Josephus, who was an eyewitness of Jesus Christ, states that Moses had a Negro (Ethiopian) wife prior to Zipporah. Josephus gives details by saying that Moses, while living in Egypt as the general of the army, led an invasion against Ethiopia. Following his conquest, the beautiful Tharbis, daughter of the Ethiopian king, promised to marry him if he showed kindness toward her people. Moses vowed to honor this request, and the wedding proceeded. Josephus' comments are found in the following source: "The life and Works of Flavius Josephus," by William Whiston, pp. 79-80, 1046. 1957.

The Negro-Ethiopians who resided in Arabia, for some mystic reason, frowned on circumcision; however, the Jewish Philo and Josephus both agreed that the practice of circumcision among the African Negroes was broad and very primitive, especially in the Land of Ethiopia and Egypt. Josephus went on to say that circumcision was learned by the Greeks from the Africans. Herodotus, Man, Vol. 5, p.175. supports Josephus.

Ex. 2: 16-22; 4:25-26; 18:24; Num. 12:1; Jer. 13:23.

PHINEHAS: "NEGRO"

Phinehas was a grandson of Aaron, son of Eleazar the high priest and great-Nephew of Moses (Ex. 6:25).* He manifested great zeal and was the third high priest of the Hebrews during and after the Exodus for nineteen years. The youthful Phinehas first appeared in Biblical history at the critical moment of the promiscuous idolatry of Shittim, where his faith and energy secured the cessation of the plague that was destroying the nation (Num. 25:14-15). For this he was honorably rewarded by the special approbation of God-Jehovah, and was given the promise that the high-priesthood should remain in his family forever. His posterity, with the exception of an interval from Eli to Zadok, was at the head of the priesthood until the destruction of the temple (Num. 25:10-13).

In retrospect during the life of his father Eleazar, the God fearing Phinehas held the position of superintendent of the Levites, and later became the high priest (Josh. 24:33), in which capacity he is presented as rendering the oracle of God to the nation during the entire war with the Benjamites (Benhamites), in regards to Gibeah (Judg. 20:28). Phinehas' grandfather Putiel was a descendant of the Ethiopian priest Jethro, whereas his Negress grandmother was an offshoot of Joseph.

The verse which ends the book of Joshua is ascribed by tradition to Phinehas, as the description of the death of Moses at the closure of Deuteronomy is to Joshua. The grave of Phinehas, which is shown at the village of Awertah, about four miles Southeast of Nablus, is a great place of resort to Jews, Samaritans and Christians.

*Phinehas was a Black or Nubian (Ethiopian). The name Phinehas is pure Egyptian meaning Negro or black skinned. The Jewish Babylonian Talmud: Sotah 43 Associate Phinehas' grandfather Putiel as a descendant of the Ethiopian Jethro. The above information is found in the following sources: The Ancient History of the Near East, Hall, pp. 408, 423, 435. 1920; Encyclopedia Biblica Cheyne, Vol. 3. p. 3304. 1902; Babylonian Talmud (Sotah 43a, Sanhedrin 82b; 9:9, 27b); and Encyclopedia Judaica, Vol. 13. pp. 466, 1415. 1971.

Ex. 6:25; Ezra 8:2; I Macc. 2:26, 53.

GERSHOM AND ELIEZER

Gershom and Eliezer were sons of Moses and Zipporah (the Cushite or Ethiopian); they were born in Midian during their father's forty-year refuge. When Moses returned to Egypt to free the Israelites, Gershom and Eliezer did not follow, but remained in Arabia with their mother and grandfather. They later joined their father, following the Exodus from Egypt.

Gershom and Eliezer were of mixed blood. Their mother was ink-black in color, for she was an Ethiopian (Negro).

According to M. Fishberg, the Biblical Cushites were Negroes, with whom the Jews freely mingled. Fishberg says, "The ancient Hebrews possessed largely Negro features such as woolly hair, dark skins, thick lips that folded, large heads, and projecting jaws." Fishberg's comments can be found in the following source: "American Anthropologist," Vol. 5, p. 89. 1903; and "The Jew," pp. 117, 120-134, 146-149, 174, 178, 181.

The Roman historian Tacitus says, "The Hebrews were people of Ethiopian origin (Book V, Chap. 2). Tacitus lived about 55-120 A.D. He wrote several books, and is considered to be one of the world's greatest historians.

Ex. 2: 21-22; 18: 2-4; I Chron. 23: 14-17; Hab. 3: 7.

HOBAB: "BELOVED"

The Ethiopian Hobab was the son of the Midian priest Jethro or Raguel; brother of Zipporah and brother-in-law of Moses. When the Israelite nation left Mt. Sinai in pursuit of Canaan, Moses pleaded with Hobab not to return with his father Jethro, but to remain as a chief scout, since he was knowledgeable of the area. Hobab honorably accepted this request, for which Moses was highly gratified (Num. 10:29-33; 11:4).

Hobab, Zipporah, Jethro and other Ethiopians whom resided in Midian (Arabia) were descendants of Ham through Cush (Gen. 10:6-8; Num. 12:1; Judg. 1:16; 4:11; II Chron. 21:16; Hab. 3:7).

The Arabian Ethiopians (Blacks) are also called Kenites. Further research has defined the word Kenite to mean Kemite, Kamite or Hamite, as well as "Smith" or expert metal workers of copper, since the Hebrew letters N and M were interchangeable. Hob- of Hobab means Hom or Ham, since the ancient letter B- of Hobab, was exchanged for M.

In ancient times, Arabia and all territories below the 45th parallel, west of China and east of Africa, were not called the "Middle East," but "Northeast Africa" or "Ham (as Hawaii and Alaska are called the United States or North America," by the Negro children of Ham, who settled those regions. They named the land after their God I Am (Cham) or Elohim (Eloham), which is the same as saying "Ham!" Volney says: "The Ethiopians had colonies all over Iraq-Arabia, as far as Persia. Mr. Baird and Dillon says: "Arabia was first called "Cush," and was often translated "Ethiopia." The book of Jasher calls Midian "the Land of Cush" (Gen. 14:5; Josh. 10:13; II Sam. I:18; Jasher 25:5; I Chron. 4:40; II Chron. 21:16; Hab. 3:7; The Original African Heritage Study Bible (Northeast Africa), pp. ix, xi. 1993; Volney"s New Researches on Ancient History, Volney, p. 179. 1856; The Family Bible, Baird and Dillon, 1884; and The Assyrian Grammar (B = M) , Delitzsch, pp. 35, 104, 112, 115-116. 1889).

JETHRO OR RAGUEL: "SUPERIORITY"

Jethro or Raguel (Reuel) was a Negro-Ethiopian Midianites shepherd-priest who resided in Arabia. He was the father of Zipporah and Hobab, grandfather of Gershom and Eliezer, and father-in-law of Moses. When the Israelites were at mount Sinai (Horeb), Jethro counseled Moses to select deputies to judge the tribes and share the burden of government with him, whereby the nation of Israel would be divided into units of thousands, hundreds, fifties, and tens with a leader over each unit. This advice, which was accepted by Moses, resolved much of his burden.

It is believed by some scholars that because of Jethro's local knowledge and devotion to Yahweh, prompted Moses to request his presence with Zipporah and Hobab during Israel's journey to Negro-Canaan. The Ethiopian Heber, who was a great descendant of Jethro through Hobab, was also a citizen of Negro-Canaan. From the word Heber (the same as Eber), derived the word Hebrew! (Judg. 4:11). While dwelling in Negro-Canaan, the Colored Ethiopians (same as Kenites) occupied a district called Chusi, the same as Cush, meaning Black or Ethiopia (Judith 7:18).

The word Jet- of Jethro means "Black," "Jet-black" or "Negro," whereas Ra- (Re) of Raguel indicates Egypt's Sun-God "Ra," who was none other than Ham.

Some scholars insist that the "Arabian Sheikh Jethro" was a Yahwistic priest, who introduced the Yahweh cult to Moses and Aaron. Referring to Exodus 6:3; 18:11 as a basic, the name Yahweh was unknown to Israel until the time of Moses' affiliation with his Ethiopian father-in-law, whom Moses and Aaron studied with! This concept constitutes that the Hebrew religion has Ethiopian (Midianites) roots; a belief based upon evidence that the name Yahweh is not a Hebrew word as preached by today's clergymen, but Egyptian! According to Park-Taylor and Baron, the names Yah, Weh and Yaho originated in Egypt.

The above information is found in the following sources: The Anchor Bible Dictionary; Doubleday, 1992; (Yahovah)= Yahweh: The Divine name in the Bible, G. Park-Taylor, pp. 49, 71. 1975; and A Social and Religious History of the Jews, Baron, Vol. 1, p. 352. 1952.

Ex. 2:18, 21-22; 3:1, 4:18; 18:1-27; Num. 10:29, 31, 33: Judg. 1:16.

VI

THE INTRUSION OF CANAAN

Sihon: "Rooted Out"

Sihon was a Hamitic Amorite king of Heshbon, the chief city of Sihon; he conquered the Moabites and became ruler of their land. When Israel requested a safe passage through his kingdom, Sihon rejected their request. Instead, he gathered all his people to suppress Israel. They fought at Jahaz, where Sihon was overthrown. His defeat was a triumph for Israel. They took all of his settlements and divided them among the tribes of Ruben, Gad and Manasseh.

Rabbi Epstein says, "The nations of Africa strongly disfavored the Jewish occupation of Canaan, by declaring to Alexander the Great that the Land of Canaan was originally African soil;" as it is written, the Land of Canaan with the coasts thereof, Canaan was the father of the people (Babylonian Talmud: Sanhedrin).

*In ancient times, Africa was the largest Continent, consisting of all territories below the 45th parallel, west of China and east of the Red Sea. The regions of Israel, Lebanon, Jordan, Syria, the Hittite Empire, Ararat, the Arabian peninsula, Iraq, Kuwait, Persia (Iran), Afghanistan (once part of Persia), India, Pakistan (once part of India), were not called the "Middle East," or "Asia," but "Northeast Africa" or "Ham," by the Negro children of Ham, who settled those regions. Volney says: "The Ethiopians had colonies all over Iraq-Arabia, as far as Persia," whereas Maclear agreed by saying: "Ham's children occupied Africa, the peninsulas of Asia, India and Arabia;" He went on to say that Cush settled Babylon.

During World War II the Near East, the same as Northeast Africa, was renamed "Middle East" by European corespondents. The title "Middle East" is a corrupted phrase applied to avoid the usage of "Northeast Africa." In the future the name Africa will vanish, later inheriting the corrupted term relating to the "Middle East." Presently, all of Northern Africa, including Sudan and Somalia are geographically renamed "Middle East" The Original Africa Heritage Study Bible, 1992: ix, xi, also Special Contributions and Appreciations; Volney's New Researches On Ancient History, 1856: 179; Maclear, A primer of old Testament History, 1969: 4; www.fctp.couk/whatismiddleeast.asp; www.Nigerdeltacongress.com/barticles/blackman.htm; www.godonthe.net/wasblack.htm; and freearabvoice.org/yesWeSupportPeace.htm).

Gen. 10:16; Num. 21:13-27; Deut. 1:4; 29:7-8; Josh. 13: 8-19, 15-28.

BITHIAH

Bithiah was a daughter of Pharaoh Seti I and sister of Ramesses II.* She accompanied the Israelites during the Exodus and became wife of Mered the Judahite, an ancestor of Jesus the Christ. The princess' matrimony with Mered indicates that he was probably a person of some distinction. The couple had several children who settled in the Negro Land of Canaan (I Chron. 4:1, 18).

It is obvious to believe that Jesus who was from the tribe of Judah visited His African relatives through Bithiah while residing in Egypt (Ho: 11:1; Ps. 68:31; Matt. 2:13-15).

Some scholars have alleged that Bithiah was the same princess who rescued Moses form the Nile. Bithiah's brother Ramesses, who was a pure black African with thick lips and a broad nose, became the fourth Pharaoh of the Nineteenth-Egyptian Dynasty. The flamboyant Ramesses was a warlike, industrious and energetic King who ruled Negro-Egypt for sixty-seven years. He had over two-hundred wives, ninety-six sons and sixty daughters.

I Chron. 4:1, 18.

OG: "GIANT"

King Og was an Amorite ruler of the strategic city Bashan, which was well-fortified with high walls and a ready army. Og never dreamed such an insufficient force as Israel could annihilate him, so he prepared for battle and met them at his chief city Edrei. There he fought, expecting a major victory, but instead experienced the agony of defeat. His territories, like Sihon's, were separated among the tribes of Israel.

King Og was one of the last remnant giantlike kings. His bedstead amazed Moses: its dimensions were thirteen feet by six feet, and it was made of iron (Deut. 3: 11). He had an enormous build!

Og, like Sihon, was a black, a great descendant of Ham, through Canaan (Gen. 10: 6, 15-16).

The Hebrew guerilla warfare of Canaan triggered great resentment, causing hundreds of thousands of Negro Canaanites to exile to Africa.

*"We are exiles who were rulers of Canaan, but were pushed from our land by Joshua the robber. We have come to reside here."**

The only modern tribe, like the Negro Biblical Rephaim (Gen. 15: 18-20, a tall tribe of Negro giants), known to be of giant stature is the Negro "Watusi" now living in east-central Africa. The average height of these people is over seven feet and six inches. There are no other races on earth which grow to such heights.

Since the Land of Canaan (now called Palestine) was territorially adjoined to Africa, many black giantlike Canaanites fled the land during Israel's intrusion. They migrated south and settled in central Africa where they gradually decreased in height, due to crossbreeding with people of smaller stature.

*W. Whiston (1667-1752), *The Works of Josephus*, p. 110. 1981.

Gen. 10: 16; Num. 21: 33-35; Deut. 3: 1; Josh. 13: 12, 29-31; Isa. 19: 18.

RAHAB: "PROUD"

Rahab was a black woman from a Canaanite city called Jericho, which was surrounded by such popular Hamite cities as Gibeon, Beeroth and Jerusalem.

When Joshua sent spies into Rahab's city, she hid them in a thread stock on her roof. Rahab had heard about these Jews and their God who rescued them from Africa and subdued their foes in Canaan. Moreover, she knew her people could not withstand their strength, so out of fear, Rahab concealed the spies and began to bargain with them concerning security. She pleaded with them to spare her and other kinsmen during the seizure of Jericho. This request was approved by the two men in regard to her courtesy.

After the spies completed their mission, Rahab hauled them down by a scarlet thread through her window and advised them to hide themselves within the mountains for three days to avoid their pursuers. But before they departed, they cautioned her that upon their return, she should remain in her quarters with a scarlet cord hanging from her window, and that her life and her kinsmen's lives would not be spared if she revealed their business to the king. Now when Rahab confirmed all that was said, she and other relatives made final arrangements.

When the messengers journeyed to camp and notified Joshua of their experience, he instantly prepared his people to overthrow Jericho, for God had instructed him as to the manner in which to take the city. He was to march around it six times once a day. Then on the seventh day he was to encompass it seven times with the sound of trumpets and a loud shout. So when Joshua did as told, the walls of Jericho fell to the earth, and only Rahab, "the harlot," and a few kinsmen were spared.

Rahab lived among the Israelites, and there she married a Jew by the name of Salmon (an ancestor of Jesus Christ), who fathered her a child named Boaz.

Gen. 9: 18; Jos. 2: 1; 6: 1; I Chron. 2: 11-13; Ruth 4: 21; Matt.1:5.

ARBA: "FOUR"

Arba was a giant Canaanite who became the progenitor of a super giant race called Anakim. In Josh. 14:15, Arba is called the "great man" among the Anakim. His son Anak, meaning "long neck," was also instrumental in producing this giant race.

The Anakim inhabited the mountainous regions of Canaan, and their chief city was found in Kirjath-arba, later called Hebron, and it was here that the twelve Hebrew spies first saw them. The Anakim's gigantic stature caused great panic among the Israelites, as they alleged these giants as being descendants of the pre-Flood Nephilim, and when comparing sizes, the Hebrews considered themselves as grasshoppers (Num. 13:33; Deut. 1:28).* The Anakim's enormous strength (Num. 13:28-32) obviously produced the proverbial saying: "Who can stand before the children of Anak (Deut. 9:1-3)?"

When Joshua advanced through Canaan with the help of Yahweh-Elohim (Eloham), the Negro Anakim were pushed from the mountains to the coastal areas of the Negro Philistines. They soon afterward regained some of their territory, which was later reconquered by Caleb, who also seized their chief city Hebron.

The great Anakim was a Negro-giant race from Ham, through Canaan. The most popular individuals of the Anakim, besides Arba and Anak, were Ahiman, Sheshai and Talmai (Num. 13:22). There were other Negro-giant groups called Zamzummim or Zuzim, Emin and Rephaim (Gen. 14:5; Deut. 2:10-11, 20-21).

In general, the Negro Anakim were half terrestrial and celestial, since falling angels who were called the sons of God, came unto the beautiful Black daughters of Ham through Canaan, and bored children of them, who became giants, an ancient variant of "the mighty men of old" (Gen. 6:4). The name Anak is a translation of falling angels called Nephilim. King Og, Goliath and his brothers, and many giantlike Egyptians, who had six fingers on each hand and six toes on each foot, were also called Nephilim or Rephaim (Shade).

When the Hebrew first entered Canaan-Land, they did not encounter a Semitic or Caucasian race, but a Hamitic-Negro race from Canaan.

The tallest race in the world is the Negro "Watusi," now living in east-central Africa. They resemble the giants in the Bible more than any other people, with long necks and heights over seven feet and six inches. The Semites and Caucasians have never produced a giantlike race. Therefore, the indigenous people of Canaan, with their extraordinary stature, long necks, etc., could not have possibly been Semites or Caucasians, but were Negroes from Ham, who bored and produced these giantlike characteristics to this day.

Gen. 6:4; 14:5; Deut. 2:10-11, 20-21; 3:11; Josh. 12:4; 17:15; I Chron. 11:23; I Sam. 17:4; II Sam. 21:20.

ADONI-ZEDEC: "LORD OF JUSTICE"

Adoni-Zedec was king of Jerusalem during Israel's invasion. When the cities of Jericho and Ai fell into the hand of Israel, Gibeon, a Hivite city, betrayed Adoni-Zedec by siding with Joshua. This alliance angered the king to seek vengeance upon the Gibeonites, and with four Amorite kings he formed a federation to destroy them. The Gibeonites knew they were outnumbered, so they asked Joshua for military support, which was granted.

The battle took place near Makkedah, where King Adoni-Zedec's forces took an early defeat. Israel and Gibeon, by the hand of Yahweh, slew them by the thousands. It came to pass as they fled, Yahweh cast great stones from heaven upon them, which killed more than Israel slew with her swords.

King Adoni-Zedec and the four Amorite kings fled with fear* and hid themselves in a cave at Makkedah. They were soon apprehended and slain.

The Jabins, who were Negro generals of Hazor (Josh. 11: 1), offered much resistance to the Hebrew invasion of Canaan. The latter Jabin opposed the intruders for twenty years (Judg. 4: 1–3; Psa. 83: 9).

* N. Slouschz, *Travels in North Africa.* Philadelphia: Jewish Publication Society of America, (Canaanites were Africans . . .). p. 337. 1927.

Josh. 10: 1–27.

JAPHIA: "SPLENDOR"

Japhia was an Amorite king of Lachish, who joined king Adoni-zedek's league against Gibeon (a city occupied by Black Hivites and Amorites). He was captured and executed by Joshua near Makkedah cave.

It is written in a Hebrew book called the "Babylonian Talmud" that the Negro-Canaanites in Africa made a plea to Alexander the Great to restore to them the Land of Canaan, which had been taken from their forefathers by Joshua ben Nun.*

According to the 1884 edition of "The Family Bible," pp. 1, 3, by Baird and Dillon, all of Canaan was originally part of Africa (Ethiopia), which at a later period became independent.

**Babylonian Talmud*, Sanhedrin 91-A.

Gen. 10: 16; Josh. 10: 3-27.

PIRAM: "FLEET"

Piram was an Amorite king of Jarmuth who helped four neighboring kings invade Gibeon. The group was defeated by Israel. He fled to a cave near Makkedah where he and his comrades were slain and hanged by Joshua. His body was buried in the cave in which he was captured.

Piram, Japhia and their superior Adoni-Zedek were Hamites, great descendants of Ham through Canaan (Gen. 10: 6, 15, 16).

On numerous ancient Egyptian monuments the Amorites are pictured as a tall race with black skins, woolly hair, and dark brown eyes.

Jehovah, while devastating the Amorites, says that their height was like the height of cedars, and they were strong as the oaks (Amos 2: 9; Deut. 7: 1).

Gen. 10: 16; Josh. 10: 3-27.

ADONI-BEZEK: "LORD OF BEZEK"

Adoni-Bezek was a Hamitic king of a Canaanite city named Bezek.* He conquered many petty kings, and his inhuman tactics caused much horror. He was notorious for having amputated the thumbs and toes of seventy conquered kings and forcing his captives to eat food under his tables.

When the men of Judah and Simeon made war with Bezek and Perizzite, King Adoni-Bezek was defeated and received the same treatment he had imposed on other kings. During his captivity he announced: "As I have done, so God hath requited me."

The Negro Canaanites being the children of Noe or Noah from Ham, were aware of Yahweh's entity, but chose not to worship Him. Instead, they clung to the gods of Baal, Baalot, Adonis, etc. Many of these deities were frequently praised by the Hebrews. Solomon worshipped many Negro-Canaanite gods, including the goddess Ashtoreth. The Hebrew people were basically an idolatrous race, and since the Exodus had worshipped abominable images (Deut. 9: 12, 32: 21; Judg. 17: 3; I Kings 11: 5-8, 33; 14; 8-9; II Kings 17: 9-12, 16; II Chron. 33: 7; Ps. 106: 19). In Deuteronomy 18: 10-11, Moses strictly warned the Hebrews to avoid consultation with a necromancer (A person who is supposed to predict the future by communicating with the dead; black magic-witchcraft), a warning that King Saul totally ignored (I Sam. 28: 1-25)! The expression necromancer is equivalent to the Medieval Latin nigromantia and the Greek nekromanteia. According to the Oxford English Dictionary, the term necromancer is synonymous to the words Negro, Nygra, Nigre, Negre, Nigra, Nygro and Necro. Nigrocromancy was also practiced by the Greeks.

The Canaanite religion was the religion which Israel encountered while entering the Land of Canaan. The Israelites incorporated much of the Canaanites beliefs into their culture, popular lore and literature, which has a tremendous impact upon today's Bible.

Within the Canaanite pantheon, God El is their chief God, whose title reads, "The Creator of Creatures," "The Father of Mankind," "The Bull," "The High God," and "The King," long before Abraham was born. The Israelites borrowed the title El to indicate God-Yahweh-Elohim (Eloham). They referred to God as "Creator," "Father," "Ox (Alpha)," "Lamb," "The Most High God," and "Hammeleck," meaning "King."

El was described by the Canaanites as an old man, dwelling in a remote place called "The Sources of the two Deeps," where He received suppliants and sent intructions by messengers.

Even though the Israelite religion was heavily composed of the Canaanite practices, it nevertheless possessed a character of its own, which wasn't compliant with the Canaanites. Israel's refusal to observe some Canaanite practices, was based upon its extremity to Yahwism. However, regardless of this withdrawment, the Israelite religion still had a strong background of the Canaanite culture. The borrowing of the Canaanite sacred poetry, music and architecture, was the organ of the Israelite religion.

Israel's obsession with the Canaanite religion was probably influenced by the fact of the two people speaking the same language, "Canaanite," also called Hebrew. Godbey reminds us of a Hamitic Hebrew speaking people living in Palestine about a thousand years before Abraham. Dr. William Smith identifies the Semitic language as Negritian (Negro), spoken by the Hebrews, which constituted the reason ancient historians believed them to be Hamites.

The above information is found in the following sources: The Lost Tribes: A Myth, Godbey, pp. 37, 50, 57, 61. 1930; Dr. William Smith's Dictionary of the Bible (Hebrew is Nigritian), Vol. 2, p. 985. 1890; From Babylon to Timbuktu (Hebrew is a Canaanite language), Windsor, pp. 28-29. 1986; Echoes of the Old Darkland (Hebrew is an African language), Finch, pp. 136,144.1991; Egypt's Place (the language Khamism), Bunsen, Book 5,1854; Ethiopia and The Missing Link in African History (Hebrew is African), Means, pp. 20-21. 1980; and Man and his Migration R. G. Latham (The Semitic Language is African), pp. 156-157.

R.R.Windsor, From Babylon to Timbuktu (Canaanites were Africans), p. 28. 1973.

Judg. 1: 3-7.

VII

THE NEGROES OF JUDGES AND RUTH

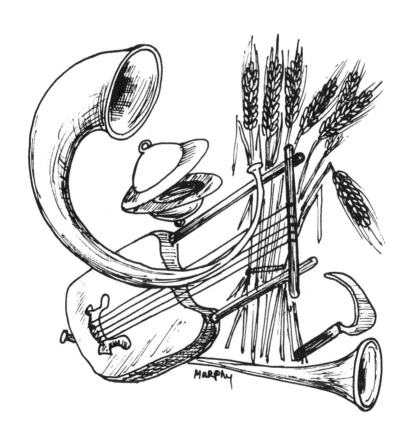

Cushan Rishathaim: "Blackness"

Cushan Rishathaim, a king of Mesopotamia while Israel commenced to sin before heaven, was steered by Jehovah to overrun Israel because of her transgressions. He governed her for eight years before being dispossessed by Othniel, Caleb's nephew.

King Cushan Rishathaim was Israel's first major oppressor following the Exodus. He was Hamitic in origin and a great descendant of the Negro "Cush," same as Ethiopia.

The Greek Herodotus, of 447 B.C., known as the father of history, clearly stated that the ancient inhabitants of Mesopotamia were Black. The Ethiopians, Persians and Babylonians, says Herodotus, were of the same family linguistically, ethnographically and historically.

According to sir Arthur Keith's research on the Mount Carmel excavations for the Royal College of Surgeons, the inhabitants of Persia and southern Mesopotamia seem to have been members of a black-skinned, wide-nosed, and woolly-haired race.

Gen. 10: 6, 15; Judg. 3: 7-10.

ZEBAH: "SACRIFICE"
ZALMUNNA: "SHADY"

Zebah and Zalmunna were two Midianite princes from northern Arabia (Ethiopians lived in Midian. II Chron. 21: 16; Hab. 3: 7. See page 40). For years they masterminded continual raids on Israel, until the people were nearly hopeless in defense. They destroyed Israel's crops and animals, making the people so weak that they fled to caves in the mountains.

The strength of Zebah and Zalmunna was similar to that of Zerah, the Ethiopian of Africa. These men were uncontrollable until there arose Gideon (who was divinely-led), who with three hundred men surrounded the camp of Zerah and Zalmunna, then attacked them with loud shouting and trumpet sounds. This sudden assault with loud noises frightened the two princes into becoming incompetent commanders. They escaped the massacre on camelback into a land near Jordan but were soon apprehended and slain by Gideon.

According to the 1884 edition of "The Family Bible" pp. 7-11, by Baird and Dillon, Arabia was first called "Cush," and was often translated "Ethiopia."

In ancient times, Arabia by land was connected to Ethiopia (Africa), but later separated by the formation of the Red Sea, leaving it solely linked to Egypt, which in modern times was completely disconnected by the construction of the Suez Canal.

Judg. 8: 5-21; Hab. 3:7.

ABIMELECH OF SHECHEM

Abimelech was of mixed blood; his mother was a Hivite and his father was an Israelite ruler who sired seventy-one sons (Judges 8: 31 mentions Abimelech's mother as a concubine from Shechem. Shechem was a country occupied by black people of Ham, Hivites. One of its earlier rulers was Hamor, the Hivite, who was a descendant of Ham. Genesis 10: 15–17, 34: 2. See page 53. Abimelech's mother was from the Hivite "stock." That is why Abimelech in Judges 9: 28 is called a man of Hamor).

After his father's death, he and his mother started a family feud against his half-brothers. He reminded her of his odds against becoming king, since he was a half-blooded Israelite. Abimelech convinced her to side with him, since he was of her race (Judg. 9: 2–3, 18), so she did, and with many kin dealt treacherously, killing sixty-nine of his brothers. This slaughter made him sole heir to the throne, except for Jotham, who escaped.

God was not pleased with Abimelech's devious ways, so He sent an evil spirit between him and his people. His influence grew weak with them, and there arose much rivalry to his throne. Naturally, with an army he found little resistance.

He killed many countrymen for trivial reasons; then one day, as Abimelech attempted to seize a tower, an unknown woman threw a millstone upon him which crushed his skull. Abimelech knew he was critically wounded, so he ordered his armor-bearer to strike him with a sword so that it would not be known that a woman had slain him.

Gen. 10: 17; Judg. 8:31; 9: 1.

DELILAH: "Poor"

From the valley of Sorek, Delilah was a Philistine woman whose glamorous beauty caused Samson to fall in love with her during the time the Philistines occupied that region. She was often approached by Philistine lords with an offering of eleven hundred pieces of silver to discover the secret of Samson's enormous strength. Delilah, after discovering Samson's hair as the source of his strength, wasted no time to inform her superiors, and as they waited in her chamber, she put Samson to sleep and shaved his head, which reduced his strength to that of a common man. The Philistines then took full advantage of Samson and made him a prisoner.

Delilah was a black woman from the bloodline of Mizraim (Egypt), the father of the Philistines.

Ludwig Kohler says that Hebrews possessed flat and pug noses, and that Samson's hair was not in locks as the Biblical translators write, but in plaits (an African custom). The 1884 edition of "The Family Bible," by Baird and Dillon, which contains the identical books of the King James Version, with additional books called Apocrypha, states in the book of Judith 10: 3, that Judith braided her hair. Jews within Samson's era were none other than the Negro type with black skins and woolly hair.

The name Samson is actually spelled Hamson (Ham-Son), since the ancient letter S was exchanged for H. The above information is found in the following source: Hebrew Man, Kohler, pp. 16, 24. 1956; and A Comparative Grammar of the Semitic Languages (S is changed to K, C and H; the S becomes Th), O'Leary, pp. 56, 59, 61-62, 89, 221. 1923.

I Chron. 1: 8, 11-12: Judg. 16: 4-20.

NAPPY DIVINE HAIR

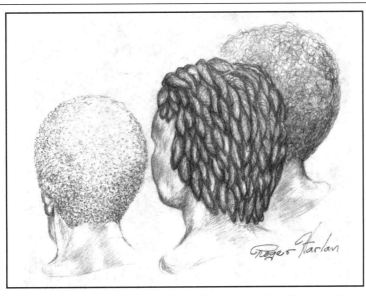

God and His Son Jesus possessed nappy hair according to Daniel 7:9 and Revelation 1:14-15. This woolly, kinky, coiled, curly, bushy, frizzy, wired, spiral, crispy, twisted, spring-like uneasy hair was styled by God Himself, whereas all the founders of the religious world, including pagan deities shared the same characteristic. Jesus was a Nazarite which according to the antiquarians the Nazarenes were accustomed to wear a parted burdensome crop of uncut long twisted plaited hair.* Such description bears a striking resemblance to the rope like braids called dreadlocks (Num. 6:2, 5; Lev. 19:25; 21:5). The two most famous Biblical characters, other than Jesus to be identified with woolly hair and dreadlocks, are Solomon and Samson (Solomon 5:11; Judg. 13:5; 16:17, 19).

*The word Nazarene was first called Nezer, meaning Neger, since the Semitic Z was exchanged for S, the S for H and the H for G. The Etruscan and Latin G was applied to replace the Greek Z. The Ancient name Neger, before there existed a great European power, meant God, King and Supreme! The Egyptians called God "N-g-r (Nigger, Negger, Neger, Niger, etc.)," before the existence of vowels.

The above information is found in the following sources: An Introduction to the Comparative Grammar of the Semitic Languages (S=H, whereas the S=Z), Moscati, pp. 35, 104, 153. 1964; Assyrian Grammar (G=M and H), Deltzsch, pp. 105, 115. 1898; A Dictionary of Jewish Surnames From the Russian Empire (G=H), 1993; Reading the Past: Etruscan, Bonfante; Hebrew Man, Kohler, pp. 16, 24. 1956; Roget's 21st Century Thesaurus (bushy means woolly), Kipfer, p. 112. 1992; Strong's Exhaustive Concordance: No. 5139-5145; Enciclopedia Universal Sopena (Negus means Negro), Sexto, Vol. 6, p. 5947. 1964; Portuguese-English Dictionary (Nego means Negro), Taylor, 1970: 440; Grande Dicionario Etimologico-Prosodico Da Lingua Portuguesa (Nego means Negar), Vol. 6, p. 2604. 1966; Cleveland Bible Commentary (Nego was also pronounced Nebo); Unger's Bible Dictionary (Abed-Nego; Nebo, a Babylonian God), pp. 2, 781.1957; Webster's New Collegiate Dictionary (Negus means King of Kings), p. 762. 1981; and An Egyptian Hieroglyphic Dictionary (N-ger-s). Budge, Vol. 1, p. 341. 1978.

BOAZ: "LOVELY"

Boaz was a half-blooded Bethlehemite whose mother was an offspring of Ham and whose father was of the Hebrew "stock."

Boaz was a wealthy landowner who capitalized in grain. One day as he toured his fields, he saw a beautiful Moabitess named Ruth gleaning his crops. He showed her considerate kindness and gave her privileges beyond that of a gleaner.

Boaz afterward married Ruth, and she bore him a son, Obed, the great-grandsire of King Solomon.

The Reverend Armistead called Boaz, a "colored man." Armistead's remarks are found in the following source: "The Negro is a Man." p. 9. 1903.

According to Barbot, Jews in Spain and Portugal were so black that whites often mistook all Jews to be black. How erroneous, he says, "The Jews in Germany and Prague are as white as their counterparts;[1] M. Fishberg, who visited Africa during the early 1900s, says that while strolling the streets of Algiers, he couldn't distinguish the Jews from the Mohammedans, and that many were of the Negro type;[2] N. Slouschz, the white Jewish rabbi, says that down the eastern borders of Algeria, settled a large group of black Jews; A Godbey said that in Algeria, in the range of 350 miles from the Mediterranean Sea, existed an area of Jews who were black as Negroes.

Ruth 4: 13, 20-22; Matt. 1: 5-6.

NAOMI: "PLEASANT"

Naomi was wife of Elimelech, mother of Mahlon and Chilion, and mother-in-law of Ruth. She left Judea in the days of the Judges with her husband and two sons because of a famine, and went to the land of Moab, where her husband and sons died. This sudden mishape compelled her to return to Bethlehem with Ruth.

Naomi was long spoken of by the women of her district, as the mother (grandmother) of Obed, the father of Jesse, who was David's father (David, the father of the Colored King Solomon). Obed was a son of the Moabitess Ruth and the Negro man Boaz, whose mother was a Canaanite Negress, named Rahab (Matt. 1: 5).

The Reverend Armistead says, "Boaz was part Negro through his Negress mother Rahab." The above information is found in the following source: "The Negro is a Man," p. 130. 1903.

Ruth 1: 1-22; 2:1-23; 3:1-18; 4:1-22.

VIII

AGE OF THE GREAT WARRIORS

GOLIATH: "SPLENDOR"

Goliath, a Philistine giant warrior who lived during the time of King Saul, was highly known for his temper, which terrified Israel. Goliath had an extraordinary physique and abilities, his height was ten and a half feet, and he could mobilize himself with an armor weighing over one hundred fifty-six pounds. One day as he and his comrades were patrolling the surrounding area, they mysteriously stumbled upon some Israelites at Ephes-dammins. The two forces camped across from one another on two mountains divided by a valley, and that same day Goliath came forth, boasting about his strength and double-daring any Israelite to challenge him. This continued for forty days before a Bethlehemite stepped forward. When the giant saw his opponent was only a child, he became disdainful, feeling it was ridiculous to send a boy to fight a warrior of his stature. He then threatened the child with a vow to give his flesh to the fowl of the air and the beasts of the field.

When the hour of showdown arrived, the lad ran toward the huge man with a slingshot that projected stones. He then whirled the slingshot above his head and released a stone, which struck Goliath's forehead, causing Goliath to fall.

The outcome of the contest saddened the Philistines as they stood watching their hero slumped over with his head in the Bethlehemite's hands. They became frightened and fled.

This fallen Philistinian hero was a descendant of Ham. His lineage was from Mizraim, whose seed produced the Philistine race.

*Herodotus said that while visiting Africa, he saw some of the blackest and tallest men of all men.**

There have been reports of seeing Ethiopians who were twelve feet tall. Probably an exaggeration, but they do support Herodotus' claim of seeing Africans who were the tallest men on earth.

The Negro children of Ham acquired exceedingly thick craniums enabling them to butt their heads and resist blows which would inevitably break any ordinary European's skull. This ability to absorb tremendous blows has been illustrated throughout the ages, particularly within sports such as boxing, which was invented by blacks along the banks of the Nile.

The great Negro pugilist Nicaeus, the brown bomber of antiquity, with his swiftness and daring, astounded the Roman empire and won fame throughout the world. Frank M. Snowden writes of a black huntsman named Olympius. He describes him as a Herculean whose name was a synonym for success, and whose victories were innumerable. The ancient Hamites were known for their strength and undaunted courage. The children of Ham have lost much of their height and strength due to mixed breeding.

The 1884 edition of "The Family Bible," by Baird and Dillon, which contains the identical books of the King James Version, with additional texts called Apocrypha, states in the book of Baruch 3: 26, that there were giants famous from the beginning, of so great stature, and so expert in war.

R. Pinney commented that the Negro giant Watusi was a heroic figure who walked with his head high, bigger than life. He rose to dominance through his own intelligence, skill and strength, becoming a powerful ruler with an army that destined him to be a master rather than a slave. But finally, because of his own arrogance and pride, he was overthrown and destroyed. Pinney's remarks can be found in the following source: "Vanishing Tribes," pp. 46-47. 1968.

*The Negro Sabeans, who were descendants of Seba through Cush, are mentioned in Isa. 45: 14 as tall men.

Gen. 10: 6, 13-14; 1 Chron. 1: 8, 11-12; 1 Sam. 17: 1.

AHIMELECH: "FRIEND OF THE KING"

Ahimelech was a friend of David during the antagonism of King Saul. One evening, Ahimelech and Abishai were confronted by young David concerning an intriguing plan to enter Saul's camp while he lay asleep. This plan was favored by Abishai, but Ahimelech, knowing the king's strength, opposed it and chose not to journey with them.

Ahimelech was a Hittite, a descendant of Canaan's second son "Heth."

The Negro Hittites were described by the Egyptian and Assyrian monuments as a great race of the North, whose shrewd army was feared for its valor and size, capable of coping with Assyria, Egypt or any earthly power. The Hamitic Hittites were a sturdy race of men, mostly pictured as beardless. During the Israelite intrusion of Canaan, Joshua was unable to subdue them; neither was David, Solomon, nor any other Judaen king. The black Hittites remained a powerful nation during the Jewish transportation to Babylon as captives, and retained this prominence for an additional two centuries.

Gen.10: 6, 15; I Sam. 26: 6-7.

URIAH: "JEHOVAH IS LIGHT"

Uriah was a Hittite living in Jerusalem as one of David's captains. Not a Hebrew, but a worshipper of Jehovah, as can be verified by his name. He was a descendant of Canaan's second son Heth, whose name is interpreted as "Hittite."* Uriah was very loyal to king David and probably was one of David's finest fighting men. He and his superior officer Joab, were at Rabbath fighting the Amonites while his beautiful black wife, Bathsheba, remained in Jerusalem.

One day as she proceeded to bathe, King David saw her from his rooftop and commanded her presence. When Bathsheba appeared, he seduced her and she conceived a child. David knew Uriah was her lawful husband and felt guilty about his action. So he fetched Uriah from battle and questioned him about Joab and their situation. Soon he sent him back to Rabbath with a sealed letter to Joab which read; "Put Uriah on the forefront of the hottest battle and retire ye from him that he may be smitten and die." The following day, Uriah fell dead by David's order.

This faithful man had fought many battles for King David and obeyed orders without question. But his beautiful wife, whom King David loved, cost him his life.

Culture and History of the Black Experience (Sept. 1974 issue of "The Message Magazine"), Uriah, a son of Ham, p. 6.

II Sam. 11: 14-27.

CUSHI: "ETHIOPIA"

Cushi, a servant of David who was named after his country Cushi, was a foreigner serving in the king's army under Joab.

When David's favorite son, Absalom, revolted against him, Cushi was among Israel's army which crushed the young man, soon afterward resulting in the death of Absalom. Cushi was ordered by Joab to run the plains and notify David concerning his son's tragedy.

Ethiopia led the world in mathematics, engineering, medicine, and agriculture. For centuries Cush kept an edge over emerging powers in government, war and conquest. Historians credit it as a land of heroism and brilliance.

The Greek Herodotus and Homer both agreed that Ethiopians were remote, and their empires were extraordinarily wide places where the sun never set.

II Sam. 18:21–32.

Subay: "Officer"

There were several black officers serving within David's army and hundreds of thousands of warriors who helped Israel in neighboring wars. Following the Davidic-Solomonic period, Israel also had several African allies. One was Ethiopia (II Kings 19: 9).

In ancient times there was a steady political relationship amongst the black people of Africa and Israel.

The Negro Ethiopians had developed a giant civilization about 200 years before Abraham (father of the Hebrew race) was born (Gen. 10: 6, 8, 10), over 1,000 years before the first book of the Bible was written. The Negro Egyptians who learned much of their civilization from their southern cousins,"the Ethiopians," were at the height of their glory when the Hebrews (who at that period had no country or government of their own, and were living in a relatively savage state) chose to reside in Egypt (Gen. 45: 17-20, 46: 5-6, 47: 1, 11, 27). Not long afterward, the Negro Egyptians enslaved the Israelites (Ex. 1: 1-14) and kept them in bondage for 430 years. Only forty years following the Exodus from Egypt was Israel able to form her own nation and government in the Land of Canaan, a land that was preowned by the Negro Canaanites (Gen. 10: 6, 15-20; Ex. 33: 1-2; Josh. 3: 10). Centuries later, David and Solomon formed Israel's first empire, which lasted four hundred thirty years following the death of Solomon.

Much of Israel's rudiments of war and government were borrowed from "Ham" Africa. The dark-skinned Moses, who for forty years had thought of himself as a Negro (the son of a black Pharaoh), studied the social, political and natural sciences of Egypt (Acts 7: 22), knowledge that he later passed on to Israel.

ISMAIAH: "YAHWEH HEARS"

Ismaiah was a Gibeonite warrior who joined David's military at Ziklag. He soon became a member of David's thirty mighty men, and afterward their captain.

The Gibeonites were from a great city called Gibeon (Josh. 10: 2), which was inhabited by the Amorites and Hivites. During Israel's early intrusion of Canaan, these Gibeonites became the first Blacks to serve under the slave-curse pronounced on Canaan.

The Negro-Canaanites were a powerful, renowned people of a magnificent civilization that had stood the test of ages, previous to Abraham, who was the father of the Hebrews. When the Israelites reached Kadesh-Barnea, under the leadership of Moses, spies were sent into the land. Their report to Moses described the Canaanites as being strong with walled cities that were great (Num 13: 28). Moses and Joshua perceived the Negroes of Canaan to be rich and superior, a leverage Israel attained three centuries later under the reign of Saul, David and Solomon.

The name Amorite literally means "high one," however, the word is generally suppose to mean highlanders (Num. 13: 29; Deut. 1: 7, 20; Josh. 10: 3). In the Tel-el-Amana tablets, as well as in the Babylonian and Assyrian texts, the name is recorded "Amurra," whereas the country being "Amurri." The Egyptians called the word, "Amur," whereby the Hebrews, "Emer" and "Amir," and the Sumerians, "Mar.Tu." The Babylonians, as far back as the great Akkadian leader Sargon, referred to Palestine and Syria as the land of the Amorites. The name Amorite is the same as the Amorites who invaded Mesopotamia and Syria about 2000 B.C.

During the period of the Tel-el-Amarna (1400 B.C.), the domicile of the Amorites was described as inland territory, located north of Canaan, however, in the Old Testament, and in some secular material, the Negro Amorite appeared to be the majority in the land of Canaan, having applied their name to the entire population of the country (Josh. 24: 8). The Tel-el-Amarna letters defined Amurri as Palestine-Phoenicia.

The Negro Amorites also dwelled east, north and south of Canaan. In northern and southern Canaan the Amorites and Hittites were interlocked; even with the Hebrews as they frequently intermixed (Ezra 9: 2; Ezek. 16: 3).

The Amorite's last hostile battle with Israel occurred near the waters of Merom (Josh. 11: 1- 14). They were at complete peace with Israel during the era of Samuel (I Sam. 7: 14). Solomon levied on the Amorites and other Canaanite nations a tribute of bond service (I Kings 9: 20-21), and following his era, the remnant Amorites were rarely mentioned.

God-Elohim spoke of the Amorite as having the height of the cedars, and were as strong as the oaks (Amose 9: 2; Deut. 7: 1).

On the Egyptian Monuments the Amorites are depicted as a tall people with black skin, woolly hair and dark brown eyes.

The most noticable black Amorities in the Bible are Og (king of Bashan), Sihon (king of Heshbon), Japhia (king of Lachish) and Piram (king of Jarmuth).

Gen. 10: 15-17; Josh. 9: 3-9, 11-2 7; 10: 1, 6; II Chron. 12: 1,4.

IX

DIPLOMATIC AND SOCIAL DEALINGS AMONG AFRICA, THE CANAANITE NATIONS, AND ISRAEL

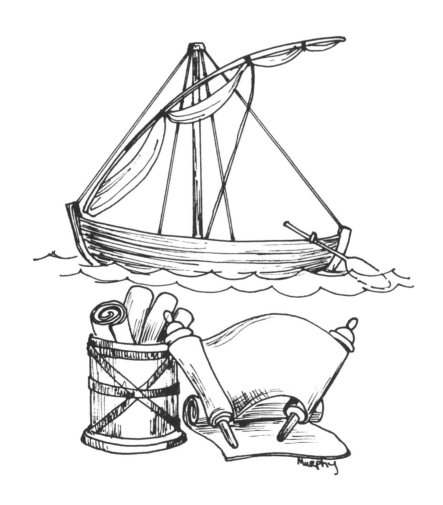

ARAUNAH OR ORNAN: "ARK"

Araunah was a Jebusite land proprietor who sold King David a threshing floor upon which to erect an altar. The purpose behind this sale was to better David's relationship with God after suffering pestilence for his transgressions.

Araunah received six hundred gold shekels (seventy-seven hundred thirty-two dollars and thirty cents) from this affair. He was a black man, of the lineage of "Jebus."

It is popularly believed that the great altar of Solomon's Temple later stood on the exact spot occupied by this threshing floor. Today the famous Mohammedan Mosque, Dome of the Rock, covers a sacred rock which many held to have been Araunah's threshing floor. This rock is about forty-five by sixty feet in dimension, and projects above the ground at heights from four to six or seven feet.

Gen. 10: 6, 15-16; II Sam. 24: 18-24; I Chron. 21: 15-28.

SOLOMON: "PEACEFUL"

Solomon, the king of Israel throughout Israel's finest years of prosperity, was a son and successor to King David. His lineage can be scripturally traced as far back as Rahab the "black Canaanite," or harlot, who was a descendant of Ham's fourth-born Canaan. Solomon was annointed king at Gihon by his stricken father's request. He rose to power when Israel was an empire, with a desire to serve God as had his father David. When the Lord appeared to him in a dream, saying: "Ask what I shall give thee," the young king asked for an understanding heart to judge his people and to discern between good and bad. This choice by Solomon prompted God to bless him beyond his wishes. Solomon was granted riches as well as wisdom.

As years passed, Israel became a strong nation and enjoyed a Golden Age, culturally, under Solomon. Her wealth increased because of Solomon's ties with God and his wisdom in social and political affairs. He made several significant steps toward bringing about Israel's recognition by improving mobility, installing copper mines, and organizing a building program to increase the number of houses, palaces, and temples throughout the empire. He also married many strange women to expand his monopoly on foreign soil.

Solomon was full of wisdom, and people came from far away to see and question him. He excelled in subjects such as literature, science and political policies.

The Proverbs are accredited to him. Solomon was even an authority on the nature of trees, beasts, fowl, and fish. He was also a commercial wizard who took advantage of weak as well as strong countries to better his economy. Israel's empire remained powerful until Solomon's death but never experienced such a great culture after the Solomonic period.

Solomon was one of Judah's earliest kings to have Negro blood in his veins. His great-great, etc., grandmother was Rahab the "black Canaanite," who was an offspring of Ham (Gen. 10: 6, 15; 45:17; Num. 13: 17; 21: 3; Josh. 2: 1; 6: 1; 17, 23, 25. She married a Jew named Salmon, having a child named Boaz, who was an ancestor of David, Solomon, Jehoram, etc. (Ruth 4:21-22; Matt. 1: 5-6; Luke 3: 31-32. Jehoram, with his Negro strain, married Athaliah, who was a daughter of the Negress (Hamitic) Jezebel, and her Jewish husband "Ahab" (Gen. 10: 6, 15; II Kings 8: 25-27). Athaliah and Jehoram were of Negro ancestry through Rahab, Jezebel, etc., from Ham. Their royal lineage continued in that family before David and after the "Messiah" (Gen. 10: 6, 15; Josh. 2: 1; 6: 1, 17, 23, 25; Ruth 4: 21-22; Matt. I: 5-6; Luke 3:31-32).

Solomon's glamorous black wives played a major role to his downfall (I Kings 11: 5, 33). His wish to serve their gods generated a split between him and Jehovah. The intermarriages between the two races were not an unusual circumstance (I Kings 11: 1, 13, 31-33; Ezra 9: 1-2). The most severe laws throughout Israel failed to prevent or curtail black and Jew matrimony.

Gen. 10: 15; II Sam. 12: 10, 24; I Kings 1: 37-39; 3: 5-13; 4: 32-34; 11: 1; II Chron. 2: 1; Matt. 1: 6-7.

QUEEN OF SHEBA: "OATH"

The Queen of Sheba was a black woman who resided in Africa and Arabia.* She was an Ethiopian by blood, land, and culture, an admirable descendant of Ham's first son, Cush, same as Ethiopia (Gen. 10:7). The Jewish historian Josephus mentioned her as Queen of Ethiopia and Egypt. The Bible addresses her as "Queen of Sheba" in honor of an Arabian country (Sheba), in which Ethiopia dominated during her reign. When talk of Solomon's wisdom spread abroad, this queen, being a woman of respect, did not accept such outrageous news! She felt that Solomon's reputation was overexaggerated, and thus, for assurance, made a triumphant trip to commune with him. The king welcomed her with honor, granting her full rights to survey his riches. But the queen doubted Solomon and began questioning him to see if he could measure up to his reputation. He answered all of her questions and she became satisfied. They exchanged gifts and she returned to her own land (Axum, the capital of Ethiopia's empire). The queen is noted for this famous remark: "The half was not told me." She was remembered by the, Savior during His teaching. He called her the "Queen of the South."

The Ethiopians also called Sheba, "Diana," a term that gradually worked its way into Europe. The Greeks and Romans worshipped Sheba as a Goddess, they called her "the black Minerva," "Artemis" and "Diana."

*The land "Sheba" (modernly known as Yemen) of southern Arabia was a colony of Ethiopia during the Queen of Sheba's reign. Though her royal palace existed in Ethiopia, the queen ruled her kingdom from both territories.

The nation Ethiopia and the Land of Sheba were under one monarchal rule. This single government was probably constituted in respect of kinship, since both countries were of the same ethnic background, "Ethiopians." During the scattering of Babal, some of Ham's children journeyed north and south of Arabia; three of them were Raamah, Sheba and Dedan, descendants of Cush (Gen. 10:7; II Chron. 21:16). It was Sheba who populated the southern peninsula and later built the wealthy country called "Sheba" (Isa. 60:6; Ezek. 27:2-23), which remained popular during Solomon's empire.

The Arabian writer Hamdani, who lived during the 10th century, states in his manuscript that the Queen of Sheba's mother was an Ethiopian (Black) named Ekeye. According to Hamdani, the queen lived in Africa and Arabia, but mostly in Africa.

Gen. 10:7; 1 Kings 10:1-13; II Chron. 9:1-12; Matt. 12:42.

REHOBOAM

Rehoboam was a son and successor to king Solomon and also a great descendant of Rahab the "black Canaanite," through Boaz, who was David's great-great-grandfather.

Rehoboam was crowned in Shechem (a country formerly owned by black people) before all of Israel. In his early succession he became confronted with his late father's old rival Jeroboam concerning a relief of heavy taxation and labor imposed on Israel under Solomon. After hearing Jeroboam's plea, he went to consult with the old men who once stood before his father, concerning what decision he should make. They advised him to speak good words to his people in order to keep them as faithful servants. But Rehoboam frowned on their counseling and decided to consult with friends with whom he had grown.

They advised him to show no mercy on the people, and when he addressed the congregation three days later, he spoke harshly to them, saying: "My little fingers be thicker than my late father's lions, and now whereas my father did lade you with a heavy yoke I will add to your yoke; My father hath chastised you with whips, but I will chastise you with scorpions." When the people heard these words, they became disappointed and rebelled against his rule, thus causing his empire to split. While Rehoboam reigned in Judah, his opponent Jeroboam became king of Israel, and there were wars between them all of their days.

Rehoboam reigned for seventeen years, and because of his sins God delivered wrath upon Jerusalem by the hand of Shishak.* When he passed, his son Abijam succeeded him.

*Shishak's army was composed of Libyans and Ethiopians. It can be assured that during this invasion of Palestine, many Jews were transported to Egypt and Ethiopia. There is archaeological evidence of Shishak's invasion of Palestine. A section of a stele found at Megiddo commemorated Shishak's victory; also, a sculpture on a temple wall at Karnak Egypt, lists over one hundred and forty cities or villages that Shishak conquered.

I Kings 12: 1-23; 14: 21-31; 15: 24; 22: 50; II Chron. 12: 1-16; Josh. 2: 1; 6: 1; Ruth 4: 21-22; Matt. 1 :5-8.

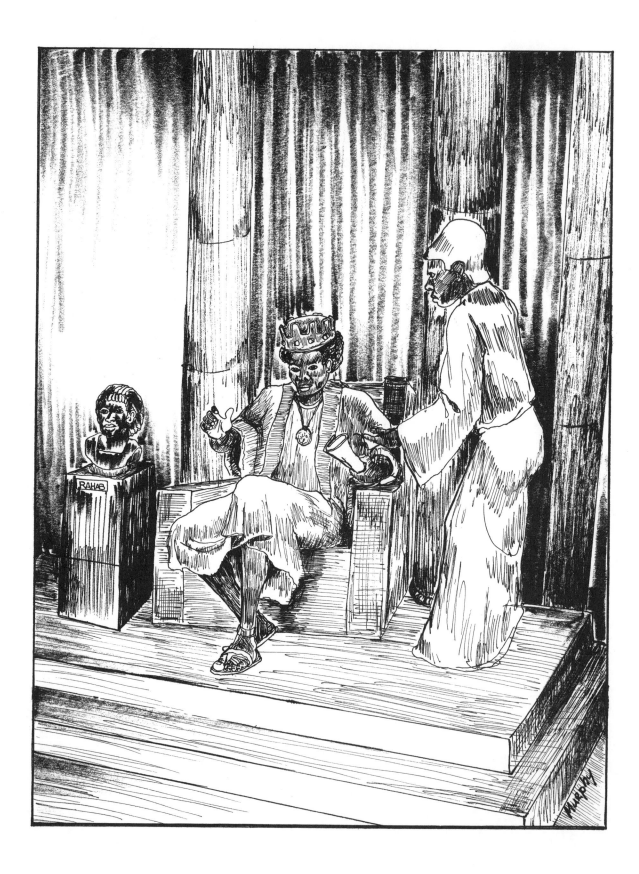

ABIJAH OR ABIJAM

Abijah was the son and successor of his father Rehoboam. His mother was called Micaiah or Maacah, who was a Colored woman, being the granddaughter of Absalom. Absalom's father (King David), grandfather (Jesse) and great-grandfather (Boaz), were descendants of the Negress Rahab.

Abijah, being the second king of the divided kingdom of Judah, tried vigorously to reunite the empire, which had separated under his father Rehoboam. Thereby, with four hundred thousand mighty men, he engaged in war with Jeroboam of Israel and won victory, but was unable to unite the kingdom, since the people of Israel, through the influence of Jeroboam, chose to remain separate.

Abijah lived recklessly, as had his father, by allowing corruption to manifest in the land. His heart, throughout his three-year reign, was not complete with God (I Kings 15: 3). Upon his death his son Asa succeeded him.

Asa begot Jehoshaphat, and the great Jehoshaphat begot Jerhoram. These royal kings' lineage can be traced as far back as Rahab the "black Canaanite," or harlot.

I Kings 14: 31; 15: 1-8; II Chron. 12: 16.

HIRAM: "NOBLE"

Hiram, a black king of Tyre or Phoenicia, a Zidonian during the age of David and Solomon, arose in the same land as Queen Jezebel, and was a descendant of Canaan's first son, Zidon. His land was known for its professional craftsmen and commercial control over lumber in Lebanon. He is remembered for his architectural skill, displayed during a twenty-year period of designing palaces and temples for God at Solomon's request. Hiram was a businessman as well as a king. He knew his country mastered the sea in trading; therefore, he formed a league with Solomon to man his navy. This new alliance placed Jewish sailors under Phoenician leadership to better both countries' commercial advantages. He even persuaded his daughter to marry Solomon to better secure their relations. Not only did he show remarkable diplomacy but capitalized on the trading along the Mediterranean Coast.

While the Phoenicians traded with the Greeks, the Greeks had no alphabet; as a solution, the Phoenicians taught them their alphabet. The Greeks transmitted this to the Romans, the Romans to the Germans, and the Germans to the British.

This same alphabet, with modification, is used by the modern world. It is an heirloom from the old Hamitic lore of the Negro-Canaanites.

Two of Phoenicia's most influential black rulers were Tabnit and his popular son Eshmunuzar II. They were pure Negroes with marvelous thick lips, flat noses, and fully developed almond-shaped eyes.

Gen. 10: 15; I Kings 5: 1; 11: 1; I Chron. 22: 4.

HADAD: "MIGHTY"

Hadad was a young prince of Edom ("Esau") who with friends, was exiled to Egypt ("Mizraim") because of an invasion by David's general Joab. While in Egypt, the Pharaoh treated Hadad well and gave him his sister-in-law to wed. She blessed him with a son named Genubath, who was reared among the Pharaoh's sons.

When Hadad heard of the deaths of David and Joab, he quickly returned to his own land and afterward became an adversary of Solomon.

Hadad was a black man who was descended from a family of royal dukes (Gen. 36: 15-19). His forefather was a Hebrew named Esau (brother of Jacob) who married three black women, Judith, Bashemath, and Mahalath. These women were considered the mothers of the Edomite race (Gen. 10: 6, 15; 26: 34-35; 27: 46; 28: 9; 36: 1, 9, 43).

Judith and Bashemath were Hittites, same as black Canaanites, since they were descendants of the black man Canaan (Gen. 10; 6, 15; 26: 34-35). Mahalath was a mixture between Jew and Negro (Egyptian) blood. She was the daughter of the half-breed Ishmael (Gen. 28: 6-9; 36: 1, 9, 43).

I Kings 11: 14-22.

SHISHAK

Shishak was a king of Libya who subjugated Egypt and formed a Libyan Dynasty. While in power he exhibited mercy to Jeroboam by granting him asylum from Solomon. Shishak later became a legendary king who defeated Solomon's son Rehoboam by invading Judah and removing great treasures from Jerusalem, including Solomon's gold shields. He governed Egypt from 935-914 B.C.

Shishak was a Negro from the lineage of Ham's third son Phut.

Shishak's army was composed of Libyans and Ethiopians. It can be assured that during his invasion of Palestine many Jews were taken captive to Egypt and Ethiopia. There is archaeological evidence of Shishak's invasion of Palestine. A section of a stele found at Megiddo commemorated Shishak's victory; also, a sculpture on a temple wall at Karnak Egypt, lists over one-hundred and forty cities or villages that Shishak conquered. Jeroboam's refuge to Africa wasn't an unusual circumstance among Jews. For Jews had regularly reinfiltrated Africa since the Exodus. Such massive migration "back to Africa" resulted from the constant internal strife and external invasion from Assyria, Babylon, Persia, Rome, Greece, Turkey, etc., Jeremiah (Jer. 44: 1, 8, 12-15, 24, 26-28), Zephaniah and Amos (Amos 9: 7) spoke of Jews being scattered throughout the Negro continent "Africa." Egypt, Ethiopia, Uganda and Kenya were swarming with black Jews. Zephaniah says, "From beyond the rivers of Ethiopia my suppliants, even the daughter of my dispersed, shall bring mine offering (Zeph. 3: 10)." This verse indicates that Jews were multiplying in Africa.*

*W. Whiston, *The Life and Works of Flavius Josephus,* p. 261.

Gen. 10:6; I Kings 14: 25-28; II Chron. 12: 1-12; Ezek. 27: 10.

NECHO

Necho II was an Egyptian King of the twenty-sixth dynasty. Like the main Egyptian branch, Necho was an African by blood, a great descendant of Ham.

During the reign of King Josiah, Pharaoh Necho launched a major invasion against the Babylonians, in hope of restoring Syria and Palestine to Africa (since both regions were anciently administered by Egypt). During his journey through Canaan, Josiah hastily attacked him at Megiddo, but was severely wounded and returned to Jerusalem where he died. Necho's encounter with the Judaens was brief as he pressed forward to engage a campaign with Nabopolassar (a Babylonian conqueror). After successfully defeating Nabopolassar, Necho began to focus attention on the successor of Josiah "Jehoahaz" whom he later deposed and replaced with Eliakim (Jehoiakim). Some four years afterward at Carchemish, Necho's military suffered a disastrous defeat by the Babylonians under the command of Nebuchadnezzar (Jer. 46: 2). Following this defeat, Necho fled homeward and made no other attempt to reestablish the Egyptian influence in Asia.

According to the Greek historian Herodotus, who is styled as the father of history, Necho was the son of Pharaoh Psammentichus. Following his succession, Necho built a great military with an extraordinary fleet, which he largely used on the Mediterranean and the Red sea. Necho sacrificed an enormous sum of money and thousands of lives, as he made a fruitless effort to join the Red Sea and the Nile by a canal. He ordered the first African circumnavigation, by dispatching ships completely around Africa.

The scientist C. F. Volney states that the first Egyptians were real Negroes of the same race as all the natives of Africa. It is generally noted, because of mixing for many centuries among the Greeks and Romans, that they have lost much of their black color. Nevertheless, they still hold indisputable resemblance to their original ancestry. C. F. Volney's comments are found in the following source: "Voyage to Syria and Egypt." Paris, 1787.

II Kings 23: 29, 30; II Chron. 35: 20–25; Jer. 46: 1–2, 6, 10.

HOPHRA

Pharaoh Hophra was the second successor of his grandfather Necho. He reigned in Egypt during the time of Nebuchadnezzar King of Babylon and Zedekiah King of Judah. Hophra and Zedekiah formed an alliance for protection against the Babylonians. However, when Nebuchadnezzar came up against Jerusalem in 587 B.C., Hophra heavily crippled his forces driving the aggressor from Palestine. Nevertheless, Hophra in honor of his victory took Zidon and Tyre from Zedekiah and returned to Africa with great spoil. Such untimely withdrawal disappointed Zedekiah and assumably caused the war-weary Judaens to become immensely vulnerable to the Babylonian war thrust.

When Nebuchadnezzar executed his final offensive upon the Kingdom of Judah, Hophra, in spite of the alliance, appeared to have made no effort in stopping the devastation of Jerusalem (Jer. 37: 1-5). Finally Hophra, after an unsuccessful expedition within the Land of Phut (known today as Libya) was dethroned by his army as was prophesied by Jeremiah (Jer. 44: 30). This formidable pharaoh had ruled Egypt for twenty-five years.

The Greek Herodotus (484-425 B. C.), who is styled as the father of history, plainly described the Egyptians of his day as, "burnt skinned, flat nosed, thick lipped, and woolly haired."

The Latin historian Ammianus Marcellinus, who lived about the era of Caesar Augustus, states, "...the men of Egypt are mostly brown or black with skinny and desiccated look." The above information is found in the following source: "Ammianus Marcellinus," Book XXII, para. 8 (24).

Lucian (120-180 A.D.) speaks of a well learned Egyptian scribe named Pancrates, as being tall, flat-nosed, with protruding lips and thin legs. This information is found in the works of Lucian.

Diogenes Laertius (333-261 B. C.) says the following about Zeno, founder of the Stoic School, "Zeno son of Mnaseas or Demeas was a native of Citium in Cyprus, a Greek city which has taken in some Phoenician colonies." In his Lives, Zeno is depicted as having a twisted neck. Appolonius of Tyre says that Zeno was black, tall and gaunt (very thin, bony, with hollow eyes and a starved look), hense the fact that according to Chrysippus in the First Book of his Proverbs, certain people called Zeno an Egyptian vine-shoot. This information is found in the following source: "Diogenes Laertius," Book VII, i.

Henry M. Stanley says, "On the sculptures of Egyptian monuments on the face of the Sphinx, in the features of the most ancient mummies and in those of Egyptian and wooden and stone statues, I saw the Afro-Asiatic type as clearly as I see it in the faces of the fellaheen and nobles of the present day." Their color, he said was "dusky, dark, dark-skinned" and their hair "varying from coarse, straight, black to curly, crinkly, wooly." The above information is found in the following source: "North Amer." Vol. 170, pp. 656 et seq. 1900.

"The Egyptians, though healthy, large and robust were clumsy in their forms and coarse in their features. Like other African tribes they were wool-haired, flat-nosed, thick-lipped, and if not absolutely blacks, very nearly approaching to it in color." This information is found in the following source: "Speciments

of Ancient Sculpture Society of Dilettanti," Vol. 1.

Higgins write, Dr. Pritchard has most clearly proved, as I have stated .... that the ancient Egyptians were Negroes. He observes the Greek writers always mention the Egyptians as being black in their compexions." The above information is found in the following source: "Anacalypsis," Vol. 1, p. 434. 1836 & 1992.

The Greek dramatist Eschylus (Aeshylus, 525-456 B. C.) in his "Supplices," makes Danaus say that he knew the approaching ship was Egyptian because "The crew may be distinctly seen with their black limbs that appear from their white garments (Pindar, Solon and Herodotus who visited Egypt, made similar comments)." The above information is found in the following source: "Collect Works Trans." Blomfield, pp. 272. 1840.

A. Block, in reference to the Egyptians says, "This characteristic is nothing else but atavistic proof of the Negroid origin of the Egyptian and consequently of their African origin. It is the same with the enlarged base of the nose and its lesser height." Block says the Egyptians were Negroes, as seen in the fulness of their lips. This information is found in the following source: "Bull. et Mem. Soc. Anthrop," pp. 393-403. 1901.

The Scientist C. F. Volney say, "All of them are puffy-faced, heavy-eyed, a thick-lipped, in a word, real mulatto faces. I was tempted to attribute this to the climate until, on visiting the Sphinx, the look of it gave me the clue to the enigma. Beholding that head characteristically Negro in all its feature that this race of blacks who nowaday are slaves and the objects of our scorn is the very one to which we owe our arts, our sciences and even the use of spoken work..."The above information is found in the following source: "Voyage to Syria and Egypt," Vol. 1, pp. 74-77, Paris. 1787.

Jer. 37: 1-5; 44: 30.

X

NEGRO PRIESTS, KINGS, AND QUEENS OF ISRAEL, JUDAH, AND PHOENICIA

ETHBAAL: "FIRE"

Ethbaal, father of Jezebel, was a King of Zidon and high priest of Astarte.

With a position equivalent to that of a pope, he accumulated the maximum power to execute and replace his brother Pheles, who had been king. Ethbaal ruled Zidon over three decades, partly under the influence of his daughter. It was she who encouraged him to recognize Baal as a national god.

This priest and king was a black man, a descendant of Ham's grandson Zidon.

According to E. Pittard, the skulls of the Phoenicians were distinctly Negroid. Their noses were flat at the end, and their mouths were wide with thick lips. The museum in Carthage, says Pittard, that held the tomb of the priestess of Tanit, bore Negro characteristics. The buried woman was of African origin. Pittard's comments can be found in the following source: "Les Races et L'histoire," pp. 108, 409-410. Paris, 1924.

I Kings 16: 31; I Chron. 1: 8, 13.

JEZEBEL

Jezebel was a beautiful black woman from Tyre of the Zidonians (Phoenicians). These Zidonians came from Canaan's first son Zidon.* Jezebel was Queen of Zidon during her father's reign as priest and king. She was very energetic and persuasive, often desiring things to go her way. When a proposal came from King Ahab of Israel, she accepted and became his queen.

This new position as Queen of Israel allowed Jezebel to acquire excessive power throughout the land. Some of Israel's heaviest influence was exerted by her. She introduced Baalism to Israel, which turned them from Jehovah to idolatry. This false image polluted all of Israel and caused many God-sent prophets to be slain. Jezebel herself had over eight hundred dedicated prophets to worship the Hamitic Baal. Her influence spread tremendously before Elijah (one of the remaining prophets) entered the scene. This prophet opposed her immoral regime and demanded a challenge of God's power against that of Baal. When the people saw no life in the Hamitic Baal against the power of God, Jezebel's influence lost favor. Her power structure took a final blow by Jehu, as he seized her city and demanded her eunuchs to throw her from a chamber.

Before her burial, there was nothing to be found but the skull, the palms of her hands, and the soles of her feet (II Kings 9: 35-36). This queen and the Hamitic Baal plagued Israel for more than forty years.

*B.H. Warmington, Carthage (Phoenicians were descendants of Canaan). p. 16. 1960, 69.

Gen. 10: 6,15; I Kings 16: 31; 18: 21; I Chron. 1: 13.

AHAZIAH OF ISRAEL: "SEIZURE"

Ahaziah, a son of Ahab and Queen Jezebel and brother to Athaliah, became Israel's eighth king following his father's tragic death at Ramoth-Gilead (I Kings 22: 34, 37).

Ahaziah was heavily influenced by his parents' idolatry, which caused him to suffer untold misery. His strength declined when Moab rebelled to free herself from paying tribute; however, Ahaziah offered no resistance but instead turned to Judah's king to form an alliance in sea merchandise, which later ended in ruins.

Nothing seemed to work well for young Ahaziah, and one day as he toured the roof of his palace, he became seriously injured from falling through a lattice. After realizing the extent of his injury, he sent a messenger to Baalzebub (false god) of Ekron to seek information concerning his convalescence. Ahaziah's choice to recognize Baalzebub angered God, and before the messenger reached his destination, he was stopped by Elijah the prophet, and instructed to return to Ahaziah and inform him that he would not recover from his bed and would soon die. Following this prophecy, Ahaziah was nobly succeeded by Jehoram.

II Kings 1: 1-6; II Chron. 20: 35-37.

JEHORAM OR JORAM: "GOD IS EXALTED"

Jehoram, a son of King Ahab and Queen Jezebel, and brother to Athaliah, became a successor of his brother, who died childless.

Jehoram was a friend of the prophet Elisha, who had predicted victory for him against the Moabites. He obeyed the prophet's counseling and became a successful king, but later, as things seemed to prosper for Jehoram, he departed from Elisha and began to worship idols. This act of reversion was the beginning of his misfortune, for it was not long afterward that he and his nephew Ahaziah united to seize Ramoth-Gilead from King Hazael of Syria. It was during this campaign that Jehoram received wounds which affected his judgment to command. Jehu, the son of Jehoshaphat, took charge and persisted to resist Hazael while Jehoram retired to Jezreel to cure his wounds.

When the fighting deescalated, Jehu, with a company of men, marched to Jezreel. There Jehoram and Ahaziah readied their chariots to meet him and resume command, but instead were surprisingly confronted by death from Jehu's bow. Jehoram was shot through the heart as his nephew outwitted the ambushers and journeyed to Samaria, but was later captured and returned to Jehu.

II Kings 3: 1-2, 18; 8: 28-29; 9: 14-16, 21-24, 28; II Chron. 22: 9.

AHAZIAH OF JUDAH: "JEHOVAH SUSTAIN"

King Ahaziah, son of Athaliah, was pursued and wounded by Jehu's army as he attempted his second escape.* From then, he managed to surpass Gur and went as far as Megiddo, where he died of his afflictions. His corpse was carried to Jerusalem and buried in the city of David.

Jehu was the founder of the Fifth Dynasty of the kingdom of Israel, son of Jehoshaphat (II Kings 9: 2). His appointment to the kingly office, his appearance at Jezreel, his destruction of the family and court of Ahab, and his slaughter of the idolators in the temple are recorded in the books of Kings. He reigned twenty-seven years and was succeeded by his son Jehoahaz.

II Kings 9: 27-28.

ATHALIAH: "BAR OF THE LORD"

Athaliah was the daughter of Ahab, king of Israel and his Zidonian wife Jezebel, and granddaughter of Omri, who was Ahab's father. She married Jehoram (a descendant of David and ancestor of Jesus Christ), king of Judah, and bore him a son named Ahaziah. After the death of Jehoram,* Ahaziah ruled Judah evilly with Athaliah's counseling as Ahab had counseled his house. When Ahaziah met death by the hands of Jehu, Athaliah immediately murdered his children in order to become sole ruler of his throne. She reigned over Judah for more than six years before realizing that one of her granchildren had escaped her bloody massacre. When Judah became aware of this grandson and heir to the throne, they sought to execute Athaliah. She cried in protest: "Treason, treason," but was slain that very day.

Jehoram died in agony of an incurable disease of the bowels. His people made no burning of him, like the burning of his fathers. They buried him in the city of David but not in the sepulchres of the kings.

I Kings 16: 28, 30; II Kings 8: 16-18, 26; 11: 1, 14-16; II Chron. 22: 2-3.

Mattan: "Gift"

Mattan was a priest of the Hamitic Baal. He was slain before the altars following the death of Athaliah, daughter of Ahab and Jezebel.

The Hebrews subdued the Canaanites physically, but having no store of mental endowments, were overcome by the intellectual civilization of the natives, aided by that of the Phoenicians. In adopting the civilization of the Negro Canaanites, the Hebrews also adopted their religious systems. There were several Hebrew kings who held control over the children of Canaan (Ham), but were unable to resist the worshipping of their gods (the Hamitic Baal, Elohim, etc.). Solomon was a prime example of this (I Kings 11: 5, 33). Israel as a nation was conquered by the religion (idolatry), laws, and general civilization of the Negro Canaanites, who were intellectually stronger.

II Kings 11: 18; II Chron. 23:17.

JEHOSHEBA

Jehosheba was a granddaughter of Jezebel and the wife of Jehoiada, a high priest.* She was able to save one of her brother's offspring when Athaliah, her mother, was arresting and murdering them for political purposes. This sole survivor was secretly obscured in the temple of God by Jehosheba and her husband until he became of age to rule Judah.

*Jehoiada was high priest at the time of Athaliah's usurpation of the throne of Judah (842–836 B.C.). He married Jehosheba, daughter of King Jehoram and sister of King Ahaziah (II Chron. 22: 11), and when Athaliah slew the royal seed, he and his wife stole Joash from among the King's sons, hid him in the temple and eventually placed him on the throne. The destruction of the Negro-Canaanite worship and the restoration of the temple were affected by Jehoiada. He died about 792 B.C.

II Kings 11: 1–3, 12; I Chron. 1: 8, 13; II Chron. 22: 11–12.

JOASH OR JEHOASH: "GOD-GIVEN"

Joash, the surviving son of King Ahaziah, reigned at an early age with Jehoiada, the high priest, to counsel him. The beginning of his rule benefited Judah as he ripped down false temples to promote the appropriate worship of God. Joash lived a good life, but when Jehoiada died, other informers led him to break the law and serve graven images.

His morals became so fragile that God sent prophets to warn him, but he listened not, which brought God's wrath against his people. Zechariah the priest even spoke against his evilness but was stoned in return, for the king had forgotten Jehoiada and slew his son. The people and his servants grieved, disapproving of Zechariah's death. They conspired and murdered Joash as he lay in bed.

Joash was taken to Jerusalem and buried in the city of David, as was his father.

II Kings 12: 1; II Chron. 22: 10-11; 24: 1.

AMAZIAH: "STRENGTH OF GOD"

Amaziah was the son of Jehoash or Joash and great-great-grandson of Queen Jezebel. After eliminating his father's killers, he organized a huge army to retrieve Edom, which had rebelled from Judah during the reign of his grandfather Ahaziah. To be certain of a clear victory, he hired outside help with one hundred talents of silver, but was warned by a prophet not to depend entirely on an army, that God was his assurance.

Amaziah, being moved, promptly sent the men he had hired back to Ephraim and attacked Seir (Edom) with only Judah. When he returned home, his heart became wicked. For in due time he had forgotten God who had led him in battle, and chose to worship the gods of Edom.

For a second time a prophet approached Amaziah, reminding him of his defilement, and even foretold the king's calamity if he didn't revert. However, these warnings were not heeded as Amaziah became boastful and made war with Israel. He was defeated and taken captive, but was still allowed to remain as king. He outlived Israel's king fifteen years without having any desire to worship God.

Finally, Amaziah lost favor with his people and fled to Lachish. There he was apprehended by his own servants and slain. His body was mounted on horses and escorted to the city of Jerusalem to be buried with his fathers.

II Kings 14: 1-3; II Chron. 24: 27; 25: 1.

UZZIAH: "GOD'S STRENGTH"

Uzziah was a son and successor of Amaziah and a fourth generation descendant of Queen Jezebel. He ascended the throne at sixteen and built a strong nation, militarily and economically. Young Uzziah obeyed the law; therefore, God blessed him, and Judah became prosperous.

His first accomplishment was building and restoring Eloth to Judah. Later he ventured into Gurbaal and carried on a small skirmish with Arabia and the Mehunims. After returning, he waged another war with the Philistines by ripping down the walls of Jabneh, Ashdod, and Gath, and then constructing his own cities in their land.

Uzziah's huge army would patrol areas often to display its power and insure peace.

The prince was known abroad for his success and inventions. He built large towers in Jerusalem that were well fortified. He was also noted for his agricultural techniques and his designs of machines that could throw arrows and stones through space.

Uzziah ruled Judah faithfully, but as he increased in power, his heart became like that of his father, for he violated the law of God by burning incense upon the altar. When Azariah the priest cautioned him of his sin, Uzziah arose in anger and oppressed the clergy. This brutal behavior provoked God to infect him with leprosy. He was afterward quarantined from his people while Jotham, his son, reigned as regent until Uzziah's death, and later became ruler.

II Chron. 26: 1.

Jotham: "God is Upright"

Jotham was the son of Uzziah and Jerushah, daughter of Zadok. During his decree the king entered not the temple and did little to stop corruption therein, although he himself feared and accepted God.

Jotham resumed some of his father's policies to improve Judah's security and standard of living. The high gate for the house of God and the wall to protect the city of Ophel were erected by him. He also built cities in the mountains, including castles and towers in the forest.

Following Jotham's building program, he engaged in war against Ammon, who at that time probably revolted in order to free herself from paying fees enacted by Uzziah. Jotham won conquest, and for three years forced payment of large concessions.

This servant never forsook God and like his father lived prosperously. He reigned for sixteen years and when he passed, he was buried in the royal tombs.

II Kings 15: 5, 32; II Chron. 26: 8, 23; 27: 1.

AHAZ: "TAKES"

Ahaz was a son of Jotham and seventh-generation descendant of Athaliah, daughter of Queen Jezebel. He governed at twenty; however, he chose not to walk with God but rather, to serve Baalism.

His idolatry provoked God to torment him with outside invasion. Rezin, king of Syria, made an assault and abducted large numbers into captivity. Pekah, king of Israel, conducted a more detrimental attack by slaying one hundred and fifty thousand men in one day. Zichri of Ephraim murdered his son, the house governor, and a close advisor, and the Philistines invaded cities and villages south of Judah.

All of these afflictions were placed on him because of his transgressions. Nevertheless, Ahaz's heart turned not to God; instead, he sought help from Tilgath-Pilneser, King of Assyria. This king welcomed and supported Ahaz for a price almost beyond his means; not only did Ahaz drain the church treasury, but became a bondsman to him as well. He even accepted their gods and had pagan altars mounted in Jerusalem while the temple of God was banned from worship.

Ahaz never recovered from idolatry, and when he died he was not buried in the royal sepulchres. His reign was similar to that of his ancestor Jezebel.

The invasion and harassment of Judah, especially under the reign of Ahaz and Hezekiah, forced a huge number of Jews to find permanent residence in Ethiopia, Egypt, etc. (Isa. 11: 11; Amos 9: 7; Zeph. 3: 10).

II Kings 16: 1; II Chron. 27: 9; 28: 1.

HEZEKIAH: "STRENGTH OF GOD"

Hezekiah was the son of Ahaz and a ninth-generation descendant of Queen Jezebel. He reigned over Judah as she underwent oppression by Sargon II of Assyria. His main goal was to free his land from this barbaric leader, who was a former ally to his father. His people had not only been oppressed but had worshipped idols as well. This vanity displeased God until Hezekiah took immediate action to dismantle idols from Holy areas. This reformation guided his kingdom back to God and caused God to find favor with him.

When Sargon died, Hezekiah revolted to ease restraints placed on him by the Assyrians. He and Sennacherib (son of the late Sargon) later developed some understanding to prevent further tyranny. Hezekiah promised to pay Sennacherib annual tribute to guarantee peace, which lasted temporarily.

Sennacherib's greed for increasing power kept him from honoring his agreement, as he threatened to overrun Judah in a letter he had sent to Hezekiah, stating that Israel's God could not deliver Judah from his wrath, that she (Judah) would soon fall as had other nations. This message shook Hezekiah to pray before God, asking Him to permit not such things, that all kingdoms would know that there is but one God. Jehovah heard him and and soon afterward sent an angel to eradicate Sennacherib's army with a plague.

Hezekiah was one of the last good kings and had similar manners to that of David as he walked uprighteously to bring about peace. He was also an ancestor of Zephaniah, who was Judah's ninth prophet.

One of Sennacherib's earlier attacks on Judah was resisted by a Negro named Tirhakah, who was the Pharaoh of the twenty-fifth Egyptian dynasty during the Ethiopian period. The Jews had high regard for the Negroes and constantly sought alliances with Ethiopia and Egypt (II Kings 19: 9; Isa. 37: 9; Jer. 37: 1-5; 44: 30).

II Kings 18: 7, 14-16; 19: 14, 35; II Chron. 28: 27; 29: 1; 31: 1; 32: 1; Zeph. 1: 1.

Manasseh

Manasseh, a son of Hezekiah, reigned at the age of twelve, becoming Judah's fourteenth king and a tenth-generation descendant of Queen Jezebel.

His heart was evil like those of past kings, and once again his people experienced a moral breakdown. For Manasseh had sinned by establishing various heathen alters and idols in the house of the Lord. He totally rejected Jehovah and resorted to sorcery, witchcraft, wizards, and strange spirits. He had many prophets and citizens slain because of their reluctance to support his false doctrine.

Manasseh's iniquity exceeded that of the heathens, insomuch that God became provoked and warned the people of their misdeeds, but they hearkened not. Their king continued to break the law until God turned them over to the children of Assyria where Manasseh was taken captive. As a prisoner, he realized all of his wickedness and prayed to Israel's God for deliverance. His grievance was heard, and after a year in Babylonia he was restored to Jerusalem as King. He quickly rebuilt old walls to protect his people and assigned officers of war to patrol Judah's boundary. Graven images and vile altars were ejected from the temple, for Manasseh's heart had refrained from corruption and under his new jurisdiction the people followed accordingly. Manasseh reigned in Judah for fifty-five years, longer than any other Judaen king.

The name Manasseh was also applied to a black skinned tribe. The ancient Hebrews were viewed as Blacks or Hamitics. The above information can be found in the following sources: "The One "Primeval Language," "The Fall," Forster, p. 330. 1854; and "Dr. William Smith's Dictionary of the Bible (the Hebrews were viewed as Hamites)," Vol. 2, p. 985. 1890.

II Kings 21:1; II Chron. 33:1-20.

AMON: "TRUE"

Amon was a son of the half-heathen King Manasseh, and eleventh-generation descendant of Queen Jezebel. He ruled at the age of twenty-two, but did not observe the laws of God.

Amon's reign was similar to that of his father's early reign. Like Manasseh, he clung to those things which displeased God, by reinitiating the use of graven images to the people. This behavior of Amon caused strong division between him and his servants. They hated him and became quite fed up with his idolatry. Nevertheless, the king grew worse, and the servants took council and slew him in his own house. Amon's corpse was honorably buried in the garden of Uzza beside his father.

The title Amon, first called "Amen," originated from the African continent (1989 B.C.) about 1,350 years before the Colored Amon of Judah was born. The god Amon was the Negroes' chief deity of heaven and earth, streams and hills, and as a demiurgos, the creator of beings. Amon was anciently called Amen or Amen-Ra by the Ethiopians, Egyptians, Libyans, Arabians and other Negro stocks, whose worship would often motivate repetitious cheers "Amen, Amen," a name (word) now cherished by the Judaists and Christians.

The early translators and revisers frequently altered the name Amen to Amon, Amun, No-Amen, and No (Jer. 46:25-26; Ezek. 30:13-16; Nah. 3:8), so that the original form Amen wouldn't interfere with the Judaic and Christian concepts. Etymologically, the term Amen derived from the African priests, meaning Ham (Black), Kam, Cam or I Am. Let it be acknowledged that the Semitic letter H was interchangeable with the Anglo K (Kh); the K with C (Ch), and the C with I.*

*Fausset says: "Ammon (Amon), the God of North Africa, is akin to Ham (Aman) "the Nourisher," or "Hamon," the Sun God, or Amon, or Amen.... Noah's youngest son." Fausset also says: "Inscriptions call him Amon-Re, "Amon the Sun..." A human figure with a Ram's (Sheep or Lamb) head, seated on a chair."

The above information is found in the following sources: Englishmen's Critical and Expository Bible Cyclopaedia, pp, 269, 513. 1880; A Commentary, Critical and Explanatory, on the Old and New Testaments (Amen means Amen-Re, Amon and Ham), Fausset, Vol. 1, pp. 551, 700. 1870; Oxford English Dictionary (Hamy-Ne means Amen), 20 Vols., 1989; Jewish Family Names (Amon means Hamon), Guggenheimer, p. 28. 1992 ; The African Origin of Civilization (Amon means Kham), Diop, p. 149. 1974; A New System (Ham was Amon), Bryant, Vol. 1, p. 3. 1807; and Jones' Dictionary of Old Testament Proper Names (Amon, Hum, No-Amon means Ham), pp. 29, 138, 256. 1990.

II Kings 21: 18-24; 11 Chron. 33: 21-25)

JOSIAH: "GOD CURED"

Josiah, a son of Amon, became the sixteenth king of Judah, and was the eleventh-generation descendant of Athaliah, daughter of Queen Jezebel. He was a just man whose ways resembled those of Hezekiah.

Josiah reigned at eight, and after seeing the destruction of his father and grandfather, he feared God and wanted to be more useful to his kingdom. He tore down high places and images to bring a state of stillness to his land. All priests who did not represent God were dismissed from the priesthood. He even razed the tombs of heathen priests and had their bones burned on pagan altars. His policy was enforced throughout Israel until all idols were dismantled.

Soon afterward, Josiah became interested in cleaning and repairing the temple, so with the aid of Shapan and Maaseiah, he collected revenue from surrounding areas. The money was then turned over to Hilkiah, the high priest, and was later distributed amongst the workmen. There were many craftsmen and the Scriptures described them as faithful stewards. Near the close of their labor, Hilkiah discovered a book of the law by Moses (Deuteronomy), and when Josiah was informed of it and the penalties it foretold, he sent several of his assistants to inquire of Huldah the prophetess. According to her interpretation, evilness was to come upon Judah because of previous kings' transgressions. But Josiah, who feared God and tore down carved images, would not live to witness such afflictions.

When Josiah was informed of this, he made a covenant with God and began counseling his people concerning the book of Moses. He also recognized the Passover, and since the days of Samuel there had been none to keep such a high observance. Judah under his reign had returned to righteousness, and God was well pleased.

His rule came to an end around 608 B.C. when he lead an unsuccessful attack upon Pharaoh Necho of Egypt. In the process of this attack, he was seriously wounded and carried back to Jerusalem where he later died. The news of his death was a shock to Judah, and there was much lamentation. The citizens of Judah honored Josiah by singing songs of lamentation long after his death (II Kings 23: 29, 30; II Chron. 35: 20-25). Jeremiah and Zephaniah spoke of Josiah in their prophecies.

II Kings 21: 26; 22: 1; 23: 21-30; II Chron. 33: 25; 34: 1; 35: 1.

JEHOAHAZ: "POSSESSION"

Jehoahaz was the third son of Josiah. He became the seventh king of Judah, and twelfth-generation descendant of Queen Jezebel.

He ascended the throne at twenty-three, but did not walk with God as had his father. For Jehoahaz did evil before God and was quickly dethroned by Pharaoh Necho, who had recently slain his father. His brother Eliakim, later known as Jehoiakim, was given his seat while he himself was taken captive to Riblah in Syria,* and afterward to Egypt, where he died. He ruled Judah a mere three months.

Necho ordered the first African circumnavigation around 600 B.C., by a Negro Phoenician expedition. This expedition sailed through the Red Sea into the Indian Ocean and circled Africa. The ships returned three years later through the Mediterranean Sea.

It was some 2,100 years later that Europe was able to master such a voyage, under a Portuguese sea captain named Diaz. He rounded the Cape of Good Hope in 1486 A.D.

*Riblah was an ancient fortress occupied by Negroes called Hamathites (Gen. 10: 18). The fortress Riblah is located in Hamath Syria, at the northeast extremity of Canaan (Num. 34: II). This fortress still retains its ancient name, on the right (east) bank of the el-Asy (Orontes).

II Kings 23: 31-34; I Chron. 3: 15; 36: 1.

JEHOIAKIM: "GOD ESTABLISHED"

Jehoiakim was the second son of Josiah. He became the eighteenth king of Judah, and was the thirteenth-generation descendant of Queen Jezebel.

With the Pharaoh's help, he encountered only minor resistance in ascending the throne after his brother's removal. Even though he carried the title of king, his power was limited because of large tributes the Pharaoh demanded of him.

When the king of Babylonia ended a war with Carchemish, he launched an assault on Jehoiakim and took him with many vessels from the house of God to Babylon. Later for some mysterious reason, he was released and restored to his throne as a subject to Nebuchadnezzar.

Conditions such as these disturbed Jehoiakim, where thoughts of paying any more tribute or being a puppet became intolerable. He wanted to be a free king in order to enjoy its full privileges. Therefore, when Babylon and Egypt began to engage in neighboring wars, he rebelled against Nebuchadnezzar. However, such a rebellion did him little good, for God was not pleased with his evil heart and directed even more wrath against him. The Chaldeans,* Syrians, Moabites and Ammonites tormented his land regularly with raids.

He finally met a catastrophe at the hands of the children of Ammon, and there was no honorable burial for him, nor did Judah mourn over his death.

*Habakkuk describes the Chaldeans as a bitter and hasty nation, which shall march through the breadth of the land to possess the dwelling places that were not theirs (Hab. 1: 6-10).

II Kings 23: 34-37; 24: 1-6; I Chron. 3: 15; Jer. 22: 18-19; 36: 30.

JEHOIACHIN: "GOD APPOINTED"

Jehoiachin was the son of Jehoiakim. He became the nineteenth king of Judah, and was the thirteenth-generation descendant of Athaliah, daughter of Queen Jezebel.

Jehoiachin began his reign at eighteen and did deeds which were evil in the sight of God. After reigning for three months and ten days, he was beset by an invasion by Babylon and was placed in prison. His kingdom lost its most valuable possessions following his surrender. Tremendous wealth was extracted from the temple, and ten thousand men and women, including craftsmen, warriors, captains, and officers joined him in captivity.

Jehoiachin was held prisoner for thirty-six years, until the death of Nebuchadnezzar. However, following his release he chose to reside in Babylon as a government official under his liberator rather than return to his kingdom.

The long period of captivity resulted in the molded and frequent misleading of the Israelites, relating to history and individuality. Jews in strange lands were often exposed to false teaching that left hundreds of thousands confounded, baffled and mystified. Brainwashing was commonly used to assure division or disunity among captive Jews. Under Babylonian authority, Jews of the new generation were lectured that a Babylonian named Hasisadra was saved from the flood and not Noah, that Noah was the progenitor of the human race, not Adam; also, that the story of Abraham, Sarah and Lot was mythical. These and other false teachings engulfed the Israelis, causing untold numbers to adopt new customs and pseudoreligions. Even during their release to return to Jerusalem, the Jews continued false worshiping. The practice of false worship was nothing new to the Hebrews, for Abraham's father, Terah, while living in the old Babylonia, served graven images (Josh. 24: 2).

II Kings 24: 11-16; II Chron. 36: 8; Jer. 22: 30; 52: 31-34.

ZEDEKIAH: "JUSTICE OF GOD"

Zedekiah was a son of Josiah. He became the twentieth and last king of Judah. His reign reverted the land back to heathen practice insomuch that God was not pleased.

Zedekiah was put on the throne by Nebuchadnezzar to replace Jehoiachin, his nephew, who was then taken captive. The king of Babylon made Zedekiah swear by God to formulate and preserve an alliance which he later found quite difficult to observe. Like his brother Jehoiachin, he saw no future in being a puppet, so he rebelled against the Chaldeans, but was unable to withstand their strength.

The Babylonians hurriedly responded with counterattacks until the city was fully besieged. Zedekiah, being powerless, tried to escape but was apprehended. He and his sons were sent to Nebuchadnezzar at Riblah. There he was reminded of the alliance he failed to keep, and because of his offense, witnessed his sons' murder. Zedekiah's eyes were plucked out, and he was bound with fetters and transferred to Babylon where he died.

Zedekiah was the last king of Judah to have Negro blood in his veins. His great-great-great, etc. grandmothers were Jezebel and Athaliah, who were daughters of Canaan, Ham's youngest Son (Gen. 10: 6, 15; I Kings 16: 31; II Kings 8: 16-18, 24-26).

Many scholars view Zedekiah as weak and careless, who held a position beyond his ability. The King with all of his interest in public affairs, seem to have lacked the military and diplomatic skills as a ruler. Zedekiah as a private citizen might have merited a respectable career, for he was amiable religiously inclined, but in the Davidic line he exhibited no strong rod to rule (Ezek. 19:4). One of Zedekiah's most fatal faults was neglecting advice from some of the wisest minds of his era. The Scriptures calls attention to the remarkable manner in which the fate of Zedekiah fulfllled two apparent prophecies of Jeremiah and Ezekiel. "Thine eyes shall behold the eyes of the king of Babylon, and shall speak with thee mouth to mouth, and thou shalt go to Babylon (Jer. 34: 3) and "I will bring him to Babylon, to the land of the Chaldaens; yet shall he not see it, though he shall die there (Ezek. 12: 13)."

Israel's downfall created the Assyrian territory just north of Judah. The Assyrians following a conquest over Israel, brought captives into Israel from Babylon, Cuthah, Avva, Hamath and Sepharvaim. The Assyrian king Sargon wrote: "I settled there people from countries which I myself had conquered, and I placed my officer as governor over them and imposed on them the tribute as for Assyrian citizen." The new population, obviously a minority, for only a small proportion had been exiled by Sargon or earlier by Tiglath-pileser III, intermarried with the remaining Israelites. The Judaeans came to regard this mixed population as no longer true Hebrews, and they are the Samaritans. Actually, neither the Judaeans nor the Samaritans could claim unmixed racial heritage (Ezra. 9: 2).*

*The Samaritans were definitely a hybrid people of Ethiopian and Jewish origin. The Talmud called these people Cutheans, meaning Ethiopians. The term Samaritan is also spelled Hamaritan and Kamaritan, since the ancient letter S was exchanged for H or K.

This information is found in the following sources: Aid to Bible Understanding, Watchtower Bible, p. 405. 1971; Wonderful Ethiopians of the Ancient Cushite Empire, Houston, pp. 22, 121; An Introduction to the Comparative Grammar of the Semitic Languages (S = H and K), Moscati, pp. 38-39, 104, 153. 1964; and The Life and Works of Flavius Josephus.

II Kings 24: 17-20; 25: 1-7; I Chron. 3: 15.

XI
KINGS AND CLERGYMEN OF ETHIOPIA

ZERAH: "Sunrise"

Zerah was an Ethiopian commander of an army of one million men and three hundred chariots, which signified Ethiopia as a world superpower during King Asa's reign of Judah. The ingenious Zerah was well known for his superior tactics and numerous conquests. There is much suspicion that he over powered many cities with his vast army, which was well-organized and highly disciplined. When the Kingdom of Judah was enjoying its long period of peace, Zerah felt it was time to upset such comfort by making war with Asa. The two Kings met in the valley of Zephathah at Mareshah, and there they clashed! The audacious Zerah with his impregnable military immediately crippled Asa's strength, which made a victory seem impossible for the Judean. Asa, after realizing the devastation of his army, frantically cried to God for spiritual support, which moved God to smote the Ethiopians, which in turn forced General Zerah to flee the valley, leaving great spoils before Judah.

Zerah, the great Ethiopian war strategist, having the largest military mentioned in Scripture, can be compared with the Egyptian Pharaoh Ramesses II; they both pushed their luck beyond limits. The legendary Zerah is also recognized by scholars to have once conquered and ruled Egypt as Pharaoh.*

The Egyptian historian Manetho, and also a priest under Ptolemy I, said that Zerah was a Pharaoh of the Eighteenth Egyptian Dynasty.

The Ethiopian rulers also used the title, "Negus," meaning King of Kings. The title Negus is equivalent to Nego, the same as Nebo, the Ethiopian-Babylonian God, whereas Nego (Nebo) means Negro, Black, Niger or Nigger. The ancient Egyptians called God "N-g-r (Nigger, Negger, Neger, Niger, etc.)," before the existence of vowels.

The Colored Ethiopians, the Negro-Egyptian Hagar and her half-Colored son Ishmael were the original parents of the Arabic people and nations: Arabia's earliest ancestors were people of the Negro race. Thus, study is proving that ancient and modern Arabia's Negro-mixture is indisputable (II Chron. 21:16; Hab. 3:7).

The above information is found in the following sources: Enciclopedia Universal Sopena (Negus means Nego), Sexto, Vol. 6, p. 5947. 1964; Portuguese-English Dictionary (Nego means Negro), Taylor, p. 440. 1970; Grande Dicionario Etimologico-Prosodico Da Lingua Portuguesa (Nego means Negar), Vol. 6, p. 2604. 1966; Cleveland Bible Commentary (Nego was also pronounced Nebo); Unger's Bible Dictionary (Abed-Nego; Nebo, a Babylonian God), pp. 2, 781. 1957; Webster's New Collegiate Dictionary (Negus means King of Kings), p. 762. 1981; An Egyptian Hieroglyphic Dictionary (N-ger-s), Budge, Vol. 1, p. 341. 1978; and The Book of Sothis, Manetho, chap., 6.

II Chron. 14:9-13; 16:8; Rev. 19:16.

TIRHAKAH: "EXALTED"

Tirhakah was an Ethiopian prince during Sennacherib's uprising to overthrow King Hezekiah of Judah. He became an ally of Hezekiah to prevent Judah any further harassment by the Assyrians. The Judaens at that time were weak, and their military lacked the stamina to sustain Sennacherib's force. Tirhakah out of mercy tried to help Judah by attacking the aggressor, but was unable to annhilate him. Instead, the young prince suffered innumerable casualties that forced him back to Egypt, where he became a temporary ruler through his uncle Shabaka, the acting Pharaoh.

About 691 B.C., Tirhakah became the third Pharaoh of the Twenty-Fifth Egyptian Dynasty during the Ethiopian period. His control over Egypt and Ethiopia gave him unlimited power, which he in turn cunningly used to batter the Assyrians during a second campaign. Folllowing his victory, the flamboyant Tirhakah began to boast to the world, proclaiming himself to be the greatest monarch on earth. Nevertheless, several years later Tirhakah suffered a severe defeat at Memphis by Esarhaddon (son of Sennacherib), which forced him to flee Egypt to Napata (capital city of Ethiopia), where he remained until his death in 663 B.C. He was succeeded by his nephew Tanwetamani.

During the life of Hezekiah, Ethiopia and Assyria existed as super-world powers (similar to modern-day world powers). The Ethiopian Tirhakah and the Assyrian Esarhaddon are noted in history as ingenious rulers. Each had a strong desire to rule the world, triggering a bitter twelve-year rivalry resulting in Tirhakah's withdrawal from Egypt.

Tirhakah's glorious rule won him notoriety, as the Jews watched him galloping across the battlefield to aid Hezekiah. The Egyptians and Ethiopians loved and never forgot him, and even Esarhaddon, in honor of Tirhakah, had his portrait engraved on a stele in Sinjirli. The diplomatic and military prowess of Tirhakah was long remembered and respected.

II Kings 19: 9; Isa. 37: 9.

EBED-MELECH: "KING'S SERVANT"

Ebed-Melech, an Ethiopian eunuch, was a high minister during the era of Jeremiah the prophet. When Judah was experiencing her dilemma, Ebed-Melech was probably one of King Zedekiah's advisors since his private residence gave him free admission to the king's chambers. This servant was a holy man who feared God and did not practice falling behind in his obligations. When Jeremiah was taken into custody and thrown into a dungeon, Ebed-Melech did not waste a moment in reaching the king for his release. There he informed Zedekiah of the injustice placed on Jeremiah and the condition of his safety as a prisoner. The king yielded and Jeremiah's life was spared. This courtesy by the Ethiopian merited him a promise that he would not be captured when the city of Judah was seized at the hands of King Nebuchadnezzar.

For centuries Ethiopia diligently sent her prophets, priests, laymen and scholars to the temples of Israel. Ebed-Melech and his kinsmen were worshippers of Judaism, a ritual that was introduced to Ethiopia by the Queen of Sheba, following her visit with Solomon.

E. G. White, in his book, "The Great Controversy," comments that in the regions beyond the sovereignty of Rome, there existed for hundreds of years masses of Christians who remained nearly entirely free from papal corruption. They were surrounded by pagansim, but continued to acknowledge the Bible as the sole authority of faith and held firmly to many of its truths. These followers of Christ believed in the continuity of the law of God and observed the Sabbath. The Ethiopians had enjoyed freedom in the practice of their faith centuries before Rome realized their existence.

Jer. 38: 7–13; 39: 15–18.

AN ETHIOPIAN PRIEST

There were many Ethiopian priests living in Judah around 899 B.C. Ethiopia did not come short of adopting and spreading Judeo-Christianity. For centuries her people were well-aware of the coming of the Messiah long before Abraham, Moses and the first book of the Bible was written (Ps. 87:1-7; Dan. 3:25; Jer. 38:7-13; 39:15-16).

Following the Crucifixion many Ethiopians broke away from Judaism to serve Christ, and even today Ethiopia is the world's oldest Christian nation (Ps. 68:31; Jer. 13:23; Acts 8:27).

For centuries the Negro family of nations recognized Israel and Yahweh, long before the children of Japheth (Europe) broke away from heathen worship (Acts 17:23; I Cor. 12:2; I Thess. 1:9). The Egyptians who were ethnically mixed with Ethiopian, worshiped Yahweh for seven centuries, before their cousins the Black Cyrenians (Phutites) spread Christianity to the Greeks, and administered the anointing of Saul (Paul) and Barnabas (Isa. 19:21-25; Acts 11:20; 13:1-3).

In the late A.D. 300s, the Roman empire began to accept Christianity under certain provision, such as the right to include paganism within the Christian assembly. The Euro- pagan calendar was welcomed in the Christian arena: January honoring the Roman god Junus; February (Februs) observing purification and the month of the dead; March respecting Mars the Roman god of war; April (Aprilis) indicating the time for fertility; May was named for Maia, the Roman female deity of spring; June (Juno)revering the patron god of marriage and gathering; July was named after the god King Julius Caesar; August was named after the god King Augusta Caesar; September (Septem) representing seven; October (Octo, month of Halloween) indicating eight; November (Novem) standing for nine; December (Decem, Jer. 10:3-5, XMAS tree) exemplifying Saturn, the god of harvest. Sunday was a day sacred to the Sun for unethical practices, which rehearsals were contrary to the ancient Christian beliefs (Ps. 84:11; Mal. 4:2); Monday recognized the moon goddess; Tuesday was for the observance of god Tyr; Wednesday was for god Mercury; Thursday was in honor of Thor, the god of thunder; Friday represented the goddess of marriage, love and housewifery; Saturday acknowledged the god of agriculture, etc.* Israel, two-thousand years before the birth of Christ, had observed the Negro-Ethiopian Babylonian's months: Nisan, Jyar, Sivan, Tamuz, Ab, Elul, Tisri, Marchesvan, Casleu, Tebeth, Shebet and Adar, an observance that still exist to this day.

About the turn of the 4th Century, Christianity became the official religion of the Roman empire. Europe's final conversion was probably attributed to pagan scholars who sponsored massive alteration of the original Bible in order to suit their own fancies. During this process many ethics, words, pages and books were discarded and renamed; Bereshith (Genesis), Shemoth (Exodus), Vayyikra (Leviticus), Bemidbar (Numbers), Debarim (Deuteronomy), etc. The books of Jasher, Enoch or any other textual matters reflecting Africa as the Mother of Judaism, Christianity and Islamism, were labeled by the Orthodox and Euro- Christian clergy as books not inspired by God; an old deception that violates Revelation 22:18-19. One of the earliest names for the Bible was called "The Books of Ham," "Chamash" or "Hamash." In many modern Jewish libraries, the Torah (Bible)is still called Hamash, indicating Ham, Pentateuch or Five, nevertheless, Five symbolizing the five books of Moses, whose name (Moses) was not Hebrew, but Africa-Egyptian.

*The Bible oppose the use of pagan deity names (Ex. 23:13; Ps. 16:4).

ZEPHANIAH: "GOD'S SECRET"

Zephaniah, the son of Ethiopia, was a royal figure and Judah's ninth prophet prior to the reign of King Josiah. He was a sensitive man who opposed outside customs, which were decaying Judah's religion. Zephaniah tried persistently to awaken Judah about future catastrophes through which all nations would be punished for their negligence to observe God! He was one of the last Old Testament prophets to preach punctiliously.

Zephaniah was from the lineage of Hezekiah, a great descendant of black Jezebel through her daughter Athaliah, who married into the Davidic line; possibly his great-great grandson.

It was the early blacks who spread Christianity throughout idolatrous Europe (Acts 11:20; 13:1-3). Soon after the death of Jesus, the Ethiopian "Queen Candace" and her eunuch (Acts 8:27) established Christian churches throughout Ethiopia and other nations (Acts 8:27,37). During this same period, Europe was under a pagan empire. Rome for the next three hundred years opposed Christianity and continued to worship Janus, Juno, Vesta and a thousand other gods. Ethiopia was not a partaker of this infidelic worship, for her people, before adopting Christianity, were worshipers of Judaism, as was Israel, and had exercised this religion for some seven centuries. The Negroes were the earliest prophets, priests and scholars of Judaism and Christianity.

The prophet Zephaniah, whose name means "Jehovah Hides" or "Protect," was one of the minor prophets, who lived about 621 B.C. His character and style were similar to Jeremiah's, during which early years they were contemporaries. His subsequent life is unknown.

The book of Zephaniah has three well defined divisions. Chapter one describes the coming Day of God-Elohim, which will bring overwhelming disaster upon Judah and the universe, a period when the Christian hymn Dies. Chapter two broadens the understanding of the punishment, especially toward certain foreign countries as Moab, the Philistine cities, Ethiopia, Ammon and Assyria with its capital Nineveh. Chapter three focuses upon the coming judgment of nations, purification and Israel's freedom, following the second grief upon Jerusalem. This Day reflect Elohim's (Eloham) mercy to spare a holy remnant who will finally enjoy peace. Zephaniah closes with a song of joy, sung by the remnant.

The prophet's rallying cry was perpetuated by the Scythians' invasion of Palestine. He perceived this intrusion to be God's wrath on Judah and all humanity to repent. Zephaniah forcasted a destruction "Day of the Lord," when the wicked would be punished. This theme is a central element in Biblical prophecy. The prophet predicted that a few would be spared of God's anger, and would be preserved in Jerusalem and the rest of Judah. There God would gather them and they would accept His rule.*

The Scythians were a cruel barbaric nomadic people, who scalped their enemies and used their skulls as drinking cups. These fierce warriors, who were a branch of the White race, identified themselves as the youngest of all the nations in the ancient world. According to the Scythian tradition, these diseased (syphilis) vampire-like warriors would suck the blood from the first person they killed in battle.

Zeph. 1:1.

195

MICHAEL AND GABRIEL

Michael and Gabriel are two of the four archangels mentioned in the Judaeo-Christian Scriptures. Their prime commitment is to act as instruments of God, and to execute His commands. They are recorded in the Bible as God's agents in administering the affairs of the world, and in protecting the welfare of individuals, as well as all of mankind. The names Michael and Gabriel originated from the Negro-Chaldeans, and were unknown to the Isrealites prior to the Captivity.

Michael, who was also called Metatron by the Jews, is described as a guardian angel of the Jewish nation, and is portrayed in Rev. 12:7-9 as a warrior leading an army of angels. According to Scholem, Michael's secret name is "Kemos," which is the same as Ham-God, since Kem- of Kemos means Ham, whereas -Os of Kemos means God!

Gabriel was sent by God to announce to Zacharias the future birth of John the Baptist; also to the Virgin Mary concerning the birth of Christ. He was also sent to Daniel to explain his visions. The Jews called Gabriel "Hamon," which means noisy or Ham.

According to the Bible, angels are spirits, whereas in Zachariah 6:1-7, one of the four spirits of God symbolized a black horse, which could have been either Michael or Gabriel, since the Hebrews called Michael, "Kemos," and Gabriel "Hamon," names which are historically and biblically defined as Black, deep black, swarthy or Ham. The Jewish Sholem Asch mentioned a Black angel with black wings.

The above information is found in the following sources: Calmet's Dictionary of the Holy Bible (Hamon means Ham), Taylor, p. 55.1849; The Legends of the Jews (Gabriel was called Hamon), Ginzberg, Vol.6, p. 363.1968: Jones' Dictionary of Old Testament Proper Names (Ham means Hamon, noisy and Black), p. 138.1990; Anacalypsis (Chaldeans were Negroes), Higgins, Vol.2, p.364. 1836; The Jewish Encyclopedia (Metatron was called Michael), Vol. 1, p. 94 .1901; Jewish Gnosticism, Merkabah Mysticism, and Talmudic Tradition (Metatron or Michael, was called Kimos or Kemos), Scholem, pp. 46 47. 1965; Young's Analytical Concordance to the Bible (Kem means Ham), p.443.1982; A Dictionary of Surnames (Os means God; see Oswald, Nicholas, Michael and Micka), Hodges, 1988; The Facts on File Dictionary First Names (see Nicholas), Dunking, 1984; Language Monographs (Mi means Black): Hittite Glossary (6-9), Sturtevant, p.45. 1930-1; Moses (Black Angel) Sholem Asch, p.503.1951; and A Book of the Beginnings (Mi means Am), Massey, Vol. 2, p.581. 1995.

Luke 1:11-22, 26-31; Dan. 8:16; 9:21; 10:13, 21; 12:1; Heb. 1:7, 14; I Thess. 4:16; Jude 9.

XII

Highlights of Blacks
During the First Century

THE WISE MEN: "MAGI"

The Wise Men were astrologers (stargazers) who journeyed to Bethlehem to greet the Savior. They carried gold, frankincense, and myrrh as gifts to the newborn King. Gaspar, Balthazar (a Black), and Melchior fell down and worshipped the Messiah and were later warned by God in a dream not to return to Herod (known as Herod the Great), who had inquired about the Child's whereabouts, but to return to their own land.[1]

The Ethiopian Balthazar dwelled in a lucrative nation called "Sheba," located south of Arabia. The Land of Sheba was part of the African-Ethiopic dominion. The Negro children of Cush, same as Ethiopia, had occupied and developed Arabia for some three centuries before the Semitic influx, three-and-a-half centuries before the half-breed Ishmael was born.

In the Books of Isaiah (43: 3) Ezekiel (27: 22-23), Jeremiah (6: 20), and Psalms (22: 10), Sheba is ranked among the richest nations of the earth. Balthazar, next to King Solomon, is acknowledged by many scholars as the second most celebrated black king in the Bible, since he is associated therein with the Child-Christ (Messianic birth, Matt. 2: 1).

Ps. 72: 10; Isa. 60: 6; Matt. 2: 1.

HEROD ANTIPAS: "PRAISE THE SKIN"

Herod Antipas was a ruler of Galilee during the era of John the Baptist and Christ. He, like his predecessors of the throne of Judea, was a potent member of a black political family.

Herod was highly ambitious, lavish and clever. His extravagance and cunning made him well-known in Rome, even to the extent of receiving gifts from emperors.

Tiberias Caesar granted Herod many favors; in return Herod built a seaport in honor of Tiberias (John 6: 1, 23).

Herod, with all of his slyness, seems to have met most of his opposition from John the Baptist (known as "the voice of one crying in the wilderness"), who publicly denounced the tetrarch for eloping with his brother Philip's wife Herodias (Matt. 14: 3–4; Mark 6: 17–18). Herod quickly imprisoned John and afterward had him beheaded by an intriguing plan of Herodias and her daughter (Matt. 14: 1–12; Mark 6: 1–29). It was not long following John's death that Herod Antipas met Jesus prior to the crucifixion, but their meeting was brief, since Jesus refused to perform miracles or hold a conversation with him (Luke 23: 8–11).

The Herods were called Idumean (name of an early region they settled), or Edomites (another form of the name Esau, who with three black wives became the father of the Edomite race). They were black people of the Hamitic strain.

Blacks and Semites are a blend of one people, for they intermingled (Gen. 16: 1–3, 16; 34: 1–10, 16; Judges 3: 5–7) form Negro-Egypt to modern times.

Gen. 10: 6; 26: 34; 27: 46; 28: 9; 36: 1, 9, 43.

MARY: "THE BLACK MADONNA"

Mary was the mother of the Immaculate Christ (the Son of God and Savior) and a distant relative of David, Solomon and Nathan through her father Heli. Heli, David, Solomon and Nathan were of the lineage of Boaz, who was a direct son of Rahab, "the Negress Canaanite," or harlot (Ruth 4:13, 20-2; Matt. 1:5-6; Luke 3:23, 31-32).

In the summer of B.C. 2, the angel Gabriel was sent to Mary with a message from Jehovah, announcing that she would conceive and give birth to the long-expected Messiah (Luke 1:26-35). During her pregnancy, Mary spent many days with her cousin Elizabeth, who at that period was pregnant with John the Baptist. Mary's future husband Joseph, after being assured of the truth (concerning her pregnancy) during a visit by an angel of God, married the Virgin. The Scriptures say: "He knew her not till she had brought forth her first born Son: and he called His name Jesus (Matt. 1:18-25)."

The Black Madonna was the greatest mother who ever lived. Besides the honor of being a favorite before God, the Black Madonna exhibited superb love as she faithfully watched and nursed her Child; showed concern for His safety and whereabouts (Matt. 2:13-14; Luke 2:40-52); followed Him during his earthly ministry; watched Him as He was taken and nailed to the cross for the redemption of mankind; and after His ascension continued to spread His teachings (Acts 1:13-14). The Black Madonna was truly a woman among women. Jesus' last request to John as He hung on the cross was to take care of His mother (John 19:25-27).

Mary is still adored throughout the religious world as a Hammoleketh-Queen, symbolizing "Mother of the Master." The Hebrews called her, "Miriyam" and "Mirijam," whereas the Persians, "Mariham."

For centuries people throughout Europe (Italy, France, Switzerland, Spain, etc.) in nearly every home and Cathedral had paintings and sculptures of Mary and Christ as Blacks. However, during the Napoleonic empire, "hundreds of thousands" of black paintings and statues of Mary and Christ were mobbed or burned, and replaced by white ones. In "Bulletin Societe Historique et Archealogique du Perigord," Rupert the Benedictine (1125 A.D., nearly seven centuries before Napoleon) says that in his day paintings of Mary were dark and black, Vol. 24, p. 80. 1897.

The 1979, May 4 issue of the Washington Post, states that the pictures of Mary the Madonna during the earliest centuries of Christianity were painted black, according to scholars, it was during the Renaissance (Michelangelo) that it became popular to portray the mother of Jesus with features of an Italian Virgin (a European woman)

Actually the concept of the Africoid "Black Madonna" (Isis) with her God-engendered Child (Horus), far predates Judaeo-Christianity, and prevailed throughout the antiquities.

The remaining European and Asian countries to honor the Black Madonna or Virgin Mary, are Poland, Spain, France, Portugal, Italy, Romania, Lithuania, Malta, Luxembourg, Ireland, Hungary, Switzerland, Sicily and Russia. There are over 700 documented Black Madonna sites throughout Europe and Asia. This doesn't include the ones hidden in vaults, and replaced by white ones (our Lady of the Hermits, Raber, 1959; The Spring 1994 issue of "Russian Life" (magazine);" The June 11, 1979 issue of Time Magazine (Poland); and The Feasts of Rus).

JESUS: "SALVATION"

The life and story of Jesus cannot be fully told. His existence can be found from Genesis to Revelation since He is Alpha and Omega (the first and last, Rev. 1: 11). His earthly maternal genealogy can be traced from Adam to Noah and Ham (The Prophet Daniel during a dream and vision, saw an anthropomorphic figure of God, same as Jesus (Phil. 2: 5-11), with woolly hair, colored arms and feet. St. John in Revelation gave a similar description of a vision of Jesus (Dan. 7: 9; 10: 6; Rev. 1: 14-15; 4: 3; John 10: 30; 14: 9).

Jesus was God in an earthly body (John 10: 30; 14: 9; Phil. 2: 5-11). He was not a "pure Jew" of the flesh for there were many Hamitic Blacks in His earthly geneaology, such as Rahab the harlot (also Rahab the Canaanite) who was Jesus' great-great-great grandmother. She survived the seizure of Jericho (a fortress ruled and occupied by black Hamites of Canaan, Ham's youngest son) and later married and bore a child called Boaz from an ancestor of Jesus named Salmon (Ruth 4: 21; Matt. 1: 5). Another black ancestor of Jesus was Jezebel, who became Israel's first black Zidonian queen by marrying the Jewish leader Ahab. They had three royal offspring but only Athaliah (daughter of Jezebel) married into the Davidic line from which came Mary, His mother. Jezebel's Hamitic blood with many other descendants of Ham continued in that family before and after Jesus.

According to the Scriptures, from Abraham (father of the Davidic line) up until King Solomon, Hebrews of that lineage took many black sons and daughters of Ham to be their mates (Gen. 16: 1-3; 34: 21; 38: 2-3; Judg. 3: 5-6; I Kings 11: 1-2; Ezra 9: 1-2; 10: 14, 16-19, 44; Matt. 1: 5-5). The Holy Seed in which the "Messiah" descended became Negritized some four thousand years before His birth (Ezra 9: 2).

Jesus throughout the ancient world was called Ham-Ashiah and Hammelech, meaning Savior and King.

Let us not overlook that Jews spent over four hundred years as slaves under the sovereign of Negro-Egypt (Ham) where there occurred extensive miscegenation. Furthermore, they were carried off into captivity by Babylonia, Assyria, Greece, Rome, etc. The Jewish Professor Einstein said that all people are mixed (See the *Saturday Evening Post*, October 26, 1929).

St. John said that Jesus' feet were like fine brass as if they had been burned in a furnace (Rev. 1: 15). Brass is yellow-brown, but when it has been burned the color changes to very dark, near black. Like Daniel and John's descriptions of Jesus, St. John portrays a dark-colored man with Negro "kinky hair" (lamb's wool).*

The Jewish people, during and prior to Christ's time, were black-skinned with Negro features. These genetic traits (through cross-breeding) extended largely from their four hundred years of slavery in Negro-Egypt, with extensive interbreeding amongst Negro-Canaanites after departing from Ham-Africa.

*The word burn in Hebrew and Egyptian means Ham (Black), whereas brass or copper in hieroglyphics, is pronounced Kam, the same as Ham. The words niello and melaconite means black brass or copper.

Matt. 13: 54-55; Luke 4: 22; Matt. 12:9, 15; 22: 45; John 7: 42; Rev. 12: 5, 13.

THE GOOD SAMARITAN

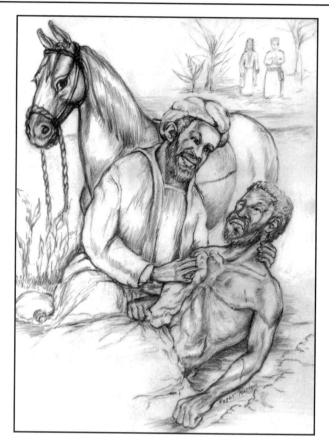

The Good Samaritan is merely a parable used by Jesus to exemplify the deed of a good neighbor. This Ethiopian-Cuthean (a half Black and Jew, which constituted a Samaritan) was described by the Messiah to exemplify the finest example of an individual coming to the rescue of a neighbor. The Messiah's description of this heroic Samaritan began when a certain man traveled from Jerusalem to Jericho, and fell among robbers who stripped and wounded him, then departed, leaving him half-dead. Now, by coincidence, a priest, then a Levite traveled the same dangerous road, but when seeing the wounded man, both went on the opposite side and continued their journey. However, when a certain Samaritan traveled the road and saw the wounded man, he immediately showed mercy by approaching him, and commenced to attend his wounds. He then mounted the wounded man on his beast and brought him to an inn for care, whereupon the next day during his departure, the Good Samaritan gave the innkeeper two pense, and asked him to nurture the man; promising to compensate the innkeeper upon his return, if the injured man's expense exceeded the two pense.

The moral of this parable is to illustrate that a neighbor isn't necessarily a person living in ones community. The cruel negligence of the priest and Levite regarding one of their own people was total contrast to the Samaritan's behavior concerning his afflicted enemy. This Ethiopian-Cuthean who was a member of a race despised and rejected by the Jews, truly demonstrated the perfect model of a Saint.

Jesus used the oppressed Negro-Samaritans as a genuine example of how a Saint should behave, particularly the story of the ten lepers (Luke 17:11-19).

Following the death of the Savior, these Black Samaritans at one time were forbidden to read the Bible or teach it to their children. Their homes and assemblies were mobbed and many suffered terrible massacres, with increasing atrocities for minor offenses. They were regarded as eternal enemies by the Christians, Muslims and some Jews; and even when they converted, they were still denied the same privileges from bureaucrats. This brutal hatred and Holocaust against the Negro-Samaritans continued even after the collapse of the Byzantine and Ottoman Empires (1453-1922 A.D.).

In 1934 there existed only 206 Samaritans, a number that increased to 430 in 1970. One of the reasons for this growth stemmed from marriages between the Samaritans and the Jewish women. *

The name Samaritan is actually spelled Hamaritan, since the ancient letter S was exchanged for H; naturally the translation of Ham- of Hamaritan means Black or Negro. The Samaritan also called themselves Shamerim or Shemerim (Shemer, I Kings 16:23-24), whereas Sham- of Shamerim also means Ham, since the Hebrews on many occasions spelled Ham, "Hham;" whereby the capital letter H was substituted with S.

*The Jews intermarriage with Ethiopians (same as Cush or Cuth), sprung forth a peculiar people called the Samaritans (Cutheans by the Jewish historian Josephus). The Negro-Samaritans were originally from Assyria or Babylon, the land of their forefather Nimrod, who was the son of Cush and grandson of Ham. The intermarriage between the Ethiopians and Jews gradually amalgamated the two groups into one race. This old matrimonial practice was also exercised in the Jewish priestly lineage (Ezra 4:2; Neh. 13:27-28).

The Jewish writer Moscati, says: "The Assyrians, Babylonians, Hebrews and Arabs were of one people." How ironic that the name Israel was once called Samaria, and that the Negro-Samaritans would often call themselves Hebrews, a claim that caused a bitter strife between the two groups (Isa. 9:9-12; Ho. 8:5; Amos 3:9; Ezek. 16:53). When Jesus was asked if He was a Samaritan with a demon, He denied having a demon, but wouldn't deny Himself as a Samaritan (John 8:48-49).

Dictionary of the Bible (They intermingled with the Israelites. Their descendants were Samaritans, described by the Hebrews as Cutheans), Hastings, pp. 195, 880. 1973; Eerdmans Dictionary of the Bible (Josephus called them Cutheans. They claim their descent from Ephraim and Manasseh), p. 1159. 200; A New System (Cuthites were Ethiopians), Bryant, 1807; and Encyclopedia Judaica (The Rabbis called Cutheans, "Samaritans." The people of Babylon, Cutha, Hamith and Israel, developed the Samaritans), Vol. 5, p. 1176; Vol. 14, pp. 724, 727, 737-738. 1971.

Gen. 10:6; II Kings 17:24, 30; Luke 10:29-37.

SIMON OF CYRENE

Simon, a black man, helped the Messiah bear His cross to Mt. Calvary. He was probably visiting Israel preceding the trial and crucifixion, since blacks themselves had their own synagogue in Jerusalem. Simon was presumably standing among the crowd as Jesus struggled with the cross near him. There he was compelled to share Christ's burden toward the place of the skull. Nothing more is said about him, except for the mention of his two sons Alexander and Rufus, who became leaders in the Christian church. The Apostle Paul saluted Rufus because of his devoted ministry and for laying his life on the line for Paul.

It was these Negro-Cyrenian Phutite Jews who spread Christianity to the Greeks (Acts 11:20; 13:1-3).

Simon and his brothers were (Cyrenians or Libyans) called Hebraist Jews (a person studying Hebrew rituals); from this with other documentation, we know that Africa had black Jews (including from Abraham) over two thousand years ago.

The Jewish philosopher Philo (40B.C. to 40 A.D.) says that in his lifetime, there were one million Jews living in central and Northern Africa. Godbey, in his book called "The Lost Tribe: A Myth," states that millions of Negro Jews lived in Africa.

Matt. 27:32; Mark 15:21; Luke 23:26; Acts 6:9; Ro. 16:4, 13.

SIMON THE CANAANITE

Simon was one of Jesus' twelve Apostles, who was honorably called a Canaanite because of his descent from Ham through Canaan (Gen. 10:6).*

The Apostle Simon, prior to meeting Christ, belonged to a faction called the Zealots, whose objective was to expel Romans from Palestine by advocating armed revolution. However, after becoming a follower of the Messiah, the converted Canaanite changed his stance and became an Apostle of God's love (I Cor. 14:12). The "Hamitic" Simon was a Jew by nationality and culture, not through genealogy, since he was a descendant of Ham.

The Negro Canaanites dominated Palestine, which was originally called the Land of Canaan, years before Abraham or any of his descendants existed.

The Apostles or Disciples without a doubt were Blacks. When a great multitude went to arrest Jesus and couldn't recognize Him among His Disciples, was evidence that the Disciples' complexion and hair resembled Jesus,' whom happen to be black with woolly hair. The name Simon was also applied to other Negro Characters, such as Simon called "Niger," who was a teacher and prophets at the church of Antioch, Simon Peter and Simon of Cyrene who carried the Jesus' cross. The name Simon is actually spelled Himon or Hamon, since the ancient letter S was exchanged for H (Matt. 10:4; Acts 13:1; Dan. 7:9; 10:6; Rev. 1:14-15).

Gen. 10:6; Matt. 10:1-7; 26:47-48; Mark 3:18-19; Luke 6:12-16; Acts 1:12-14.

SIMEON THAT WAS CALLED NIGER
AND LUCIUS OF CYRENE

Lucius and Simeon were chosen men of God who were teachers and prophets of an Antioch church located in Syria, about three hundred miles north of Jerusalem. They suffered threats and persecution following the crucifixion of Jesus but chose to sustain themselves through their preaching, which proved them worthy leaders in the Church.

Lucius was from Cyrene, which is in the northern part of Africa. He, like Simon the Cyrenian, also supported the black Church established in Jerusalem. Simeon the Niger was also from Africa, but from a different region called Niger.*

These two men ordained Barnabas and Saul by the demand of the Holy Ghost (Acts 13:1-3). Saul, who later acquired the name Paul, ministered to more of the Gentile nations than any other saint! It is certain that the roles Lucius and Simeon played triggered a momentous change in the religious world.

*From the word Niger derived the European words Negrum, Negre, Negrillo, Nigrito, Negrus, Negro, nigger, etc. The Ethiopian royal title "Negus;" which means King, is a synonym of the Portuguese word Nego, meaning Negro. The derogative word nigger, is linked to the words Negro, Nego, Niger and Negus, meaning King; see the following sources: Oxford English Dictionary (see Negus), Portuguese-English Dictionary, by Taylor, p. 440; Grande Dizionario Della Lingua Italiana, p. 322; Cassell's Spanish Dictionary, by Funk & Wagnalls, p. 1163; Origins Etymology Dictionary, pp. 431-432; Dr. William Smith's Dictionary of the Bible, Vol. 1, p. 4. 1890; Enciclopedia Universal Sopena (Nego means Negus), Tomo Sexto, Vol.6, p. 5947. 1964; and Kleins Comprehensive Etymological Dictionary of the English Language, p. 1037.

Christianity was largely developed on the continent of Africa. Ethiopia aided the early birth of Christianity, while all in Europe were worshiping Caesar, Odin, etc.

The Vulgate was the Latin version of the Bible. The name is equivalent to Vulgate edition (the current text of the Holy Scripture). The history of the earliest Latin version of the Bible is lost.

All that can be affirmed is that it was written in Africa in the first century. In the fourth century a new version by Jerome was universally accepted, but was refuted within that era by the African scholars.

St. Augustine, a black born in northern Africa in 354 A.D., set the moral doctrine of the Christian Church.

Acts 6:9; 8:27-39; 13:1; Ro. 16:21.

THE EUNUCH: "A SEEKER"

This prime minister was sent to Jerusalem under the authority of Queen Candace of Ethiopia. His main task was to seek knowledge concerning the new religion that revolutionized Israel, and then to return to his own land. (Ethiopians then were under Judaism, while at the same period Europe was worshiping idols). He journeyed over a thousand miles across Africa before reaching his destination. While there, he gathered Biblical material regarding Christ and His divine will.

When his visit to Jerusalem came to an end, the eunuch mounted his chariot and traveled toward Gaza with a roll, which contained the fifty-third chapter of Isaiah. It was this chapter he was reading when Philip the Evangelist approached his chariot, questioning him about his understanding of the Scriptures. He informed Philip that he obtained no values in what he had read and asked him to explain the material to him (since he only knew Judaism).[1] So, the Evangelist did accordingly, and when they saw water, the Ethiopian received baptism. This eunuch left Ethiopia as a queen's treasurer, but it is almost certain that he became a more important figure when he returned to his land. Today Ethiopia still upholds the Christian faith which was instituted by this prime minister nearly two thousand years ago.

E. Ullendorff, in his book, "Ethiopia and the Bible," says that the Eunuch under Candace was called Candacis.

The British writer C. F. Rey in his book, "Unconquered Abysinnia" (Ethiopia), declares that Ethiopia was a great nation when the first book of the Bible was written, and was practicing Christianity while Europe was still worshiping Thor and Odin (Acts 17: 23; I Thess. 1: 9).

The American writer J. H. Shaw, in his book, "Ethiopia," states that Ethiopia had instituted Christian churches throughout its land long before William the Conqueror set foot in England and a thousand years before Columbus discovered the New World.

Acts 7: 23–39.

Roger Harlan

QUEEN CANDACE: "QUEEN MOTHER"

Candace was a queen of Ethiopia around the time of Christ. Her name is royal, as she is descended from a long line of Candaces. She is accredited with bringing Christianity to her country by sending her high treasurer to Jerusalem to enquire upon the new religion of Christ.

Some scholars believe the name Condace, which means Queen Mother, was not a personal name, but rather a dynastic title such as Pharaoh, Caesar, Herod and Ptolemy, since all Cushite Queens bored the title Candace.

According to Reisner, in his book called "Anglo Egyptian Sudan," all Candaces, like the Pharaohs of Egypt, were buried in pyramids. The name Candace is found in a ruined pyramid in ancient Ethiopia (Lipsius. Denkmaler, V 47; Cailliaud, plate XLVI). One of the pyramids in ancient Meroe bared a picture of a Candace which can still be seen at Kaga.

The Candaces were the first women to ever rule a country without any interruption for seven hundred years (350 B.C. to 350 A.D.). One of the most remarkable Candaces of Ethiopia reigned during the era of Alexander the Great. Other than carrying the title of Queen, she also commanded Ethiopia's army, and several times led her country into decisive battles, even against Alexander in 332 B.C. During that campaign, the Queen was able to stop the conqueror, forcing him to return to Egypt. To protect his fame, Alexander made no other attempt to conquer the children of Cush.

In 24 B.C., the Ethiopian Candace Amanirenas repelled an invasion by the Roman governor and general Gaius Patronius. She devastated three Roman legions, sacked southern Egypt, and set fire to Thebes. In addition, Amanirenas defaced a statue of Emperor Augustus Caesar by detaching the head, then bringing it back to Ethiopia as a prize, latterly burying it in the doorway of an important building as an act of disrespect (Keating, Nubian Twilight, p. 70). Augustus, who was disappointed with defeat, vowed to lay his arms aside if Amanirenas would negotiate a peace settlement, which she accepted. During the negotiation, the Emperor through frustration, reluctantly gave the Queen everything she demanded. The Greek writer Strabo stated: "Amanirenas won."

The Virgin Queens of Ethiopia were also called "Negeste Negestate," meaning Queen of Kings. The title is also a synonym to Nega, meaning Black-female, Negress, Niger, Nigger, Ham or Hammoleketh (I Chron. 7:17, 18), whereas today's Kings uses the title "Negus," to indicate King of Kings. Moreover, the title is equivalent to Nego, Negro, Black, Niger, Nigger, Ham or Hammelech (Jer. 36:26). The above information is found in the following sources: Unger's Bible Dictionary (Abed-Nego; Nebo, a Babylonian God), pp. 2, 781. 1957; Cleveland Bible Commentary (Nego was pronounced Nebo); Enciclopedia Universal Sopena (Negus means Nego), Sexto, Vol. 6, p. 5947. Webster's New Collegiate Dictionary (Negus means King of Kings, ruler of Ethiopia), p. 762. 1981; and The Portugese English Dictionary (Nega and Nego means Negress and Negro), Taylor, p. 440. 1970.

Ancient Africa was as popular in culture and power as today's leading nations. Africa gave the world writing and arithmetic, buildings of stone, and the fundamentals of war and government, ideas which Europe, the Western Hemisphere, Asia, and other nations borrowed to construct their own civilizations. For ages Africa was a continent of inventors who gave the benefits of its culture to the world.

Acts 8:27: Rev. 19:16.

RUFUS AND ALEXANDER

Rufus and Alexander were sons of Simon the Cyrenian, who was ordered to bear the Messiah's cross. These two faithful servants became leaders in the Christian church. The Apostle Paul saluted Rufus because of his devoted ministry and for laying his life on the line for Paul.

It was these Negro-Cyrenian Phutites who spread Christianity to the Greeks (Acts 11:20; 13:1-3).

The term Rufus in Old Latin means Niger or brown. The ancient Greeks defined Rufus as "deep" and "dark-colored," whereas the Spaniards, "dark-brown." The modern term is defined as red, which is the same as black, since the color black and red are equally the same. Let it be acknowledged that when blood is caught in a vessel, it becomes cool, afterward drying up, leaving a black solid mass or clot. However, if removing that scab, solid mass, or clot to a moisured environment, or water; that same black scab, through maceration, will turn red again. The above information is found in the following sources: The Origin Of Races and Color (red and black can produce one another), M.R. Delany, pp. 23-24, 32. 1879 & 1991; and Language Monographs (Rufus means Niger): Hittite Glossary (1-5), E.H. Sturtevant, p. 10. 1930-1.

Mark 15:21; Luke 23:26; Ro. 16:13.

XIII

ABSENCE OF AFRICA'S THEOLOGICAL HISTORY

EXPOSITORY COMMENTS I

May the readers be reminded that Noah's youngest son Ham (Ham, Egypt's Amen or Amen Ra, India's Om and Greece's Zeus) was used by God to populate the world with Hamitic people. This man was created for a special purpose but has not been honored as have his brothers Shem and Japheth.

For centuries, instead of putting him in his respective place, world scholars and authors displayed Ham as an underdog. It is strange that such a man—who fathered the Egyptians, Ethiopians, Libyans, and influenced the Israelites and Arabians through crossbreeding, as well as fathering the African-Americans (who were kidnapped from the land of Ham, "Africa")—has received only minor recognition. Ham's descendants who have become legends include Ramesses, Solomon and the Ethiopian Queen of Sheba (Sheba, Artimis or Diana to the Greeks; just Diana to the Romans).

The Bible clearly states the origin and history of the black race, but through time, black people have not been properly recognized among the children of Ham or linked with Japheth or Shem. In Genesis 9: 18-19, Noah's three sons Shem (Semitic or Hebrew), Ham (Hamitic-Black or Negro) and Japheth (Caucasian or European) are mentioned as being the fathers of people and nations. It is known that Ham was a continuous father of the Colored race, which mixed over the centuries with other races.

From 90 A.D. in Jamnia; 325 A.D., in Nice, Turkey; 1553 and 1611 A.D. in England, up until modern times, changes have been made within the Bible that conceal the black identity. This occurred in European Bible translations, western revisions and teachings from some clergymen and scholars.

When the first book of the Bible was written, the Negro nations were mentioned before any other nation of man (Gen. 2: 11-13), and they existed even during and after the Roman empire (Acts 8: 27: The Negro Egyptians, unlike their Ethiopian brothers, collapsed under Greece and Rome).

The exploitation of Bible translations and revisions was not aimed at discarding man's inquiry of salvation whether he be red, white or yellow. The primary purpose was to minimize the black identity in Europe, North American and other lands. Not only were words and verses extracted from the Scriptures, but also entire books were omitted. (About eighteen books, largely involving the African literary contribution within the area of reincarnation, were removed from the Koin Bible, considered the original Bible of that period, 50 A.D. to 100 A.D.).

The modern-day Catholics, who have 73 books in their Bible, the Protestants with 66 books, and the Jews with 39 books, have still not agreed on the number of books the Bible should have.

Some contemporary Hamites or Blacks, chiefly those of Europe and America, seem to remain blind to the origin of the Bible, and to take no stand as to their Biblical heritage. That race which seeks knowledge of itself, will have to find and nourish that knowledge within itself, not depending on others who may overlook or discredit it!

Was Abraham Prejudiced?

Why did Abraham refuse to allow Isaac to marry a daughter of Canaan, "Ham" (Gen. 24: 32; 28: 1)? Was Abraham prejudiced? It may seem as though he was, but as a clean-hearted servant before God, it is very obvious that he was not prejudiced. God did not tolerate such sin, especially from his chosen leaders. When Miriam spoke against Moses concerning his Negro-Ethiopian wife, God became angered and cursed her with leprosy. Prejudice is a sin, and when the heart is full of love, prejudice is unknown.

Abraham himself was married to a black woman from Egypt (Gen. 16: 3), which clearly indicates his true feelings toward intermarriage. It was not the intermarrying to which he objected, but the concern of a promise made to him regarding his people's future. God had made a covenant with him that his seed should multiply as the sand in the sea, and that from them should arise a great priest (Jesus). Also, that the land upon which he stood (which belonged to the black Canaanites) should one day belong to his people (Gen. 15: 12–16, 19–21; Ex. 33: 1–2). He knew his seed could not become full owners of the land if he allowed them to mix. So, the patriarch's favor of separation resulted from consideration of land rights, and the fulfillment of God's promise, not prejudice!

Regardless of Abraham's warnings, the Hebrews or Jews still intermingled their seed with the Negro Canaanites.

Abram

When Abram harkened to the voice of God and ventured from Haran to Canaan, God blessed him and made his offspring heir to the Land of Canaan. God knew that Abram and his seed would live and deal among the descendants of Ham; therefore, God changed his name from Abram to Abraham (Gen. 11: 26; 12: 1–6; 15: 13, 18–21; 17: 5–7).*

*J. Ballou, *The Oahspe Bible* (The third syllable of the name Abraham derives from that of black Ham), p. 327. London, 1882.

Hidden Facts About Blacks

The Bible has been translated several times and during the translations many blacks were excluded from the Scriptures or camouflaged as being of other ethnic groups. Even though the Bible speaks of Canaanites and Egyptians as being Hamitic (black-skinned people), they are often looked upon in American and European history books and movies as light-skinned, blue-eyed blonds (Japhites).

Anthropologists' study of Egyptian statues and skeletons, such as Ramesses II, show their facial features to be those of a Negro. The Greek historian Herodotus said, "There were not too many Pharaohs in Egypt who did not have kinky hair and black skin." Cleopatra,* was always portrayed as a black African Queen.[1] The great dramatist Shakespeare called her *schwarthy,* which still means *black* in German. The Roman writer Cornelius Capitolinus praised her beauty and dark skin.

Awareness of Biblical heritage awakens Blacks to see that they of all people were first used by God (Gen. 2: 13). Also, the Bible speaks more of the seed from Ham than from Japheth. After the 1960s, many revised or paraphrased editions of the Bible deny black Americans, or other Blacks around the world, any spiritual-historical connection with Ham by saying that he (Ham) populated Africa but was not black, and that Blacks did not descend from him.

Since the beginning of earlier times, from ancient Ethiopia and Egypt, Blacks (Negroes) played significant roles in developing nations and civilizations. When the world was relatively uncivilized, the African Negroes were already working mathematics, using an alphabet, building pyramids, palaces, homes of bricks, temples, yielding crops, raising livestock, and melting metal that was molded into other objects such as tools, weapons and utensils. Blacks also excelled in the fields of arts, literature, merchandizing, science, engineering, medicine, politics, religion, etc. Those ancient civilizations lasted for thousands of years, longer than any civilization known to man. It reached its peak and subsided long before Europe was born.[2] There were others like Mali, Songhay and Ghana that produced some of the finest universities and political structures in the world,[3] where at one time, untold numbers from abroad would visit Africa to seek knowledge. For centuries Blacks were in the "highlight" of all progress.

Cleopatra's father Ptolemy XIII, sometimes called Ptolemy XI, was labeled "The Bastard," since he was a son of a Negress mistress of Ptolemy Lathymus. A picture of him in Lepsius K. Denkmaler's reference book on Egyptian and Ethiopian art, printed in 1849 by R. Lipsius, Berlin, Germany, portrays him with Negro lips. P. Elgood, "The Ptolemies of Egypt," p. 175. 1938.

THE INTERMARRIAGE BETWEEN BLACKS AND HEBREWS

Abraham, the father of Ishmael and Isaac, slept with a black woman named Hagar. She bore him his first son, Ishmael. Hagar was Sarah's handmaid from Egypt.

Notice the name of Ham's second son Mizraim is interpreted as "Egypt" (Gen. 10: 6; 16: 1–3, 16).

Shechem, a black prince, married Dinah, Jacob's daughter (Gen. 34: 1–8, 12).

Esau, the brother of Jacob, married Judith, Bashemath, and Mahalath, who were Negro women. Isaac and Rebekah did not approve of Judith and Bashemath because of their "pure" Negro origin (Mahalath was a half-breed from the half-breed Ishmael). Rebekah feared them because of a poor relationship with Esau. Mahalath was more accepted, since she was Isaac's niece by his mixed-blood brother Ishmael (Gen. 26: 34–35; 27: 46; 28: 9).

Moses, the Israelite leader, married a Negro (Cushite, same as Ethiopian) woman. She was a descendant of Ham's first son, Cush (Gen. 10: 6; Num. 12: 1).

David married a black woman named Bathsheba (Solomon's mother). She was the former wife of Uriah the Hittite, who was a Negro cavalryman in David's army. The Hittites were a dark race from Ham's grandson Heth (Gen. 10: 15; I Chron. 1: 13; II Sam. 12: 9).

Solomon, being black himself, married hundreds of Negro princesses. These women were daughters of kings or Pharaohs. They came from royal families, since King Solomon was man of legend. The Egyptians, Hittites, and Sidonians were offspring of Ham's sons and grandsons Heth, Mizraim, and Sidon (I Kings 11: 1; I Chron. 1: 8, 13). The Edomites were also descendants of Ham through Judith, Bashemath, and Mahalath.

THE NINETEENTH EGYPTIAN DYNASTY

Ramesses I
Seti I (2)
Ramesses II (1)
Merneptah
Amenmesses
Seti II
Siptah

EGYPT

Some scholars advocate that Egypt is called the land of the black because of its soil. Egypt is called the land of the black because of the black people who walked on the soil.

WHAT HAPPENED TO BLACK DOMINANCE?

How is it that Negroes, who discovered science, engineering, medicine, and fine arts—once living on the highest order, mastering the world's highest economy and diplomacy for thousands of years, long before Europe was born—now find themselves on the lowest echelon?[1]

Once the richest people on earth with vast resources (including diamond mines still existing today) located throughout Africa now in the twentieth century find themselves poverty stricken, living in some of the most deplorable areas (ghettos and slums) around the globe!

To have reached such heights in world dominance, what could have occurred at a later period to cause such a great civilization to collapse? What could have happened to the "Negro-African race," to make its members embarrassed of their own color when over three-fourth of earth's population, who are non-white, share this color?

Black supremacy existed from the Biblical architectural Nimrod (Nimrod, Hercules to the Greek) to the historical military "genius" Hannibal. Many historians have documented that during the fall of Hannibal, black supremacy ended.

CANAAN'S CURSE

One thousand years after the curse on Canaan, the first Negro nation out of seven to fall under the curse was Gibeon (Amorites and Hivites, Deut. 7:11; Josh. 9:2-3, 7, 15-16, 21-27:10-12).

When Israel left Egypt as slaves to subjugate Canaan, Joshua and his successors could not eliminate all of the Canaanites; therefore, millions of them remained in the Land of Canaan for centuries. As time passed, the land was invaded and ruled by the Greeks (Javan) and Romans (Gen. 10:1-5). Those invaders were Europeans, the children of Japheth.

The curse on Canaan's offspring ended around 450 A.D., following Rome's withdrawal from Palestine; no longer were the Black Canaanites under a Japhite or Hebraic rule. The Canaanites as a race gradually lost their identity through mix-breeding among the Hebrews (Gen. 34:21; Judg. 3:5-6).

Centuries later Europe, North America, etc. invaded Africa and took many citizens for slaves. They proclaimed themselves to be the fulfillers of a curse (placed on Ham: the Canaanites, children of Ham), which had been consummated over twelve centuries before their time in the Land of Canaan. Remember, the curse only applied to the Black African Canaanites, not the African Blacks of Cush, Mizraim and Phut (Gen. 9:24-25).

WERE CANAANITES SEMITES?

Many scholars have referred to Canaanites as being Semites. However, this can be a misleading appellation, if not thoroughly explained. For instance, since Canaanites dwelled among Israelites (following Israel's departure from Egypt to Canaan), they were able to learn the Semitic language, customs, and laws. From such encounter, scholars could assume that Canaanites were Semites only by culture but not through genealogy, since they were descendants of Ham.

The name Canaan or Canaanite only applied to the original people of the Land of Canaan. They called themselves Canaanites because they were offspring of the Black man Ham's youngest son, Canaan (Gen. 9:18, 22). The Jews, after seizing Canaan, never called themselves Canaanites, but rather addressed their race as Hebrews, Israelites, or "of the seed of Abraham" (John 8:33; Ro. 11:1; II Cor. 11:22; Phil. 3:5; Jonah 1:9).

The Jewish female would use the term "Hebrewess or Israelitish" (Jer. 34: 9; Lev. 24: 10), while the black female used the term "Canaanitess" (I Chron. 2: 3).

*N. Slouschz, *Travels in North Africa*. Philadelphia: The Jewish Publication Society of America (Canaanites were Africans), p. 337. 1927.

Were There Black Semites?

There were many black-skinned Semites from Shem.[1] Abraham, Isaac, Jacob and their descendants up until Gehazi (Gehazi, a black-skinned man who was changed white with Naaman's leprosy. The leprosy became part of his genes; therefore, all of his offspring were of white complexion and were looked upon as having black skin originally—II Kings 5: 27).

There is Scriptural evidence to support this fact, but first it should be noted that Egyptians during that era were coal black. According to Gen.10: 6, the man Egypt was Ham's second son, which made the Egyptian people Africans by blood.

When Joseph was sold to the Africans (Egyptians) as a slave, years later he gained his freedom and became a governor of Egypt. Such a position gave him full authority over Egypt's food supply, which meant that all outsiders who wanted to buy had to first consult with him. When Joseph's ten brothers came to Egypt to buy corn, they did not recognize him.

If Hebrews had been white, then Joseph's brothers could have so easily recognized him among so many black-skinned Egyptians. But during their meeting, Reuben and his brothers thought Joseph to be another Egyptian (since Egyptians and Jews were of the same color). This can be proved from a report to their father, Jacob: "The lord of the land spoke roughly to us (Gen. 39: 1; 42: 1–30)."

When the Pharaoh of Egypt ordered the slaying of every Hebrew male baby, Moses was secretly hidden in a basket in the Nile. He was soon found and adopted by Pharaoh's daughter and then became a member of Pharaoh's household. The Pharaoh at that time hated Hebrew babies; therefore, if Moses had been a white child, he would have easily been discovered. To see a white-skinned baby playing with a group of black babies would have aroused much suspicion from the Pharaoh.

Moses' concealment was not so difficult because of his dark skin (Ex. 4: 6–7). He was a black Hebrew living among "black Egyptians."[2]

The thirteenth chapter of Leviticus also verifies the fact that Hebrews were black in color, as they were warned regularly about white bright spots appearing in their skin or hair turning white or yellow from leprosy (Lev. 13: 4–5, 10–11, 30–33, 36–37). It is clearly understood that Hebrews of that epoch were not born with white complexion or white-yellowish blond-looking hair. White hair was found only in the elderly when prior discovery, if not from old age, merely meant a sign of leprosy. All people who bore such characteristics, other than white hair from old age, were pronounced unclean and segregated. According to Jehovah, black hair was a positive sign of good health; also the darkening (including freckles) of the skin, found in the white leprosy, was a signification of healing (Lev. 13: 30–31, 36–37, 39)!

THE HIGHLIGHTS OF "HAM" AFRICA

In Gen. 2: 11, Africa is mentioned first of all lands. The name Havilah is the same as Cush or Ethiopia; Ethiopia is located on the continent of "Ham" Africa (Gen. 10: 6–7; Ps. 105: 23–27; 106: 19–23). Africa is the "Mother" of the earth since it is the creation spot of Adam and Eve (Geographically, Eden was located in Africa). It was Africa that pioneered the world in medicine, science, engineering, fine arts, religion, etc.* Abraham visited Africa, while at a later period, his grandson Jacob and the entire Hebrew race resided there (Gen. 12: 10; 47: 1). The great Israelite leader Moses and the black Lady of the South, "The Queen of Sheba" were born on the continent of Africa (Matt. 12: 42). Jesus lived most of His childhood in Africa (Ps. 68: 31; Hos. 11: 1; Matt. 2: 13–15). Following Christ's crucifixion, the first nation to become Christianized, other than Israel, was Ethiopia of Africa (Acts 8: 27). Africa held the last known "recorded seed" (Haile Selassie of Ethiopia) of King Solomon and Makeda "Sheba" through their son Menelik I. The blood of Solomon and Makeda reigned in Africa, "Ethiopia," for nearly 3,000 years. Selassie died in 1974.

*J. Hiernaux, *The People of Africa* (Behaviors, ideas, objects, knowledge and beliefs, and their development began in Africa), p. 1. 1975.

DIVINE USE OF THE COLOR BLACK

If black or dark colors had represented shame or inferiority, then why would "The Almighty Jehovah" jubilantly array Himself in the form of blackness. Abraham, Moses, David and Solomon often visualized God in the form of blackness (thick darkness), which represented Omnipotence (all powerful)! Of all the different colors of the universe, why would Jehovah commonly fashion Himself in a darkish-blackish color? During the crucifixion, darkness covered the land. Was it God, who had previously appeared in dark forms (Matt. 27: 45)?

HAMITES

May it be remembered that there are several classes of Hamite people who differ from one another in appearance and culture. Some are those who have long noses and thin lips, while those of other tribes have heavier lips and broad noses (Gen. 10: 6, 13–18).

All Blacks in Africa did not resort to tribal life; Egypt and his older brother Ethiopia formed governments that rivaled Europe's for thousands of years.

There were many Hamites who did not travel to what is perceived as Africa today, following the desertion at Babel. It is a known fact that one of Ham's sons and numerous grandsons journeyed east and west, instead of south, to what is referred to as Africa today. They dwelt in such places as Babylon, Arabia, Asia Minor (Hittite), Crete, Cypress, and Israel (anciently called Africa, or Ethiopia, as Hawaii and Alaska are called America or the United States. Texas was first called "Mexico," Afghanistan, "Iran" and Pakistan, "India") where there were many black priests, prophets, warriors, craftsmen, doctors, teachers, and kings who ruled Judah for centuries.

The Hamites and Hebrews dwelt together for centuries and there was much mixed-marrying and crossbreeding between the two races (Ezra 9: 12; 10: 14, 16–19, 44). Their relationships were unique in that they even exchanged cultures (Gen. 34: 2, 9, 16, 21; Num. 31: 9; Josh. 15: 63; Judg. 1: 21, 3: 5–6). Many Hamites were overlooked because they used Hebrew names and were called Israelites simply for being natives of the state (born and reared in Israel). This can still be observed in Russia, England, Spain, America, etc., where natives can still be traced back to Ham in Genesis 10: 6–20; I Chronicles 1: 8–13.

It has often been stated that Hebrews granted Hamites citizenship in Israel. However, let us not forget that Negroes dominated that region (Canaan-Land) years before the children of Israel left Egypt as freed slaves (Gen. 12: 5–6; 15: 18; Ex. 3: 17; 33: 1–2; Deut. 9: 27–28; 16: 12; Josh. 2: 10; 3: 10).

NOAH'S SONS AND GEHAZI

During the settlement of the Ark, Noah's two sons Ham and Shem were similar in color (dark). This likeness in skin color continued up until Gehazi, who was first a black skinned Semite but later fell under a curse by Elisha, which changed him as white as snow from Naaman's leprosy (II Kings 5: 27). That particular leprosy caused a change in his genes and chromosomes. All of Gehazi's offspring, following his experience, took unto his likeness (white complexion). But before that incident there were no light-skinned Semites by birth.

Scripture does not answer why Japheth was white-skinned. The Bible doesn't speak much of Japheth and his descendants, mainly because it records more history of the East and Africa than of Europe. However, it is certain that after the scattering of Babel, Japheth became white like Gehazi.

Isaac and Rebekah, like Noah and his wife, had sons (Esau and Jacob, who were twins) who differed in skin color. It is explicit in Gen. 25: 25; 27: 11, 23, that one son differed from the other by being red and hirsute (hairy). A similar occurrence happened some two thousand years earlier to Ham, Shem and Japheth, who had the same parents.

MELANIN

Melanin is a body chemical that produces black, dark and brown skin colors, in which to absorb the sun rays and endure tropical living.[1] It is a prehistoric body substance that is genetically found among 85 percent of the people on earth: Africans, Asians, South and Central Americans, North American Blacks and Indians, Australian Aborigines (a Negro race living in Australia)[2] Melanesians (meaning black islanders), Tasmanians (a pure black race, extirpated by English settlers), etc.

The ancient Ethiopians, Egyptians, Phutites, and Canaanites carried more of the melanin in their skins than today's Negroes. Melanin is not as prominent among Negroes in the Western Hemisphere and Europe because of mixed breeding.

EXPOSITORY COMMENTS II
MOST BIBLICAL CHARACTERS ARE BLACK

The Bible was put here for the human race, yet over ninety percent of the Bible stories and events are mainly about Hamites (Negroes or Blacks) and Semites (Hebrews or Semitics). Some of the greatest kings and queens who ever lived arose from such southern countries as Ethiopia, Egypt and Judah.

(1) Zerah, Tirhakah, Amenhotep III, and many queens called Candace were from Cush.
(2) Ahmose I, Nechoh XXVI, Akhenaton, and Ramesses II were from Ham's second son Mizraim.
(3) Jehoash, Jotham, and Josiah were lineages of Jezebel, who descended from Ham.
    God used these people for major and minor chores from Genesis to Revelation, and they adopted names and languages according to the region in which they lived.

In America, Europe, and other lands, the blackest Blacks are mixed with white blood. Conversely, whites possess some five percent of black blood in their veins.

NAMES MISCONSTRUED

There are many names used in our Scriptures which are misinterpreted as being of Jewish origin, such as Ai, Beersheba, Beeroth, Gilgal, Hebron, Jericho, Jerusalem, Joppa, Kedesh, Mamre, Salem, Sidon, Tyre, etc.*

These names were originated and used by the Negroes of Canaan long before Abraham entered the Land of Canaan (Gen. 12: 5–6); the Hebrews adopted these names following their departure from Ham (Ps. 105: 23–27; 106: 21–22). The Israelites borrowed many Canaanite laws and customs. Their ancient language and literature shows much Canaanite influence.

*W. Chomsky, *Hebrew the Eternal Language*. Philadelphia: The Jewish Publication Society of America, p. 34. 1957.

The Twenty-Fifth Egyptian Dynasty
(Ethiopian Period)

Shabaka (or Sabacon)
Tirhakah

1. A. Weigall, *Personalities of Antiquity* ("The Exploits of Nigger King"), N.Y., 1928.
2. *Herodotus, Book II* (When I visited Egypt, the priests revealed a list, consisting of 330 Egyptian Pharaohs; eighteen were Ethiopians).
3. P. Montet, *Eternal Egypt* (The skull we found near the Nile was Negroid.) p. 27, London, 1964.
4. L. Bennett, Jr., *Before the Mayflower* (Dr. Randall Mac Iver says, "How astounding, that an African black man, "Tirhakah," could fashion himself as king of the world"), p. 11.1978.
5. *Encyclopaedia Britannica* (Egyptologist Margaret S. Drower spoke of these black Pharaohs).
6. R. Mac Iver, *Ancient Races of the Thebaid* (The Negro element has existed in Egypt from ancient to modern). 1906.

Who's Who in Asia

Many of the original Asians (also Orientals) were a product of "Cush" (Cush, Apollo to the Greeks) and "Canaan," who gradually settled in the East, following the breakup of Babel (Gen. 11: 8–9). The Greek historian Herodotus, known as the father of history, spoke of the African and Asian Ethiopian; the Smith's Bible Dictionary (Holman) defines Ham as dark, and that his youngest son, Canaan lived in Asia (Canaan-Land. In ancient times, what is modernly called the "Middle East," was known as East Africa);* Professor Munro, a leading authority on Japanese life and culture, says that the people of Japan are a mixture of Negro. Their flat nose, prognathism and brachycephaly, says Munro, could be traced to the Negro.

Smith's Bible Dictionary, Holman, p. 121.

The Eighteenth Egyptian Dynasty:

Ahmose I
Amenophis I (or Amenhotep)
Thotmes I (or Thutmose)
Thotmes II
Hatshepsut
Thotmes III (3)
Amenophis II (2)
Thotmes IV
Amenophis III (1)
Amenophis IV (4)

(Akhenaton)
Smenkhare
Tutankhamen - (5)
    (Tut)
Ay
Horemhab

CAUCASUS

The Caucasus Mountains are located within Europe and Asia, between the Black Sea and Caspian. The etymology of the word Caucasus derived from Noah's oldest son Japheth, meaning Caucasian. The Negroes in Asia who dwelled in the range of the Caucasus mountains were in some instance called Caucasians, in reference to their geographical location, not geneaology. The Greek historian Herodotus called a group of these Negroes "Colchians" (a people who settled on the shores of the Black Sea in a city called Colchis). Having journeyed to Egypt on several occasions, Herodotus was convinced that the Colchians were offspring of the Africans, since their woolly hair and black skins bore a striking resemblance to the Egyptians. *Herodotus, Book II,* Chapter 104.

TRANSLATION OF THE WORD BLACK IN OTHER LANGUAGES

Arabic	Sudan (or Akhal)
Chinese	Hei
Czechoslovakian	Cerny
Danish	Sort
Dutch	Swart
Egyptian	Kem
Finnish	Musta
French	Noir
German	Schwarthy (or Moor)
Greek	Ethiopian (or Apay)
Hungarian	Fekete
Italian	Nero
Japanese	Kuroi
Latin	Nigrus (or Nigrum)
Norwegian	Svart
Polish	Czarny
Portuguese	Nego (or Preto)
Rumanian	Negru
Spanish	Negro
Swahili	Giza (or Susi)
Swedish	Svart
Turkish	Siyah

Vietnamese...Den
Yiddish ....Shuahrts
Hebrew (ancient) ....Ham (or Kam)

The words mulatto and creole are usually used to avoid the usage of the word Negro.

In the early 600s A.D., the most commonly used word throughout Europe to identify people of Africa (Ham), was the term "Moor," which meant people with black faces.

The Ethiopians, Egyptians, and other Negro nations avoided many European terms by solely identifying themselves as African or Hamites (descendants of Ham).

The Ethiopians, Egyptians, Phutites, and Canaanites were none other than Negroes occupying different regions.

THE NEGRO EGYPT, ETHIOPIA, PHUT AND CANAAN

Over 95 percent of all statues and human remains—ranging from prognathism, brachycephaly, cheekbones, nasion, the mouth, lips, pelvis, biceps, melanin in the skin—found throughout ancient Egypt, Ethiopia, Phut and Canaan, bear a striking resemblance to the modern-day Negroes.

BLACK KINGS AND QUEENS OF ISRAEL AND JUDAH

NAME	REIGN
Solomon	Israel
Rehoboam	Israel and Judah

Jezebel

Black queen of Israel, wife of Ahab. She mothered two sons and one daughter, whose offspring ruled the throne of Israel from 849–841 B.C., and Judah's from 841–587 B.C.

Ahaziah	Israel
Jehoram	Israel
Ahaziah	Judah
Athaliah	Judah
Jehoash (or Joash)	Judah
Amaziah	Judah
Uzziah	Judah

Jotham	Judah
Ahaz	Judah
Hezekiah	Judah
Manasseh	Judah
Amon	Judah
Josiah	Judah
Jehoahaz	Judah
Jehoiakim	Judah
Jehoiachin	Judah
Zedekiah	Judah

Other than being a descendant of Ham (Black or Negro), according to the United States Bureau of the Census, any person who has a small percentage of Hamite (Negro) blood, without distinction, must be classified as a Negro: by Langston Hughes and Milton Meltzer, *A Pictorial History of the Negro in America*, p. 2, N.Y. 1968.

Other Sources

Harris, Levitt, Furman and Smith, *The Black Book,* p. 88, N.Y., 1974. Random House Publishing Company, *The Negro Handbook,* p. 3, Chicago, 1966.

THE GARDEN OF EDEN

It has been revealed in the Scriptures that the Garden of Eden was located in Africa somewhere near, or possibly in, Ethiopia.[1] In Genesis 2: 7–14, following the creation of the first man,[2] the Pishon River which compasseth "Havilah" (the area Havilah was located in Africa. It attained its name from a black man named Havilah, who was the second son of "Ethiopia." Gen. 10: 6–7) is affiliated to Adam's environment. Also, the Gihon River which compasseth "Ethiopia" (same as Cush) from the Garden of Eden, is mentioned as being part of Adam's vicinity.

The Pishon and Gihon at one time were associated with the Hiddekel and Euphrates River prior to the Global Deluge. But over a long period of time there occurred a territorial change (with the help of many volcanoes, floods, and earthquakes long after the Great Flood) which separated these rivers from Africa where Eden was located.

The great Jewish historian Josephus and others have associated the Gihon River with the Nile[3] since the word Nile* is a Greek translation of the Hebrew word "Gihon," according to the *Septuagint* (the Greek translation of the Old Testament by seventy-two Jewish scholars under the orders of Ptolemy Philadelphus).

Other clues point to Africa because of its vast resources and archeologists' finding of the oldest prehistoric bones and artifacts in West and East Africa.[4]

The Greeks called the "Nile" the River of Ham.

MISCEGENATION

The early Egyptians were pure black Africans, who had thick lips and broad noses like their southern cousins the Ethiopians (Gen. 10: 6). The Egyptians lost most of their broad features from northern dominations (Europe).

Alexander the Great was one of the first Europeans (Japhites, Gen. 10: 1) to conquer Egypt, in 332 B.C. The longest European rule came from Rome, which held Egypt nearly seven centuries. While residing in Egypt, many Japhites intermingled their blood with the Hamites.[1] By this, the Egyptian people gradually lost much of their bushy-thick fuzzy-wuzzy hair and deep-black skin. This again happened with other Hamitic Negro nations, which were conquered and ruled by the Japhites.

It should also be remembered that such dominance occurred vice versa. There were several European nations which fell under black Africa's rule. Hannibal, the great "genius" Carthaginian general (Carthaginians were Negro-Phoenicians, who were descendants of Ham's grandson Sidon) plundered deep in Europe and seized Spain, Portugal, a portion of France, and made a triumphant trip across the Alps to conquer Rome. While dwelling in Europe, Hannibal and his Negro-African army intermixed their blood with the Europeans; even to this day, the people of those nations that Hannibal conquered have frizzy coiled hair and darkish skin.

Many B.C. historians believed that "Black supremacy" ended following the Hannibalic period.

There are coins of Hannibal in the British Gallery, portraying him as an African wearing earrings.

AFRICAN AERONAUTICS

There is nothing new under the sun (Eccl. 1: 9). The Africans were drawing and flying airships some 2,000 years before Da Vinci's idea of flying, 3,000 years before the Wright Brothers. The Ethiopians had developed airships that could fly a few hundred feet above ground.[1] In 1922, a model of a sailplane was found in the tomb of King Tut. In 1969, Dr. Khalil Missiha, who studies birds, while looking through a box of bird models in a Cairo museum storeroom, was startled to have rediscovered a two-thousand-year-old model of an airplane, made of sycamore wood. It looked modernistic and resembled the American Hercules transport aircraft.[2] The prophet Ezekiel, who lived about 2,500 years ago, witnessed a flying airship (Ezek. 1-3, Chapters).

THE LION OF JUDAH

From Cush came Makeda (the Ethiopian Queen of Sheba) and her historical son Menelik I, who historians of Egypt and Ethiopia claimed to have been the Son of King Solomon. Ethiopia's last monarch, Haile Selassie ("The Lion of Judah") proclaimed himself to be a descendant of Solomon and Makeda through their son Menelik I. He (Selassie) and his predecessors (Yekuno Amlak, Menelik II, and Lij Yasu) often boasted to Europeans of being the only Cushite (Ethiopian) family in the world who could trace their lineage to Solomon and Makeda. Furthermore, Solomon's lineage in the Bible can be traced to Adam.

Even today the Ethiopians call their land the region of Makeda. Historians praised the Black Lady from the South "Makeda" because of her association with Solomon. However, there were greater Negro queens prior to, and after, her.

Haile Selassie ruled Ethiopia for forty-four years, and during his entire reign Europeans' news media would address him as "The Lion of Judah" (because of his descent from Solomon, who was from the tribe of Judah).

The great Jewish historian Josephus says that the "Queen of Sheba was Queen of Ethiopia and Egypt." Josephus' remarks can be found in the following source: Josephus "Antiquitates Judaica" Vol. 5, p. 661. 1966.

Josephus' mention of "Egypt" obviously meant Upper-Egypt, known then as the southern territory of Egypt's Kingdom. From 1168-1091 B.C., Egypt was speedily declining under Ramesses IV-XII, who were all weak monarchs. Because of these weaknesses, Ethiopian troops shrewdly marched into southern Egypt and annexed it to Ethiopia under the Queen of Sheba.

DID YOU KNOW?

(1) The world's first empire following the flood was formulated and ruled by Ham's grandson Nimrod (Gen. 10: 8-10).
(2) The original Babylonians were of Ham's lineage through Cush and Nimrod (Gen. 10: 8-10; Micah 5; 5-6).[1]
(3) The country Ethiopia, of all nations, is mentioned first in the Scriptures (Gen. 2: 12-13).
(4) The whole Palestine region (Canaan-Land, Holy Land, or the land of milk and honey) was formerly inhabited and controlled by black people of Ham (Gen. 12: 5-6; 9: 18; 10: 15-19; Ex. 3: 8; Deut. 7: 1; I Chron. 1: 40).
(5) Africa was once named Ham (Ps. 78: 51; 105: 23-27; 106: 21-22).
(6) The Lord Jesus Christ once lived in Africa (Ps. 68: 31; Matt. 2: 13-15).

HAIR STYLING

The blacks of Ancient Egypt, before propagating with Europeans, used hot combs made of iron to press their thick, woolly, peppercorn hair, over four thousand years ago. Such art was commonly practiced by pharaohs and queens as well as commoners.[1] Blacks also excelled in the field of cosmetics. The first head of hair to ever exist, was Negro wool hair (Dan. 7:9).

Through Canaan, Blacks Were Members of the Davidic Line

God	Gen 1: 1
Adam	2: 7, 19
Noah	5: 32
Ham	9: 18
Canaan	10: 15
Sidon	
Jezebel	I Kings 16: 31
Athaliah	

Athaliah was the daughter of Ahab and Jezebel. She married Jehoram the king of Judah, who was a member of the Davidic line. Athaliah bore Jehoram a son named Ahaziah, whose offspring continued to reign in Judah up until Judah's captivity by Nebuchadnezzar (II Kings 8: 16, 18, 26; 11: 1; 24: 11-16; 25: 1-2, 6-11).

Jechoniah or Jehoiachin

Jechonia was a great descendant of Jehoram and his black wife. It was Jechoniah who continued the Davidic line (Matt. 1: 11-12).

Salathiel
Zorobabel
Abuid
Eliakim
Azor
Sadoc
Achim
Eliud
Eleazar
Matthan
Jacob
Joseph

Skepticism

There has been some controversy about blacks deriving from Cain. God made a promise to destroy man with a flood (Gen. 6: 17). Only Noah and his wife, his three sons, and their wives were saved by entering the Ark (Gen. 7: 7; 8: 15-16, 18). When the Ark rested on Mt. Ararat, only eight individuals disembarked from it (Gen. 9: 18).

The Scriptures don't mention Cain, or any of his descendants boarding or departing the Ark. God didn't allow him or his offspring to board the Ark. Therefore, it is evident that Cain and his seed were extinct (no longer existed) during the Global Deluge. After the flood, the only human existence on earth was Noah's family. The Scriptures tell us that it was Noah's three sons Ham, Shem, and Japheth who populated the earth (Gen. 9: 19).

There has also been debate on Adam's complexion, that he was red. It could have been possible that he was red. Redness can be found in a variety of people throughout the world. There are some red Indians; however, if one makes a closer observance, without a doubt, a blend of darkness can be seen also (The Judaica Encyclopedia, see Adam; the word Adamatu, means dark red earth).

Frank Snowden, Jr., mentions that the Greek Philostratus described Memnon as a black skinned, red-looking man![1] The Greek Statius agreed by speaking of red Negroes with copper-colored skin.[2] M. J. Hershovits says he saw African Negroes who varied in color, from brownish-black to reddish-brown.[3] Snowden mentioned the Ethiopian Lycoris as being black as as mulberry (a dark purplish-red color).

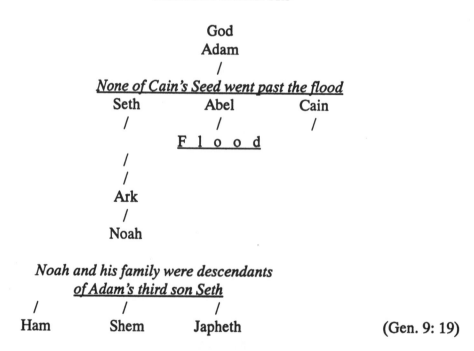

ADAMITIC SURVIVORS

God

Adam

/

None of Cain's Seed went past the flood

Seth   Abel   Cain

/   /   /

F l o o d

/

/

Ark

/

Noah

*Noah and his family were descendants
of Adam's third son Seth*

/   /   /

Ham   Shem   Japheth   (Gen. 9: 19)

The first life to depart the Ark in search of dry land was a large "black" bird called a raven (Gen. 8: 5-7), who is the first named bird in the Bible. This particular bird is viewed by naturalists to be one with the highest intelligence, fitness, and resourcefulness of almost all fowls. Its ability to fly over large territory and survive on a broad variety of food, qualified it to make the first voyage from the Ark.

God miraculously used ravens to transport food to Elijah twice daily while the prophet was hiding from Ahab (I Kings 17: 1-6); later, Jesus spoke of the raven as a model of God's benevolence (Luke 12: 24).

EXPOSITORY COMMENTS III
THE ORIGINAL HEBREWS

The original Hebrews had black skin. For centuries, they lived around black Egyptians, Ethiopians, Canaanites, and other Negro stocks. At one time Hebrews, Egyptians, Ethiopians, Canaanites, and other African tribes were very difficult to distinguish from each other, if documentary (birth record) proof was not available.[1] Usually in such situations, the Hebrews were distinguished by their dialect, dwelling area, and religion.

When Jacob sent his ten sons to Egypt to buy corn, they were confronted by a governor who was their brother (Joseph). None of them recognized him as their flesh and blood or even as a Hebrew. Reuben and his brothers thought Joseph to be another black Egyptian (Gen. 42: 30).

When Moses was rescued from the Nile River and became a member of the Pharaoh's household, Pharaoh Seti I, who passed a decree to slay all Hebrew babies, could not recognize Moses as he walked among his own sons. Moses' dark skin played a major role in concealing him, for Egyptians during that period were extremely black, and for Moses to have had white skin and straight hair would have definitely been a giveaway! For forty years he lived among the black Egyptians passing as an "Egyptian" citizen.

There were several famed historians, such as Tacitus, G. Massey, G. Spiller, etc., who claimed the original Jews to have been black in color, and that the European Jews are light because of mixed marrying into the white race (Japheth).

Another famed historian H. Norden says he saw many black Jews in Ethiopia with kinky hair.[2] The Bible also mentions Jews living in and around Ethiopia (Amos 9: 7; Zeph. 3: 10).[3]

The Hamitic (Negro) Egyptians have for some time been reclassified as Egyptian Caucasoids (white), and so have the Ethiopians (Ethiopians are still called Negroes in many encyclopedias; see Races of Man, also Ethiopia and Africa). The black heritage consists of (Ham) Egypt, Ethiopia, Libya, Tunisia, many African tribes, etc.

There are many reasons for the present Egyptian-Arabic-Jewish wars. One reason can be centered upon the "color issue"; by tradition many Egyptians and Arabs have been taught that the original Jews were dark like themselves, and the light-skinned Israeli Jews were merely European colonialists. Only within the twentieth century has the nation Israel been occupied by a light-skinned race or people. For the Ancient Jews (with whom historically the Arabs and Egyptians are familiar) were not light, but black with Negro features. There are still millions of black-skinned Jews living throughout Israel, Africa, Arabia, etc., who are the majority of our world Jews.

EUROPE'S EARLY CONCEPTION OF JESUS CHRIST

In the year of 705 A.D., a gold coin of Jesus Christ and Emperor Justinian II circulated throughout Byzantine. The full-face bust of Justinian showed him to have had straight hair. The reverse: full-face bust of Christ revealed woolly hair. The image of Christ places beyond a doubt that He was a Negro.[1] The coin was of high interest and later generated a war between Byzantine and a neighboring nation concerning its ownership, according to the Cambridge Encyclopedia Coin Collection Company.

When Pope Pius was head of the Vatican State, an official postage stamp was issued with the Virgin Mary as a Negro on it. There was a similar stamp in Spain commemorating the black Virgin and Child. If Christ were not a Negro, possessing Negroid features, then why for centuries following His death would Europe and Asia make pictures and statues of Him and Mary as being Negroes? M. Etude says that there were 230 black Virgin shrines located throughout France, and 36 elsewhere. Etude's comments can be found in the following source: *Sur L'origine des Vierges Noires,* Paris, 1937.

L. Bertrand says that the Virgin of Front-Romeu had a flat nose, and that Jesus looked like a little woolly-haired African with large ears. Bertrand's remarks can be found in Catalonia, p. 42. 1931.

THE AFRICAN PHOENICIAN

The Hamitic Phoenicians called "Eden," Jeden, Haden, Aden and Ahden. In southeast Ethiopia, there is the district of Ogaden (Og) upper (Aden) Eden.

ADAM AND EVE

Adam and Eve resided southeast of the Mediterranean Sea, in a gigantic land that is identified as the "tropics" (the hottest part of the earth). The Bible, natural history and science have clearly revealed that the original inhabitants of those areas (Ethiopia, etc.), from ancient to modern are born dark-skinned.

The Greek Herodotus of 447 B.C, known as the father of history, said very clearly that people of those regions were black, dark and brown. The tropical man, says Herodotus, "is never white." Dr. Hirschfeld who journeyed throughout the torrid zone, says, "The tropics are no place for a white skinned person, because of his insufficient pigmentation."[1]

One reason for importing Hamitic Blacks from Africa was due to the white's inability to cope with intense sun heat.

Woodruff said that in order to live comfortably in a tropic zone, a person must have black skin as an armor. (Modern-day advancements such as air conditioning, skin chemicals, and medicine have enabled whites to endure tropical living).[2]

Adam and Eve could not have been white-skinned. Observing the Biblical geographical area of their creation (Gen 2: 7-14) should eliminate such fantasy.

THE ORIGIN OF THE WORD BIBLE

The word Byblus or Biblia is a Greek word deriving from an African plant called papyrus, which grew along the Nile River during the Biblical period. The Greek pronunciation of this African papyrus (meaning paper) in their tongue meant byblus, and from the word byblus (meaning books) derived the English word Bible. The Egyptians called their sacred writings, "the books of Ham," the Hebrews, "Ham-Ash," "Hum-Ash" or "Torah (Law)," whereas the Greeks, "Pentateuch," meaning Five. The Hebrew or Semitic word Five meant Ham, Hams or Hames. This information is found in the following sources: A New System, Bryant, Vol. 5, p. 290. 1807; The Introduction of the Comparative Grammar of the Semitic Languages, Moscati, p. 116. 1964; and The Jewish Family Names, Guggenheimer, pp. 319, 350. 1992.

BEARING FALSE IDENTITIES

There are many nations and people who bear false genetic identities. From the beginning of time, Africans ("Hamites") have heavily penetrated Europe by the millions, leaving a large dosage of African blood, thus mutating such nations as Portugal, Spain, Italy and other European lands from white blue-eyed blonds to darkish skinned, brown-eyed, coiled-curly-haired heads. However, those nations and people, regardless of their Negro mixture, still call themselves Caucasoids.

The influential writer Freyre spoke of the Negro intermixture of Spain and Portugal that continued for centuries;[1] the French religious writer Schure says that Blacks intruded Europe in ancient times, but were finally expelled by whites.[2] In 1930 when Hermann Gauch, a researcher on interbreeding, called Italians half-Negroes, the Italian government arose in protest, declaring that no race on earth has kept its purity, not even the Jews. Gauch's book was later suppressed.[3]

J. P. Widney says that the ancient Negroes who largely occupied Africa once settled a much broader region and rendered more authority globally than modern Negroes. He added that traces of the Negroes are found in remote areas, even to the islands of Malaysia.[4]

J. Hawkes and Sir L. Woolley say that the Negroids (same as Negro), left a scattered trail eastward from Africa to southeast India and across the Indian Ocean to the Philippines, Australia,[5] New Guinea, Melanesia and Tasmania.

Ancient Negro remains can be found from Africa to the Fiji Islands, China, Japan, Mexico, South America, Europe, etc.

SCULPTURE AND ANATOMY

The Sphinx, which is the oldest statue known to man, bears the face of a Negro. The Sphinx was built about four thousand years ago and was visited by the French writer Count C. F. Volney in the eighteenth century. He was highly startled to see the jaws projecting beyond the upper part of the face, the broad nose, everted lips and heavy chin; his reply was that it looked strictly Negro.[1] He later wrote, "We owe our arts and sciences to the race of Negroes."[2] A Hewn stone of Pharaoh Zoser of the third dynasty, according to C. A. Diop, exhibits a strong African face with all the characteristics;[3] Dr. Reisner who studied Egyptian portraits dating about 3,000 B.C., called them portraits of Negroes;[4] Count Gurowski says that the architects, artists, mechanics . . . of ancient Egypt were definitely of Negro stock.[5]

Modern falsification (movies, etc.) has claimed ancient Egypt to have been Caucasian. However, ancient records, anthropology, archaeology and geology studies refute such claims, proving that the old and new Egypt were of Negro origin. Their physiques and monuments bear proof of that! *The Negro influence is so revealing that even an unpolished archaeologist, or a non-Bible student could see it.*

THE WAY IT WAS

Europe, from the dawn of her history, up until the French empire, had always recognized Ethiopia and Egypt as Negro nations. However, in 1798 A.D., when the French under Napoleon plundered Egypt, Europe became highly astonished to learn that the Ethiopians and Egyptians, whom they had thought to be inferior because of their sable skin and woolly hair, were actually the originators of the world's first powers.[1] Through archaeology and recorded findings, the French had reluctantly unmasked a hidden civilization of two Negro Elements, which for centuries led the world culturally in science, medicine, engineering, writing (hieroglypics) and buildings of stone, etc.

When Napoleon learned of the superiority of the Negro architecture, he became angered and ordered his soldiers to destroy the Sphinx with cannons and rifle fire. However, their attempts were unsuccessful, only managing to destroy the nose and mouth of the Sphinx. The Sphinx still stands in Egypt today.[2] Napoleon also commanded his soldiers to raise the coffins of Pharaohs under strict orders to mob, burn and disfigure their faces (usually their lips and noses).

Napoleon's expedition without question had disclosed a long buried secret about Africa and her gift to the world. European and American scholars, philosophers, etc., dropped Europe and accepted Africa as the cradle of life and civilization, agreed that western civilization was a borrowed culture from the Negroes; that great thinkers such as Socrates, Aristotle, and Plato had learned much from Africa; and that Negroes were once world dominators while Asia and Europe were relatively uncivilized.[3]

Many Black Jesus and Madonna paintings and statues throughout Europe were destroyed under Napoleon's regime.

THE MOORS

The Negro Moors conquered Europe in 711 A.D. and were the chief power there for the next 600 years. Writings and pictures described them as coal-black with Negro hair. The Moorish contribution in science and art uplifted Europe from the Dark Ages, and before the departure from Europe, the blood of the Negroes was spread immensely throughout the continent. Many of today's darkish-brownish Europeans and American immigrants are of Moorish "Negro" descent. Groups of scholars have fallaciously identified the woolly-haired, black-skinned and everted-lipped Moorish Negroes as African Caucasians, in order to disrupt any notion of a former Negro dominance in Europe.

AN ANCIENT DIVINE COLOR

The color "black" was Egypt's most sacred color![1] The ancient Greeks and others also viewed black as divine. Scripturally, the Hebrews frequently heard Jehovah's voice descending from the thick, dark clouds (Deut. 4: 11–25; 5: 22–23). David says that as God descended from above, He made darkness His secret place; His dwelling area roundabout Him consisted of dark water and thick clouds of the skies (Ps. 18: 11; 97: 2). Solomon later spoke of God dwelling in the thick darkness, referring to the clouds (I Kings 8: 10–12).

At Mt. Sinai, as Moses received the law of God to Israel, Jehovah symbolized His presence to Moses in the form of a dark, thick cloud with great thunder and lightning, the tone of a trumpet and a loud voice (Ex. 19: 16–19).

The color "black" has always been in touch with God, force, power, justice, and wisdom (Deut. 5: 22). Some of the finest judicial systems throughout the globe dress their men of justice in black! The nine justices of the twentieth-century U.S. Supreme Court wear black robes. Many priests, ministers and scholars address their congregations wearing black or dark attire.

Most heads of state, while motorcading among large populations, prefer to be seen in black limousines, which distinguish high position, honor, order, etc.

In Genesis 15: 12–13, Jehovah visited Abraham in the form of great darkness, a darkness of horror!

THE TREE OF DESCENDANTS

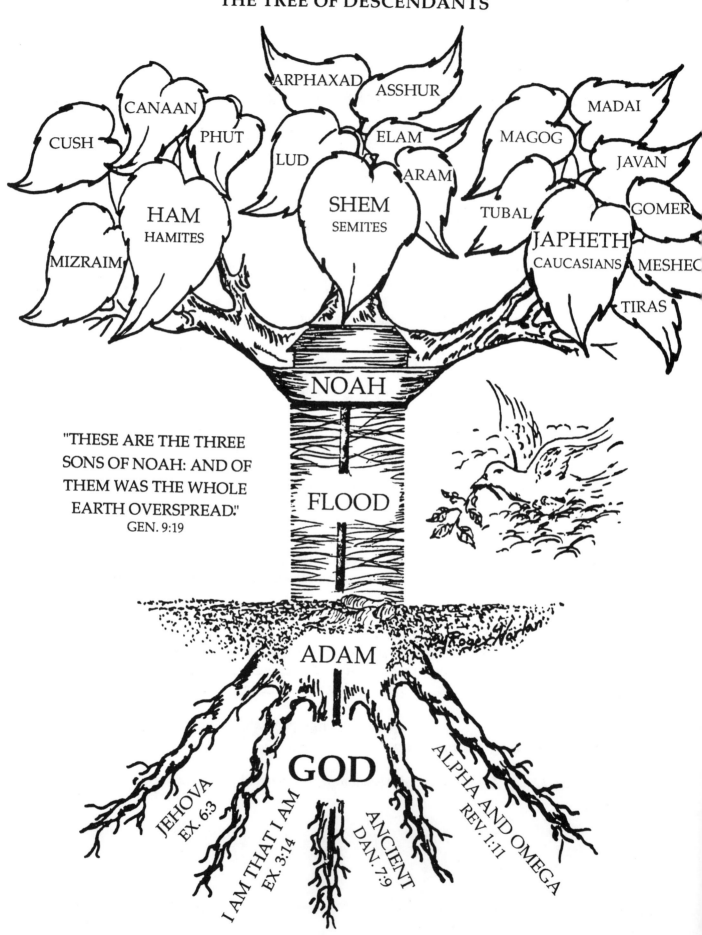

ARPHAXAD
ASSHUR
CANAAN
CUSH
PHUT
MADAI
ELAM
LUD
MAGOG
JAVAN
ARAM
HAM
HAMITES
SHEM
SEMITES
TUBAL
GOMER
JAPHETH
CAUCASIANS
MESHEC
MIZRAIM
TIRAS

NOAH

"THESE ARE THE THREE
SONS OF NOAH: AND OF
THEM WAS THE WHOLE
EARTH OVERSPREAD."
GEN. 9:19

FLOOD

ADAM

GOD

JEHOVA
EX. 6:3

I AM THAT I AM
EX. 3:14

ANCIENT
DAN. 7:9

ALPHA AND OMEGA
REV. 1:11

CHAPTER NOTES

"The worth of a people is determined in how they
honor God, the Bible and their heroes."

I. The Beginning

The Creation and the Garden of Eden

1. R. Davidson, *Genesis 1-11* (1973), 33. Gihon and Pishon, which departed from Eden, were associated with Ethiopia and Upper Egypt.

2. B. Jacob, *The first Book of The Bible* (1974), 17. The second river that departed from Eden was the Nile.

3. J. Hawkes and L. Woolley, *Prehistory and the Beginnings of Civilization* (1963), 1:1. The creature who populated the whole face of the earth is seen ascending out of Africa.

4. R. Ardrey, *Africa Genesis* (1973), 1. The home of our fathers was not in Asia, but Africa.

5. Dr. V. Robinson, *Ciba Symposia* (1940). Africa is the mother of civilization.

6. J. E. Pfeiffer, *The Emergence of Man* (1972), 4. Africa is the home of man.

7. Sir Thomas Browne, English physician and author (1605–1682). There is some African in all of us.

Adam and his Companion

1. Hawkes and Woolley, *Prehistory*, 1. The creature who populated the whole face of the earth is seen ascending out of Africa.

2. Ardrey, *Africa Genesis*, 1. The home of our fathers was not in Asia, but Africa.

3. Dr. J. F. Rock, *New York Times* (26 Nov. 1933). In China there was an unmixed Negro race who had preserved a culture for 2,000 years.

The Ark Rested on Mt. Ararat

1. F. Ratzel, *History of Mankind* (London: 1896–8), 547. A Negritic people occupied a large portion of Asia in prehistoric times.

2. P. Hasluck, *The Black Australians* (1942).

3. E. Smith, *Human History* (London: 1934), 125. The Negro race inhabited New Guinea, Melenesia, the Bismark Archipelago, the Fiji and Polynesia Islands, New Caledonia, and the American coast.

Rasaka ("Roots")

1. Edward A. Johnson, *A School History of The Negro Race in America* (1892), 9–10. Ham was the eponymous ancestor of Africa's people.

2. Herbert Lockyer, *All the Men of The Bible* (1977), 134. Blacks descended from Ham.

3. J. Ballou, *The Oahspe Bible* (London: 1882), 73. Ham was the same as Egypt and Africa.

4. W. Smith, *Concise Dictionary of The Bible* (London: 1865), 305; Ham's Blackness.

5. C. Taylor, *Calmet's Dictionary of the Holy Bible* (London: 1832), 448; Ham, deep Black.

6. Boccardo, *Nuova Encyclopedia Italiana* (1875–88), s. v. "Negri." The words *Negro, Moor,* and *Ethiopia* are different terms to identify a huge African race with black skins of Ham, son of Noah.

II. Ham and His Sons

1. C. A. Diop, *The African Origin of Civilization* (U.S.A.: 1974), 5, 71, 124. Ham was the ancestor of Negroes.

2. "Culture and History of The Black Experience," *The Message Magazine* (Southern Publishing Association, Nashville, Tennessee)(Sept. 1974).

3. *International Bible Dictionary* (1977), 182; Ham, burnt-swarthy.

4. Rev. W. S. Armistead, *The Negro is a Man* (Tifton, Ga.: 1903), 22. Ham is the father of all Black people. Ham means "Black-Negro."

5. I. Asimov, *Words in Genesis* (1962), 101. "Negro" means "Ham."

Nimrod ("Brave")

1. Davidson, *Genesis*, 103. Nimrod was the first to gain excessive power after the flood.

2. *Aid to Bible Understanding* (1971), 1227. Nimrod was a dark man.

3. P. S. Schaff, *Dictionary of The Bible* (New York: 1880), 352. Hamites dwelled in Babylonia.

4. C. A. Diop, *Black Africa* (1974), 3. Blacks formed the first civilizations.

5. G. Higgins, *Anacalypsis* (1927), 2:364. Chaldeans, who were closely related to Babylonians, were Negroes.

6. *The New American Bible* (New York: Benziger, Inc.,1970), 16.The Babylonians built the earliest skyscrapers.

7. Josiah Priest, *American Antiquities*, 56. The old Greek Septuagint Bible states that Nimrod was a giant, and that he was a Colored man.

8. Josiah Priest, Bible Defence of Slavery (1853), 54, 68-69, 283. Nimrod was Hercules.

9. Hislop, The Two Babylons (1903), 34, 45. Nimrod was Hercules.

Cush

1. L. J. Morie, *Histoire de L' Ethiope* (Paris: 1904), 1:207. Cush was born Black.

2. G. Emerson, *Pageant of India's History* (London: 1948),152. The Cushan empire included northern India, as well as Afghanistan and Bactria.

3. L. Solanks, *United West Africa at the Family of Nations* (1906), 18:1. Imperial Ethiopia was the center seat of civilization before Rome was seen on the map.

4. *Working Together* (Foreign Mission Board, Southern Baptist Convention, 1982), 13. Ethiopia is the oldest African nation.

5. S. Wolpert, *A New History of India* (1977), 72–73, 75, 89. Cush invaded India and founded dynasties for more than a century.

6. M. Ilin, *Men and Mountains* (1935), 135; tells of seeing Afghans who were as black as Negroes.

7. Purchas, *His Pilgrimage*, Book VIII, *Africa*, 511. The Negro King Ganges marched his Ethiopian army deep into Asia and subdued territories as far as the River Ganges, to which he left his name, being previously called Chliaros.

8. Higgins, *Anacalypsis* (London: 1927), 1:59. The ancient Buddhas were all woolly-haired, depressed-nosed and thick-lipped. Their builders were Negro Buddhists.

9. H. H. Johnston, *Colonization of Africa* (1905), 92; Negro princes in India.

10. J. D .B. Gribble, *History of the Deccan* (London: 1896), 1:51, 100, 104–105, 125–126, 251–262. One of India's greatest rulers was a Negro named Malik Ambar.

11. Bryant, *A New System*, Vol. 1, "Apollo" (1807), 6,81; Vol. 2 (1807), 52-53.

12. B. K. Mookadi, *Hindu Civilization*, 33. The earliest dwellers of India were of the Negritic race.

13. V. Dury, *Ancient History of the East*, 1: 21. India was first inhabited by a Black people.

Mizraim

1. Diop, *The African Origin*, xiv, 1, 63. Ancient Egyptians were Negroes.

2. J. A. Rogers, *100 Amazing Facts About The Negro With Complete Proof* (U.S.A.: 1957), 49:9, 91:14, 12:21, 47:29; Black Egyptians.

3. R. E. Dennis, *The Black People of America* (1970), 3; Negro Pharaohs from the eighth century B.C.

4. J. A. Williams, *Africa* (New York: 1969), 8. Amenhotep was Ethiopian.

5. P. Montet, *Eternal Egypt* (London: 1964), 104, 114. Joseph went to the Black Land in bondage.

6. J. Bucholzer, *The Land of Burnt Faces* (London: 1955).

7. Y. Ben-Jochannan, *Black Man of the Nile.*.

8. Nahas, "Good-for-nothing," in *Wolof* (1974), 44–45. Egyptians were Negroes to the last degree. Also see Diop, *The African Origin,* 63.

9. G. G. M. James, *Stolen Legacy,* 160. The Greeks called the Egyptians "Hoi Aiguptoi," meaning Black people.

10. S. M. Means, *Ethiopia* (1980), 53; Negro Egypt and her Black Pharaohs.

Phut (Libya)

1. R. R. Windsor, *From Babylon to Timbuktu* (New York: 1973), 1:4, 142. Libyans were Black people.

2. O. Bates, *The Eastern Libyans: An Essay* (London: 1914). Libyans looked like Ethiopians.

3. M. W. Flinders Petrie, *Royal Society of Arts Journal* (1901), 49:594. The famed Egyptologist tells of seeing an American Mulatto whose features were a striking resemblance to a statue of ancient Libya.

4. *Culture and History,* 6. Phut was the father of Libya.

5. *Aid to Bible Understanding* (1971), s.v. "Cyrene."

6. *Peloubet's Bible Dictionary* (1973), s.v. "Phut."

7. *Harper's Bible Dictionary* (1961), s.v. "Libya."

Canaan (Humble)

1. Windsor, *From Babylon,* 26-34, 106. Canaanites were all Blacks.

2. N. Slouschz, *Travels in North Africa* (Philadelphia: The Jewish Publication Society of America, 1927), 337. St. Augustine called Canaanites Africans.

III THE GRANDSONS OF HAM

Sidon or Zidon (Fishing)

1. Slouschz, *Travels,* 337. Canaanites were Africans.

2. G. Charles and C. Picard, *Daily Life in Carthage* (1961), 76, 129, 166, 214–216; Negroes in Carthage.

3. J. A. Rogers, *World's Great Men of Color,* 1:98. Phoenicians were Negroes.

4. F. Josephus, *Jewish Antiquity,* 4:67. Sidon built the city of Sidon.

5. Dr. W. Chomsky, *Hebrew: the Eternal Language* (Philadelphia: Jewish Publication Society,1957), 25. Carthaginians called themselves Canaanites.

6. *Les Races et L'historic,* 411. Skeletons discovered in Carthage were those of Blacks.

Heth (Hittite)

1. L. J. Morie, *Histoire d'Ethiopie* (Paris: 1904), 2: Chap. 5; Turkish Negroes.

2. Morgan, *History of Barbary and Algiers* (1728), 160; Negro Turks.

3. D. F. Dorr, *Round the World* (1858), 138; Negroes in Turkey.

4. *Unger's Bible Dictionary* (1972), 480, 492–493.

5. *Aid to Bible Understanding* (1971), 874.

Caphtor (Crete)

1. Windsor, *From Babylon*, 31-32.

2. A. Evans, *The Early Nilotic, Libyan and Egyptian Relations with Minoan Crete* (London: 1925). Negroes were the earliest inhabitants of Crete.

Dedan and Sheba

1. W. Smith, *Bible Dictionary* (1948), s.v. "Sheba." Ethiopians dwelled in Arabia.

2. B. Jacob, *The First Book of the Bible* (1974), 72; associates the Queen of Sheba with Ham's grandson Sheba.

3. C. A. Diop, *The African Origin of Civilization* (1974), 288. Arabia was a colony to Ethiopia, even during the Queen of Sheba's reign.

4. Lenormant, *Histoire Ancient des Pheniciens* (Paris: Levy, 1890), 260-261. The grandsons of Ham, the father of Blacks, formed the first Ethiopian empire throughout Arabia.

5. Ibid, 429–430. Negro blood spread throughout the Arabian peninsula.

6. G. Palgrave, *Essays on the Eastern Question* (London: 1872), 349-377; intermarriages between Negroes and Arabs.

7. W. Cooley, *The Negroland of the Arabs* (London: 1841).

8. E. Rutter, *Holy Cities of Arabia* (London: 1928), 2:74; the African and Arabian mixed breeding.

9. Higgins, *Anacalypsis*, Vol. 2, "Juda" (1836), 352.

IV BLACKS' INTERACTION WITH ABRAHAM AND JACOB

Melchizedec (Just)

1. *Harper's Bible Dictionary* (1961), s.v. "Melchizedec." Melchizedec is called an Amorite.

2. Windsor, *From Babylon*, 14:60, 143. Amorites were Blacks.

3. Diop, *The African Origin*, 107. Canaanites were a Black race.

4. *The New American Bible*, 20. Melchizedec is called a Canaanite priest.

5. Means, *Ethiopia*, 159. The Black priest Melchidzedec ordained Abraham.

Ishmael (Allah—God Hears)

1. Diop, *The African Origin*, 127, 136. Hagar, the Egyptian Negro woman. All Arabs are crossbreeds between Jews and Negro blood.

2. P. K. Hitti, *History of the Arabs* (1937), 382. The Negroes conquered the most powerful capital of the world, Bagdad, known then as the world's greatest empire.

Abimelech of Gerar (Father of Kings)

1. Windsor, *From Babylon,* 32. Philistines were Blacks.

2. Avenel Books, *The Family Bible Dictionary* (1963), 74.

Ephron (Dust)

1. Higgins, *Anacalypsis,* 11:364. Chaldeans, who were closely related to Babylonians, were Negroes.

2. H. G. Spearing, *The Childhood of Art* (1912), 255. Chaldeans were Negroes.

3. H. Lockyer, "Ephron," in *All the Men of the Bible* (1977), 113.

Hamor (Clay)

1. G. Speller, *Universal Races* (London: 1911), 330. Sir H. H. Johnston says, "The prejudice of Hebrews springs from their Negro strain."

2. L. F. Celine, *Bagatelles Pour Un Massacre* (Paris: 1927),191–92. Jews are a mixture of Negro . . .

3. J. K. Turner, *Schwarzchild* "Same as Blackchild," 250, 277; the Jewish Negro.

4. *The National Jewish Monthly* (May 1981); the ancient Black Jews.

5. *Encyclopedia Judaica* (1972), 6:1213; incongruity between non-white Jews,"Black Jews," and white Jews.

6. F. Boaz, *Changes in Bodily Form of Descendants of Immigrants* (1912).

7. S. Feist, *Stammeskunde der Juden* (1925).

8. A. B. Cleage, Jr., *The Black Messiah* (1968), 41. Ancient Israel was a mixed-blood, non-white nation.

Shuah (Pit)

1. Diop, *The African Origin* (1974), 107, 168; Black-Negro-Canaanites.

2. *Memoires* (1885), 5:Chap. 26, 12 Vol. The Negro and Jews can be been in a single person.

3. K. B. Aikman, *Victoria Institute Journal* (London: Jan. 1935); Bible history on race mixing.

4. O. G. Cox, *Caste, Class and Race* (1948). Jews enjoyed mixing their blood with other races.

5. P. Spear, *India* (1971), 73. Black Jews intermixed locally.

6. H. Lamb, *Cyrus the Great* (1960), 262; race mixing.

V Prior to and During the Oppression

Asenath

1. C. Williams, *The Destruction of Black Civilization* (1976), 83.The Black Egyptians turned brown and then white.

2. Weisgerber, *Les Blancs d'Afrique* (Paris: 1910), 83. In North Africa, the whitest people are mixed with Negro blood.

3. Diop, *The African Origin,* xiv, 1, 63. Ancient Egyptians were Negroes.

4. James, *Stolen Legacy,* 106. The Greeks called the Egyptians "Hoi Aiguploi" meaning black people.

5. R. T. Pritchett, *Natural History of Man,* 125. Egyptians were an African race.

6. C. F. Volney, *Voyage to Syria and Egypt* (1787), 57. The ancient Egyptians were real Negroes.

Manasseh and Ephraim

1. Y. Ben-Jochannan, *We, the Black Jews* (New York: 1984).

2. C. Jenkins, *The Black Hebrews* (1969).

3. *The National Jewish Monthly* (May 1981); the ancient black Jews.

4. *Encyclopedia Judaica* 6:1213; incongruity between nonwhite Jews, "Black Jews," and white Jews.

5. G. Speller, *Universal Races* (London: 1911), 330. Sir H. H. Johnston says, "The prejudice of Hebrews springs from their Negro strain."

Ahmose (Moon Child)

1. Windsor, *From Babylon,* 63–64. Ahmose knew not Joseph.

2. S. Birch, *Egypt From the Earliest Times* (London: 1875), 83. Nefertari was a Negress.

3. "Specimens of Ancient Sculpture Society of Dilettanti,"*Bulletins et Memories Society de Paris* 1 (1901): 393, 403. Lucian, Galen, and Block, who journeyed to Egypt at different periods, all agreed that the Egyptian's large flat nose and puffy lips were proof of their Negro origin.

4. Montet, *Eternal Egypt,* 21. They are black skinned with flat faces and woolly hair.

5. Rogers, *Men of Color,* 1:48. She was Ethiopian. Also see Rogers, 1:54; sex and race.

6. H. R. Hall, *Ancient History of the Near East,* 271. The Eighteenth Dynasty was controlled by Negroes.

Pharaoh's Daughter

1. William Whiston, *The Life and Work of Flavius Josephus* (1981), 77.

2. *The History of Herodotus* (London: 1875).

3. J. A. Rogers, *100 Amazing Facts* (1957), 49:9, 47:29; Black Egyptians.

4. E. Dean, *All the Women of the Bible* (1955), 311. Her name was Thermuthis.

5. B. Davidson, *Africa in History* (1969), 21–22. Egypt was of Negro stock.

6. Herodotus, *Book II.* The Greek Herodotus identified the Colchians, who resided near the Black Sea, to be an exact living type of the Egyptians, with woolly hair and sooty skins.)

Ramesses II (Sun Born)

1. Windsor, *From Babylon,* 6:69, 143.

2. *The Story of Egypt* (1887), 252.

3. Browns, Filzmyer, and Murphy, *The Interpreter's Commentary on the Bible* (London: 1875), 1:35-36. Ramesses was Pharaoh of the oppression and Exodus.

4. J. D. Douglas, *The New Bible Dictionary,* 4:980; Ramesses, the last oppressor.

5. Montet, *Eternal Egypt,* 104, 114. Egypt is called the Black Land.

6. Rogers, *Men of Color,* 1: xii, 11, 28, 64. Pure Blacks ruled Egypt.

7. Diop, *African Origin,* 239. Ramesses II resembled the Ethiopian type.

8. D. Cappart, *Reflet du monde* (1956). The designs on Ramesses' war helmet represented frizzy "woolly" hair.

9. Sergi, *The Mediterranean Races* (1901), 243. The features of Ramesses II showed marked resemblance to the notorious Negro King of Uganda, "Mtesa."

Moses

1. Sale, *Al Koran* (1784), 128, 257. Moses was a black skinned man.

2. T. W. Arnold, *The Preaching of Islam* (1896: Westminister), 106. Moses, according to Mohammedan tradition, was a Black man.

3. Armistead, *The Negro*, 8. Moses was a Colored man, being a Hebrew.

4. Rabbi D. G. Silver, *Images of Moses*, (1982), 5–6. Movie directors, Sunday school instructors and grandparents can be forgiven if they view Moses to have been white complected; world scholars should know better. Moses' culture and lineage suggest him to be dark.

Zipporah

1. H. St. J. Thackeray, "Josephus," *The Life Against Apion* (London: 1961), 1:231.

2. F. M. Snowden, Jr., *Blacks in Antiquity* (1970), 199, 201–202, 333. Moses's wife Zipporah was Black, she was a daughter of Ham.

3. A. S. Maxwell, *The Bible Story* (1954), 3:21. Zipporah was dark-skinned.

4. *Negro History Bulletin* (1978), 41:915. Moses married an Ethiopian.

5. Sir Thomas Browne, *Works* (1926), 3:233. The word "Ethiopian" relates to the notable nations of Negroes which are burnt and torrid.

Gershom and Eliezer

1. Origen, *Commentarius in Cantium Canticorn*, 2:360–362, 8:118. Zipporah was Black and beautiful. The Ethiopians were the blackest people on earth.

2. *Encyclopaedia Judaica*, 6:1146. The Black Jews in Ethiopia are a mixture of Hamitic and Semitic blood. There is a difference in the color of the skin.

3. Ibid., 11:1460. There are also brown-skinned Jews.

4. *The Christian Century* (1–8 July 1981), 704–706. The origin of Ethiopia's Black Jews has been traced to the early Hebrews. Scholars say they exercised ancient customs that today's white Jews fail to observe.

5. *Harper's Bible Dictionary*, s.v. "Zipporah."

6. D. D. Houston, *Wonderful Ethiopians of the Ancient Cushite Empire* (1985), 127. In Midian, Moses lived among the offspring of Ham.

Hobab

1. Houston, *Cushite Empire*, Chap. 8–10.

2. Lenormant, in *Ancient History of the East*, 2:306, 8:296.

3. Heeren, *Ethiopian Nations*, 46. Ethiopians possessed very black skin.

4. W. Cooley, *The Negroland of the Arabs* (London: 1841).

VI THE INTRUSION OF CANAAN

Og (Giant)

1. Windsor, *From Babylon* 14:143. Amorites were Blacks.

2. Hawkes and Woolley, *Prehistory* 1:55. Negroes are among the tallest of all humans.

3. A. H. Godbey, *The Lost Tribes: A Myth* (1930), 206; Canaanites in Africa.

Rahab (Proud)

1. Baird and Dillon, *The Family Bible*, 45; identifies Rahab as a Canaanite.

2. *The Black Heritage Bible* (Nashville: 1976), 9. Rahab was "Black," Hamitic.

3. Aikman, *Victorie* (Jan. 1935); Bible history on race mixing.

4. Armistead, *The Negro,* 9:130. Rahab was a Negro woman.

Piram (Fleet)

1. Windsor, *From Babylon* 14:60, 143. Amorites were Blacks.

2. Grant and Rowley, *Dictionary of the Bible*, 773.

VII THE NEGROES OF JUDGES AND RUTH

Cushan Rishathaim (Blackness)

1. W. L. Hansberry, *Africa and Africans,* 13. The word *Cushanrishathaim* is a derivative of *Cush.*

2. Ibid., 51.

3. Schaff, *Dictionary of the Bible,* 352. Hamites lived in Babylonia.

4. *The Zambesi and Its Tributaries* (New York: 1866), 526. Livingstone said that the face of the Negro reminded him of those on the statues of ancient Assyria.

5. Grant and Rowley, *Dictionary of the Bible*, 195.

Zebah (Sacrifice) and Zalmunna (Shady)

1. Cooley, *Negroland.*

2. H. and C. Black, *Encyclopaedia Biblica* (London: 1901), 1: 967. Cush is similar to Midian.

3. F. d'Olivet, *Hermeneutic Interpretation* (1915), 6, 40. Blacks possessed Arabia.

4. *New York Times* (2 Feb. 1945). Black people are identical to Arabs.

5. F. W. Hasluck, *Christianity and Islam* (Oxford, 1929), 2: 730-735. Negroes and Arabs were largely indistinguishable.

6. R. Linton, *The Study of Man* (1936), 35. The Arabian conquerors of Sicily and Spain were mixed with Negro blood.

7. E. A. Toppin, *A Biographical History in America since 1528*, 7. Arabs called their land Sudan meaning "Black."

8. A. F. Rainey, *The Land of the Bible*, 134. Cush is appellative to Midian.

9. G. Van Vloten, Abu Othman Amr Bahr, Al Djahiz (778-868 A.D.), *The Superiority in Glory of the Black Race over the White* (Basrens: Leyden, 1929). Most of the Arabs were as black as Negroes.

Abimelech of Shechem

1. *Memoires*, 5: Chap. 26. The Negro and Jew can be seen in a single person.

2. *Encyclopaedia Judaica,* 5:621; the Black and white Jews.

3. A. H. Keen, *Stanford Compendium of Geography and African Travels.* Philologists are gathering evidence that the Hamites and Semites were originally one people.

4. Ratzel, *History of Mankind,* 11:143, 246. Every form of mixing has taken place among the original Negroes and Semitic people. The entire Semitic population, living within or outside of Africa, has a Negro character.

5. *Man* (1905), 5:93; (1906), 6:14. In Whitechapel, London, the skulls of Polish Jews were measured. About thirty percent of them were Negroid.

Delilah (Poor)

1. *Encyclopaedia Judaica* 11:1088, 1090. A preserved head of hair was found in Jerusalem, over two-thousand years old, in plaits.

2. Windsor, *From Babylon,* 32; Black Philistines.

3. Deen, *All the Women.* Josephus says that Delilah was a Philistine.

4. *Harper's Bible Dictionary,* 134. Delilah is called a Philistine.

Boaz (Lovely)

1. *Description of Guinea* (1746), 9.

2. Slouschz, *Travels,* 351, 352–353.

3. Celine, *Bagatelles,* 191–2. There are no pure Jews. After all, the Jew is a Negro.

4. Rev. Armistead, *The Negro is a Man,* 130. Boaz was part Negro.

5. *Harper's Bible,* 77.

VIII AGE OF THE GREAT WARRIORS

Goliath (Splendor)

1. Windsor, *From Babylon,* 32; Black Philistines.

2. Hawkes and Woolly, *Prehistory,* 1:55. Negroes are among the tallest of all humans.

3. Van Vloten, Amr ibn Bahr, Djahiz, *Superiority.* Negroes are physically stronger than any other earthly race. A single one can lift stones of great weight and carry burdens which several whites could not carry among themselves.

4. Linton, *The Study of Man,* 41. Negroes are the tallest and the shortest of the human breed.

5. Frank M. Snowden, *Blacks in Antiquity* (1970), 8. The Negro race has the tallest groupings of mankind. The Ethiopians around 400 B.C., says the Greeks, were the tallest race on earth.

6. Pliny, *Naturalis Historia,* 23-79. The Ethiopians were over eight cubits in height.

7. G. D. Kittler, *Let's Travel in the Congo* (1965), 30. The Watusi is the tallest race in the world, whose members can reach the height of seven to eight feet.

8. V. Quinn, *The Picture Map Geography of Africa* (1964), 85; the popular giants of Africa.

9. *Lands and Peoples* (Grolier Incorporated, 1985), 328. Many Watusi are over seven feet tall.

10. L. Hughes, *The First Book of Africa* (1964), 58. The Watusi are the tallest people in the world.

11. Best and Blij, *Africa Survey* (1977), 467; the proud pastoralists.

12. R. Hallett, *Africa Since 1875* (1974), 581. The Tutsi or Watusi are remarkable for their great statures and refined features.

13. Ellen and Atitilio Gatti, *The New Africa* (1960), 13. The ancient Egyptians made statues of the Watusi to be eight feet and nine inches; the Pygmies, four feet and five inches.

Ahimelech (Friend of the King)

1. *The Family Bible Dictionary* (Avenel, 1963), s.v. "Heth."

2. *International Bible Dictionary*, 17.

Cushi (Ethiopia)

1. J. L. Hurlbut, *D. D. Hurlbut's Story of the Bible* (1969), 271–272. Cushi is called a Negro.

2. Lockyer, *All the Men*, 86. Cushi also means Black.

3. Snowden, *Blacks in Antiquity*, 170–180. Diodorus praised the Ethiopians who dominated Meroe and the adjacent land of Egypt. He regarded Ethiopians as the founding fathers of the Egyptian civilization. Lucian tells us that the Ethiopians were the discoverers of astrology and that their popularity for wisdom was great, as they were in all aspects more prudent than other men. Herodotus called the Cushites, same as Ethiopians, the most handsome people on earth. Pseudo-Callisthenes announced a Black Queen of Ethiopia during Alexander's era to be of wondrous beauty.

4. Strabo, *Astrology 3*, xvi, 2, 24–5. The Greek historian and geographer Strabo (63 B.C.–24 A.D.) says that Greece learned her method of geometry from the Ethiopians.

5. Sir F. Petrie, *The Making of Ancient Egypt* (London: 1939). The first dynasty of Egypt was of Ethiopian origin.

6. I. V. Sertima, *They Came Before Columbus*, 127–128. There were Ethiopian Pharaohs of Egypt. The manner of their burial practices give clear proof of this! Between the two, only Ethiopia would bury her kings on beds with legs, rather than in coffins. Such burial customs have been found throughout Egypt, which was a non-Egyptian practice. The Ethiopians were natives of Egypt, not foreigners.

Subay (Officer)

1. J. Huxley and A. C. Haddon, *We, Europeans* (1935), 94. The Colored Ethiopians and Egyptians were the fathers of Western Civilization.

Ismaiah (Yahweh Hears)

1. Windsor, *From Babylon*, 60, 196. Amorites, same as Canaanites, were Blacks.

2. Grant and Rowley, *Dictionary of the Bible*, 428.

IX DIPLOMATIC AND SOCIAL DEALINGS AMONG AFRICA, THE CANAANITE NATIONS, AND ISRAEL

Araunah or Ornan (Ark)

1. "Culture and History," 6.

2. *Unger's Bible Dictionary*, 77, 557.

Solomon (Peaceful)

1. Rogers, *Sex and Race*, 1:91; Solomon's Black wives.

2. Windsor, *From Babylon* 140:9; Solomon's Black wives.

3. M. Fishberg, *American Anthropologist* 5(1903): 105. Soloman was a son of a Hittite "Black" woman.

4. Silver, *Images of Moses*, 65. Ancient Jews were not bothered by Black wives—Solomon had an attraction for Sheba.

Queen of Sheba (Oath)

1. Snowden, *Blacks in Antiquity*, 202–203. Origen, Sheba was Black and beautiful.

2. Schweich Lectures, *Ethiopia and the Bible* (London: 1967), 3–4, 10, 130; Sheba, Queen of Ethiopia.

3. N. Hill, *The Intimate Life of the Queen of Sheba* (London: A. E. Marriott, 1930).

4. Josiah Priest, *American Antiquities*, 36. The Queen of Sheba, being a descendant of Ham, was a Black woman.

5. Rogers, *World Great Men of Color*, Vol. 1, "Sheba" (1972), 87.

Rehoboam

1. Baird and Dillon, *The Family Bible*, 2. Canaanites were swarts, "Blacks."

2. *The Black Heritage Bible*, 9. Rahab was "Black," Hamitic.

3. Armistead, *The Negro Is a Man*, 130. Solomon, the father of Rehoboam, was part Negro.

4. Ibid., 9, 49. Rahab was a Negro woman.

5. W. Whiston, *The Life and Works of Flavius Josephus*, 261.

Abijah or Abijam

1. Rogers, *Men of Color*, 1:98. Phoenicians were Negroids, same as Negro.

2. Slouschz, *Travels*, 337. Canaanites were Africans.

3. Windsor, *From Babylon*, 26, 31, 60, 106. Phoenicians were Blacks.

4. E. G. Wright, *Biblical Archaeology* (1960), 41. The Canaanites invented an alphabet.

Hadad (Mighty)

1. Diop, *The African Origin*, 127. Semites seem to be mixed with whites and Negroes.

2. A. H. M. Jones, *The Herods of Judea* (London: 1938), 1. Edom, same as Idumaean.

3. Baird and Dillon, *The Family Bible*, s.v. "Edom" or "Edomites."

Shishak

1. Rogers, *100 Amazing Facts*, 11:20. Shishak was a Negro.

2. Rogers, *Nature Knows No Color Line* (1957), 11. Shishak was an Ethiopian.

3. O. Bates, "The Eastern Libyans: An Essay" (London: 1914). Libyans looked like Ethiopians.

4. "Culture and History," 6. Phut was the father of Libya.

5. *The World Book Encyclopedia* (1970), 6:100. Shishak was a non-Egyptian ruler.

Necho

1. Bucholzer, *Burnt Faces.*

2. J. G. Wilkinson, *The Ancient Egyptians* (London: 1878), 1:42. The portrait of Pharaoh Amenophis III fits that of a Negro more than any other Pharaoh.

3. S. Means, *Black Egypt and Her Negro Pharaohs* (Maryland: 1945).

Hophra

1. *Herodotus.*

2. Gurowski, *Slavery in History* (1860), 5. The Egyptians were Negroes.

3. H. Johnston, *The Uganda Protectorate* (London: 1902), 3:472. The main stock of the ancient Egyptians was Negroid, and is best delineated by the modern day Somalians, Gallas, Ethiopians.

4. Flinders Petrie, *Royal Society of Arts Journal* 49 (1901): 594. The famed Egyptologist says that the Pharaohs of the Tenth Dynasty were of the Galla—a Negro tribe—type.

X Negro Priests, Kings and Queens of Israel, Judah and Phoenicia

Ethbaal (Fire)

1. Slouschz, *Travels,* 337. Canaanites were Africans.

2. Rogers, *Men of Color*, 1:98. Phoenicians, or Zidonians, were Negroids, same as Negro.

3. Windsor, *From Babylon* 28, 31, 106. Phoenicians were Blacks. They were blood related to Africans.

4. Contenau, *La Civilisation Phoenicienne,* 187. Phoenicians were none other than the Negro. Their skeletons resemble Blacks of the Congo.

Ahaziah of Judah (Jehovah Sustain)

1. Lockyer, *All the Men,* 38.

2. *Peloubet's Bible Dictionary* (1973), 19.

Mattan (Gift)

1. *Peloubet's Bible Dictionary*, 391.

2. *The Family Bible Dictionary*, 63.

Jehosheba

1. *Peloubet's Bible Dictionary*, 295.

2. *International Bible Dictionary,* 217.

Amon

1. Bryant, *A New System*, Vol. 1 (1807), 3; Ham means Amon.

2. Diops, *The African Origin of Civilization* (1974), 149; Amon means Kham.

Zerah (Eastern)

1. *Encyclopaedia Britannica.* Egyptologist Margaret S. Drower spoke of these Black Pharaohs.

2. L. Cottrel, *The Lost Pharaohs* (New York: 1951).

3. G. K. Osei, *The Forgotten Great Africa: 3000 B.C. to 1959 A.D.* (London: 1965).

Tirhakah (Exalted)

1. Rogers, *100 Amazing Facts,* 11:20. Tirhakah was a Negro.

2. L. Bennett, Jr., *Before the Mayflower* (1978), 11. Dr. Randall Mac Iver says, "How astounding that an African Black man, Tirhakah, could fashion himself as king of the world."

3. Herodotus, *Book II,* Chap. 100. When I visited Egypt, the priests revealed a list consisting of 330 Egyptian Pharaohs; eighteen were Ethiopians.

Ebed-Melech (King's Servant)

1. Schweich Lectures, *Ethiopia and the Bible* (1967), 7; Ebed-melech, a dark-skinned Ethiopian.

2. H. M. Hyall, *The Church of Ethiopia* (London: 1928).

3. Snowden, *Blacks in Antiquity,* 201–202. Ebed-melech was from a dark race.

4. F. S. Mead, *Who's Who in the Bible* (1934), 13; relates Negro spirituals to Ham.

5. K. S. Latourette, *A History of the Expansion of Christianity* (London: 1939).

6. M. Geddes, *The Church History of Ethiopia* (London: 1696).

An Ethiopian Priest

1. Schweich Lectures, *Ethiopia,* 45–58. Judaism was practiced in Ethiopia. They sang hymns, used and translated Hebrew Bibles.

2. Hyall, *The Church.*

Zephaniah (God's Secret)

1. G. Parrinder, *Africa's Three Religions* (London, 1969), 107–108; Eunuch, from Judaism to Christianity.

2. A. Weigall, *Paganism in our Christianity* (London: 1928).

3. Geddes, *Church History.*

4. E. A. W. Budge, *The Books of the Saints of the Ethiopian Church* (London: 1928).

5. Latourette, *Christianity.*

XII HIGHLIGHTS OF BLACKS DURING THE FRIST CENTURY

The Wise Men

1. *The Lincoln Library* (1971), 1:298; Black Balthazar.

2. *New Catholic Encyclopedia* (1967), s.v. "Magi."

3. *Times Weekly Newsmagazine* (30 Dec. 1972).

4. Rogers, *Sex and Races*, 1:3.

5. *Negro History Bulletin* 41 (June 1978): 915. Balthazar was a Black Ethiopian.

6. *Chamber's Encyclopedia* (1967), 8: 798.

7. *The Children's Bible* (New York: Golden Press, 1965), 354–355; Balthazar, the Black wise man.

Mary (The Black Madonna)

1. *Washington Post* (4 May 1979). Many of the earliest Madonnas were painted black, until the Renaissance (Michelangelo, 1475–1564) when it became popular to paint Mary the Madonna white.

2. Higgins, *Anacalypsis*, 11:137–139. The white Germans, Italians, Swiss, and French worshipped the Black Virgin and Child. In all of Europe, all of the Madonnas and Child-Christs were depicted as Black.

3. Massey, *Ancient Egypt,* 301–346. The Black Jesus was well worshipped throughout Europe.

4. *Sepia Magazine* (May 1975), 32; (Dec. 1980), 10–17. Jesus was Black. Following His death, before the rise of white "supremacy," people of all continents drew, painted and sculptured Him and His mother in dark colors with Negro features. The original Jews were Black.

5. Armistead, *The Negro Is a Man,* 9. Rahab was a Negro woman, David and Solomon were Colored Men.

6. A. Hyatt, *Old Civilisation of the New World,* 145. The inhabitants of ancient Central America, as those in Europe, worshipped a Black Christ.

7. J. S. Matthews, *Intermediare*, 40:129. Jesus of the ancient church of St. Paul at Citta Vecchia is distinctly Negro.

8. J. H. Matthews, *Notes and Queries,* 9 ser 111:377. ". . . I saw an image of Jesus on a worm-eaten panel, which had been cut into a Gothic shape around the fifteenth century. His Black face had been subjected to a little touch up to exhibit a Caucasoid image; however, his head remained distinctly Negroid with woolly hair."

9. C. W. King, *Gnostics and their Remains,* 2d ed. (London: 1887), 173. During the Middle Ages, the French Cathedrals displayed Black Virgin statues.

10. H. Guichenne, *La Vierge Noire de L. Abbaye de St. Victor Lez Marseilles,* 4 et seq. Statues of Black Virgins were not rare in France.

11. Bonwich, *Egyptian Beliefs* (London: 1878), 141. Europe had Black Madonnas.

12. Fraser, *The Golden Bough* (London: 1914), 9:92. Russia had two types of Virgins; one with African-Ethiopian features, the other with a reddish-brown color, having Greek features.

13. A. France, *Intermediare des Chercheurs*, 40:293. ". . . In the church of Mende (Loziere), near a small altar, there was a statue of a Black Virgin, which appears to be from the Middle Ages."

14. C. Middleton, *Letters From Rome,* 84. "I was surprised at first sight of the Holy Image, for it was as black as a Negro."

15. Roman Rolland, *Intermediare des Chercheurs et des Curieux* (Paris), 34: 193. If Christ and Mary were not Negroes, then why for centuries, did people of all continents draw, paint, and sculpture the two as Blacks?

Jesus (Salvation)

1. Windsor, *From Babylon,* 35–36. Jesus' hair was like that of Negroes.

2. R. Eisler, *Messiah Christ,* 411, 421–442. The Jewish historian Josephus describes Christ as black skinned, with average features.

3. G. Massey, *Ancient Egypt: The Light of the World* (London: 1907), 11:754; the little Black Jesus.

4. Ibid., 301, 346. The Black Jesus is well known and worshipped throughout Europe.

5. G. Massey, *A Book of the Beginnings* (London: 1881), 11:3000, 340. Black Christ.

6. Huysmans, *La Cathedrale,* 31. Mary the Negress and Christ the little Negro.

7. Higgins, *Anacalypsis,* 11:137–139. The white Germans, Swiss, French and Italians worshipped the Black Virgin and Child. In all of Europe, all of the Madonnas and Christ-Childs are depicted as black.

8. *Sepia Magazine* (May 1975), 32; (Dec. 1980), 10–17. Jesus was Black. Following His death, before the rise of white "supremacy," all continents drew, painted, and sculptured Him and His mother in dark colors with Negro features. The original Jews were black.

9. Hyatt, *Old Civilisation,* 145. The inhabitants of ancient Central America, as in Europe, worshipped a Black Christ.

10. J. H. Matthews, *Notes and Queries,* 9 ser. 111:377. "I saw an image of Jesus on a worm-eaten panel, which had been cut into a Gothic shape around the fifteenth century. His Black face had been subjected to a little touch-up to exhibit a Caucasoid image; however, his head remained distinctly Negorid with woolly hair."

11. J. S. Matthews, *Intermediare,* 40:129. Jesus of the ancient church of St. Paul at Citta Vecchia is distinctly Negro.

12. Armistead, *The Negro is a Man,* 87, 130-132, 153. Christ was of mixed blood.

13. Rolland, *Intermediare* 34:193. If Christ and Mary were not Negroes, then why for centuries, did people of all continents draw, paint and sculpture the two as Blacks?

14. A. B. Cleage, Jr., *The Black Messiah* (1968).

15. *Saturday Evening Post* (26 October 1926).

Simon of Cyrene

1. Rogers, *Men of Color* 11:13. Simon was an African.

2. S. Grazel, *A History of the Jews.* "There are over one hundred thousand Jews in Africa who are not Christians."

3. Windsor, *From Babylon,* 4:142. Libyans were Blacks.

4. W. J. Simmons, *Men of Mark* (1970), 49. A Negro carried Christ's cross.

5. J. Williams, *Hebrewism of West Africa,* 2d ed. (New York: The Dial Press, 1931).

6. *Aid to Bible Understanding* (1971), s.v. "Cyrene."

7. *Scribner's Magazine* (April, May, June, July 1929); west African Jews.

8. M. Hyman, *Blacks who Died for Jesus* (1983). Simon was Black. Negro schools and churches in the United States are named after him.

9. S. Mendelssohn, *The Jews of Africa, Especially in the Sixteenth and Seventeenth Century* (New York: 1920).

10. *Harper's Bible Dictionary*, s.v. "Cyrene."

Simeon that was Called Niger and Lucius of Cyrene

1. Rogers, *100 Amazing Facts,* 52:9, 31–32. Many of the early patriarchs of the Christian Temples were Africans. There were three African Popes of Rome.

2. *The New Catholic Encyclopedia.* Victors, Medchiades, and St. Gelasius were African Popes.

3. *Jet* (28 March 1983), 25. Victor the Black Pope, decided Easter should be held on Sunday.

4. *Libers Pontificals*, or *The Book of the Popes.* Africa had popes before Rome. There were seven popes of north Africa and twenty-seven bishops.

The Eunuch (A Seeker)

1. Parrinder, *Three Religions,* 107–108; Eunuch, from Judaism to Christinaity.

2. *The Catholic Liquorian* (Oct. 1980), 28. Africans knew of Christianity before the Europeans, and were practicing it before experiencing slavery in the New World.

3. Ibid. Monastery practice originated in Africa and was later brought to Europe by Blacks.

4. Hyall, *The Church of Ethiopia.*

5. S. A. B. Mercer, *The Ethiopia Text of the Hebrew Book of Jubilees* (Oxford, 1895).

Queen Candace (Queen)

1. G. Reisner, *Anglo Egyptian Sudan.*

2. Rogers, *Men of Color,* 2:13. Candace was an African.

3. C. Williams, *The Destruction of Black Civilization,* 133. Pyramids were first built in Ethiopia. The idea was later carried to Egypt.

4. *Harper's Bible Dictionary,* s.v. "Ethiopia."

ABSENCE OF AFRICA'S THEOLOGICAL HISTORY

Expository Comments I

1. *The Lost Books of the Bible and The Forgotten Books of Eden* (Alpha House, Inc: 1926 & 1927).

2. *The World Book Encyclopedia* (1970), 2:219–222.

Was Abraham Prejudiced?

1. Slouschz, *Travels,* 337. Canaanites were Africans.

2. Windsor, *From Babylon,* 28, 106. Canaanites were Blacks; they were blood related to Africans.

Hidden Facts About Blacks

1. C. W. King, *Antique Gems and Rings* (London: 1872), 326; describes Cleopatra as a Negress.

2. Diop, *Black Africa,* 3. Blacks formed the first civilization.

3. Bennett, *Before the Mayflower,* 19.

4. R. Ripley, *Believe It or Not* 6 (1934): 83. Cleopatra was fat and Black.

5. Lord Raglan, *The National Annual: The Future of Civilization* (1946), 49. Civilization was founded by brown-skinned people, not white. The modern-day barbarians are in the same homunculus condition that whites experienced four thousand years ago.

6. R. E. Dennis, *The Black People of America* (1970), 7. Culturally, the Africans were ahead of Europeans for thousands of years.

7. F. d'Olivet, *Hermeneutic Interpretation* (1915), 6, 40. While Blacks were dominant with sceptre of science and power, the Europeans were powerless, barbaric, lawless and lacked cultivation.

8. *We, Europeans,* 94. The wheel, building in stone, agriculture and the art of writing are the fundamental discoveries on which civilization is built. The founding fathers were not of Europe.

9. E. Schure, *Les Grand Inities,* (Paris: 1931). Whites learned two essentials from Blacks: the sacred writing of hieroglyphics and the smelting of metals.

10. *Reader's Digest* (Nov. 1982), 178. While Egypt was enjoying a lustrous worldly-wise civilization, Europeans were still living in primitive villages.

11. F. Champollion and J. Jacques, "Lettres," in *Egypte Ancienne* (Paris: Collection I'Univers, 1839), 32–32. I am ashamed to admit that, at one time, our own land Europe was last and the most dormant of lands.

12. Professor Breasted, *American Historical Review* (1929), 219. While Egypt was a civilized world, Europe was land of wilderness and slavery for some two thousand years.

13. *Black World* (Feb. 1974). All Greek science, without a doubt was borrowed from the Negro Egyptians.

14. W. Durant, *The Life in Greece* (1966), 68–69. Most Greeks believed that their civilization derived from Egypt. Simon and Schuster.

15. Herodotus, *The History of Herodotus* (New York: Tudor, 1928), 99. The root of Greek religion ascended from African cosmology.

Intermarriage Between Blacks and Hebrews

1. Windsor, *From Babylon,* 140; Solomon's Black wives.

2. Dr. M. Hirschfeld, *Racism,* (1938), 61. There is Negro strain among Jews.

3. Speller, *Universal Races,* 33. Sir H. H. Johnston says, "The prejudice of Hebrews springs from their Negro strain."

4. Celine, *Bagatelles,* 191–192. Jews are mixture of Negro.

5. H. Lamb, *Cyrus the Great* (1960), 262; race mixing.

Nineteenth Egyptian Dynasty

1. Windsor, *From Babylon,* 69. Ramesses II was very black, with thick lips and a wide nose.

2. Rawlinson, *The Story of Egypt* (London: 1887), 252. Seti I, father of Ramesses II, had Negro features.

3. Volney, *Voyages,* 74–75. Early Egyptians had black skin and woolly hair. The statues I saw looked strictly Negro.

4. Gurowski, *Slavery,* 5. The Egyptians were Negroes.

What Happened to Black Dominance?

1. Raglan, *The Future,* 49. Civilization was founded by brown people, not white. The modern-day barbarians are in the same homunculus condition that whites experienced four thousand years ago.

2. *Negro History Bulletin,* 876, 877. Imhotep, a learned Negro doctor, who lived in Egypt around 3500 B.C., was called the god of medicine. The Greeks learned much of their medical knowledge from him.

3. L. Solanke, *United West Africa at the Family of Nations* (1927). Negroes led the world in culture and conquest for centuries, while whites were still learning the fundamentals of war and government. Ethiopia conquered Egypt and formed the Twenty-Fifth Dynasty, becoming the central seat of civilization for a century and a half before Rome was seen on the map. When Europe began to flourish in civilization, the Negroes had already reached their height and begun to decline.

4. *History of Nations* 18(1906): 1. Europe was a land of nomadic barbarians, while one of the most remarkable civilizations existed along the banks of the Nile.

5. James, *Stolen Legacy.* The Greeks learned their philosophy from the Egyptians.

6. J. McCabe, *American Historical Review* (Jan. 1929), 219. Four centuries ago, when civilization was already old, Europe was inactive outside the civilized world.

7. *Black World* (Feb. 1974). All Greek science, without a doubt, was borrowed from the Negro Egyptians.

Were There Black Semites?

1. J. C. Prichard, *Natural History of Man* (1845), 145. Jews were especially dark.

2. Sale, *Al Koran* (1784), 128, 257. Moses was a black-skinned man.

3. *Natural History of Man* (London: 1848), 145; the Black Jews of India.

4. M. Fishberg, *American Anthropologist* 5(1903): 89. The ancient Hebrew is characterized as having black hair.

Melanin

1. N. Alcock, *Why Tropical Man Is Black* 30(1884): 402–03.

2. *Histoire Universelle;* Australian Negroes.

3. P. Hasluck, *Black Australians* (1942).

Expository Comments II (Most Biblical Characters are Black)

1. Rogers, *100 Amazing Facts,* 6, 50. The Bible is enormously Negro.

2. Volney, *Voyages,* 74–75. The early Egyptians had black skin and woolly hair. The statues I saw looked strictly Negro.

3. *Jet* (2 March 1978), 6. Egypt's former president of the twentieth century Anwar Sadat openly admitted that he was Black.

4. Weisgerber, *Les Blancs d'Afrique,* 83. In north Africa, the whitest people are mixed with Negro blood.

Who's Who in Asia

1. *Prehistoric Japan* (Yokohama: 1911).

2. Diop, *The African Origin,* 281. There was a Negro empire in southern China during its earlier history.

3. Rock, *New York Times* (26 Nov. 1933). In China there was an unmixed Negro race who had preserved a culture for 2,000 years.

4. *The Negritoes de la Chine* (1928). Prior to 122 B.C., prince Liu Nan spoke of a kingdom of Blacks residing in southwest China.

5. Professor Chang Hsinglang, *Bulletin No. 7* (Catholic University of Peking) (Dec. 1930). In 373-397A.D., China had a Negro empress named Li, and that around 618-907A.D., there was a black skinned people living in Lin-yi having woolly hair.

6. *Les Negritoes.* The Negroes at one time peopled all of south India and China. "China's earliest history in classic textbooks," says Imber, "spoke of Negro dwellers with black oily skins. . . ."

7. *Ainu Life and Lore* (Tokyo: 1927), 8. The Japanese Ainus show signs of Negro admixture. They have thick lips and hair, wide mouths and flat noses.

8. *La Revue Hebdomadaire* 11 (Nov. 1927): 141–162. The Chinese dynamic statesman Eugene Chen is too dark and thick lipped to be a pure Chinese. There is too much Negro in him.

9. *The Lincoln Library* 1:520. Negritos means "little Negroes."

10. H. P. Howard, *America's Role in Asia,* 162. The present emperor of Japan, Hirohito, shows a Negroid strain. He looks very much Negroid and would experience some difficulties in most southern American states.

11. R. B. Dixon, *Racial History of Man* (New York: 1923), 287–292; believed that the Japanese showed a Negro strain.

12. *American Anthropologist* 7(1909): 29. The Japanese and other dark races bear physical traits of Negro descent.

The Eighteenth Egyptian Dynasty

1. Darwin, *Descent of Man,* part 1: 172. "When I saw the statue of Pharaoh Amenophis III, I agreed with two qualified Judges that he had strong Negro features."

2. F. Shay, *National Geographic Magazine* (1925), 130. The mummy of Amenophis II, grandfather of Amenophis III is blue-black.

3. J. A. Williams, *Africa* (New York: 1969), 8. Thotmes III and his great grandson Amenophis are called "Cushites," same as Ethiopians.

4. Rogers, *100 Amazing Facts,* 50:9. Amenophis or Akhenaton IV, father of King Tutankhamen or "Tut," looked very much Negro.

5. J. G. Wilkinson, *The Ancient Egyptians* (London: 1878), 1:42. Amenophis III, father of Akhenaton, also grandfather of King "Tut," fit those of a Negro more than any other Pharaoh.

6. G. Smith, *Egyptian Mummies* (London: 1924).

7. W. R. Dawson, *Egyptian Mummies* (London: 1921), 74–75.

8. A. Lucas, *Ancient Egyptian Materials and Industries* (London: Edward Arnold & Co., 1926).

Translation of the Word Black in Other Languages

1. *Browning Society Papers* (Feb. 1980), 31-36.

2. Procopius, *History of the Wars.* Index says, "Moors, a Black African race."

The Garden of Eden

1. Hawkes and Woolley, *Prehistory,* 1.

2. A. Winchell, *Preadamites,* 158. The first man was dark or black in complexion.

3. Whiston, *Flavius Josephus,* 33.The Gihon is the Nile.

4. *Sepia Magazine* (May, 1976), 32.

5. Colonel A. Brighane, *The Shadow of the Atlantis,* 206. The German Scientist Dr. A. Herrman was convinced from research that the River "Gihon" was the Nile, and that the Garden of Eden was in Abyssinia—Ethiopia.

6. J. A. William, *Africa,* 3.

7. Dennis, *America,* 2.

8. B. Davison, *A Guide to African History* (1969), 1.

Miscegenation

1. Sertima, *Before Columbus,* 111. The Negro Egyptians intermixed with whites. Egypt was the meeting ground of races. However, the Negro element remained dominant.

2. Freyre, *Masters and the Slaves* (1966), 200–208; the Negro invasion of Europe.

African Aeronautics

1. J. Bramwell, *Lost Atlantis,* 197.

2. *Journal of Africa Civilization* 1, no. 2 (Nov. 1979).

3. Means, *Ethiopia,* 19–20.

The Lion of Judah

1. Jenkins, *The Black Hebrews*, 16.

2. *Ebony Pictorial History of Black America,* vol. 1, "African Past to the Civil War" (1971), 16–18.

3. *The Christian Science Monitor* (13 Sept. 1974).

4. E. A. W. Budge, *The Queen of Sheba and Her Only Son, Menyelek* (London: 1922).

5. *Encyclopedia Judaica* 6:943; Solomon's seduction and contract with the Queen of Sheba.

6. *National Geographic Magazine* (June 1931): 683; Ethiopian Kings, from Ori of 4,478 B.C., to Haile Selassie of 1930 A.D.

7. Priest, *American Antiquities,* 36. The Queen of Sheba, being a descendant of Ham, was a Black woman.

Did You Know?

1. Schaff, *Dictionary of the Bible*, 352. Hamites dwelled in Babylonia.

2. Higgins, *Anacalypsis* 11:364. Chaldeans, who were closely related to Babylonians, were Negroes.

Hair Styling

1. P. Perdrizet, *Bronzes Grecs de l'Egypt* (Paris: 1911), 58. Hot irons were used to take the tight curls from their hair.

2. *Specimens of Ancient Sculpture Society of Dilettanti,* 1. The Egyptians, like other Negro tribes, were wool-haired.

3. Aristotle, *Physiognomy* VI. The Greek (384–322 B.C.), who is still considered as one of the world's greatest scientists and philosophers, plainly stated that Ethiopians and Egyptians during his time were very black with (Negro) woolly hair.

Skepticism

1. Snowden, *Blacks in Antiquity*, 3.

2. Statius, *The Biology of the Negro* (1942), 27.

3. M. J. Hershovits, *Encyclopedia Britannica* XVI (London: 1960).

Expository Comments III (The Original Hebrews)

1. The Polish Count A. Gorowski, *America and Europe* (New York: 1857), 117. "Whilst visiting America I mistook the light colored Negroes to be Jews. Their complexion, thick lips and kinky hair resembled Jews in Poland."

2. T. Waitz, *Introduction to Anthropology* (1846), 47–48. All shades from light to black are found among Jews.

3. *The Christian Century* (1–8 July 1981), 704. Scholars say the Black Jews of Ethiopia are descendants of the tribe of Dan.

4. *Encyclopaedia Judaica* 5:622. In 1882 the chief rabbi of Jerusalem, R. Meir Panigel, answered an appeal to the congregation that Black Jews were true Jews.

Europe's Early Conception of Jesus Christ

1. J. H. Lewis, *Biology* 61 (1922). No other race than the Negro, or one intermixed, has kinky or woolly hair as a firm feature.

2. *Washington Post* (4 May 1979) Many of the earliest Madonnas were painted black, until the Renaissance—Michelangelo (1475–1564)—when it became popular to paint the Madonna Mary white.

3. Armistead, *The Negro Is a Man* (1903), 87, 130–132, 153. Christ was of mixed blood.

4. Eisler, *Messiah Christ,* 411, 442. The great Jewish historian Flavius Josephus, who was a witness of Palestine during the time of Christ, says that "Christ was as dark-skinned man, and the early Christians accepted this description of Him."

5. L. S. Costello, *Pilgrimage to Auvergne,* 64–73. A Black woman was worshipped as the Madonna.

6. T. Inman, *Ancient Faiths* (1867), 1:159; 2:267; the Black Virgin.

The African Phoenician

1. *We, Europeans,* 94. The whites have advanced civilization. However, the originators of civilization were of the darker race. They were highly cultivated when we whites were savages.

2. Raglan, *The Nationalist Annual:The Future of Civilization,* 40. Ancient whites were intellectually inferior. They obtained much of their culture from the dark skinned Africans.

3. D. de Rienzi, *L'Ocenaie* (Paris, 1836). While the dark race dominated culturally, our own white race was quite savage.

4. *Reader's Digest* (Nov. 1982), 178. While Egypt was enjoying a lustrous worldly-wise civilization, whites were still living in primitive villages.

5. Champollion, "Lettres," (Jan. 1929), 30–31. I am ashamed to admit that at one time, our own land Europe was last and the most dormant of lands.

6. Breasted, *American Historical Review,* 219. While Egypt was a civilized world, Europe was a land of wilderness and savagery for some two thousand years.

7. Dennis, *The Black People of America,* 7. Culturally, the Africans were ahead of Europeans for thousands of years.

Adam and Eve

1. Dr. Hirshfeld, *Man and Woman* (1935), 93–96.

2. Woodruff, *Effects of Tropical Light,* 298.

3. A. Castellani, *Climate and Acclimatization* (1931).

Bearing False Identities

1. *Masters and Slaves,* 200–208.

2. *Les Grand Inities,* 6, 113th ed. (Paris, 1931), 6.

3. *New York Times* (8 Dec. 1934).

4. *Race Life of the Aryans,* vol. III (New York, 1907), 238.

5. Hasluck, *Black Australians* (1942).

6. *Histoire Universelle,* vol. 1, 55. Speaks of Australian Negroes.

7. *Prehistory and the Beginning of Civilization,* vol. 1, 55.

8. St. Y. d'Alveydre, *Mission of the Jews.* The Ethiopians crossed the Mediterranean and invaded and conquered France. The Mediterraneans received a large dosage of African blood. Because of the Negro invasion, the Mediterraneans without a doubt have African blood.

9. Count A. Gruowski, *America and Europe* (1857), 5, 27, 175–7. The Ethiopians controlled the whites and intermingled their blood with them.

10. *Historical Miscellanies*, vol. 1 (London, 1823), 217. The French leader Napoleon's comments on Black and white children as brothers, in relating to interbreeding.

11. Professor R.B. Dixon, *Racial History of Man* (New York, 1923), 478. Negroes at one time lived in southern Russia.

12. H. Guenther, *The Racial Element of European History* (London, 1927), 65. The Negro strain is found throughout southern and central Europe, especially in Italy, France, Spain and Portugal.

Sculpture and Anatomy

1. *Voyages en Syrie,* 74–75.

2. "The Hamitic Hypothesis," *Journal of African History* (1969), 525.

3. *The African Origin of Civilization*, 204.

4. *The Negro in Greek and Roman Civilization* (1929), 12.

5. *Slavery in History* (1860), 5.

6. "Nahas: Good-for-nothing," in *Wolof,* 44–45. Egyptians were Negroes to the last degree. Also see: Diop, *The African Origin of Civilization,* 63.

The Way It Was

1. Volney, *Ruins of Empires* (1890), 16–17.

2. *Negro History Bulletin* 41 (May–June 1978), 834–835.

3. James, *Stolen Legacy.*

4. *The World Book Encyclopedia* 6 (1970): 92.

5. Breasted, *American Historical Review* (Jan. 1929), 219. While Egypt was a civilized world, Europe was a land of wilderness and savagery for some two thousand years.

6. Herodotus, *The History of Herodotus,* 99. The root of Greek religion ascended from African cosmology.

7. W. Durant, *The Life in Greece* (Simon and Schuster, 1966), 68–69. Most Greeks Believed that their civilization derived from Egypt.

8. Champollion and Jacques, "Lettres," in *Egypte Ancienne,* 31–32. I am ashamed to admit that at one time our own land Europe was last and the most dormant of lands.

An Ancient Divine Color

1. *Mythology of all Races*, 12:84, 97, 414.

2. L. Ginzberg, *Legend of the Jews* (1927), 2:303.

3. Higgins, *Anacalypsis,* 1:286, 332.

4. Ibid., 2:137, 346. The white Germans, Italians, Swiss, and French worshipped the Black Virgin, and Child-Christs were depicted as Black.

5. Massey, *Ancient Egypt,* 301, 346. The Black Jesus was well worshipped throughout Europe.

6. *Sepia Magazine* (May 1975), 32; (Dec. 1980), 10–17. All continents drew, painted, and sculptured Jesus and Mary in dark colors with Negro features.

BIBLIOGRAPHY

"A people who lack wisdom from whence they came;
possess little influence on what is to come."

Aikman, K. B. *Victoria Institute Journal*. London: 1935.

Ainu Life and Lore. Tokyo: 1927.

Alcock, N. *Why Tropical Man Is Black,* vol. 30. 1884.

American Anthropologist 5 (1903).

———— 7 (1909).

Ardrey, R. *Africa Genesis*. New York: 1973.

Armistead. *The Negro Is a Man*. Tifton, Georgia: 1903.

Aristotle (384-322 B.C.). Chapter 6 in *Physiognomy*.

Bates, O. *The Eastern Libyans: An Essay*. London: 1914.

Ben-Jochannan, A.A.Y. *Black Men of the Nile*. New York: 1978.

Bennett, L., Jr. *Before the Mayflower*. U.S.A.: 1978.

Best and Blij. *Africa Survey*. 1977.

Birch, S. *Egypt from Earliest Times*. London: 1875.

Black, H. C. *Encyclopaedia Biblica*. London: 1901.

Boaz, F. *Change in Bodily Form of Descendants of Immigrants*. New York: 1912.

Breasted, J. H. *American History Review*. 1929.

————. *History of Egypt*. 1905.

Browing. *Society Papers* (28 Feb. 1890).

Browne, Sir Thomas. *Works*. 1926.

Browns, Filzmyer, and Murphy. *The Interpreter's Commentary on the Bible,* vol. 1. London: 1875.

Bucholzer, J. *The Land of Burnt Faces*. London: 1955.

Budge, E. A. W. *The Queen of Sheba and Her Only Son Menyelek*. London: 1922.

————. *The Book of the Saints of the Ethiopian Church*. London: 1928.

Bull, et Mem. Soc. *Anthropology* (Paris) (21 Nov. 1901).

Bulletin (Catholic Univ. of Peking) 7 (Dec. 1930).

Cappart, D. *Reflet du Monde*. Brussels: 1956.

Celine, L. F. *Bagatelles Pour un Massacre*. Paris: 1927.

Campollion, F., and J. Jacques. *Egypte Ancienne*. Paris: 1839.

Charles, R. H. *The Ethiopic Version of* Hebrew Book of Jubilees. England: Oxford University Press, 1895.

Chomsky. *Hebrew: The Eternal Language*. Philadelphia: The Jewish Publication Society of America, 1957.

The Christian Century (1-8 July 1981).

The Christian Science Monitor (13 Sept. 1974).

Contenau. *La Civilisation Phenicienne*.

Cooley, W. *The Negroland of the Arabs*. London: 1841.

Cottrel, L. *The Lost Pharaohs*. New York: 1951.

Cox, O. G. *Caste, Class and Race*. 1948.

d'Alverdre, St. *Mission of the Jews*.

Davison, B. *A Guide to African History*. New York: 1969.

Davidson, R. *Genesis 1-11*. New York: 1973.

Dawson, W. R. *Egyptian Mummies*. London: 1921.

Dean, E. *All the Women in the Bible*. New York: 1955.

Dennis, R. E. *The Black People of America*. 1970.

de Rienzi, D. *L'Oceanie*. Paris: 1836.

Description of Guinea. 1746.

Diop, C. A. *Black Africa*. U.S.A.: 1974.

———. *The African Origin of Civilization*. U.S.A.: 1974.

Dixon R. B. *Racial History of Man*. New York: 1923.

d'Olivet, F. *Hermeneutic Interpretation*. 1915.

Dorr, D. F. *Round the World*. 1858.

Durant, W. *The Life in Greece*. 1966.

Dury, V. *Ancient History of the East*, vol. 1.

Eisler, R. *Messiah Christ*.

Elgood, P. *The Ptolemies of Egypt*. 1938.

Emerson, G. *Pageant of India's History*. London: 1948.

Epstein, I. "Sanhedrin." In *Babylonian Tulmud*, vol. 2.

Evans, A. "The Early Nilotic, Libyan and Egyptian Relations with Minoan Crete." The Huxley Memorial lecture, London, 1925.

Feist, S. *Stammeskunde der Juden*. 1925.

Fishberg, M. *The Jew*. London: 1911.

Foerster, R. *Scriptores Physiognomonici Graec et Latini*, vol. 1. Leipzig: 1893.

Freyre. *Masters and Slaves*.

Godbey, A. H. *The Lost Tribes: A Myth*. 1930.

Geddes, M. *The Church History of Ethiopia*. London: 1696.

Goodspread, E. J. *How Come the Bible*. U.S.A.: 1981.

Grazel, Solomon. *A History of the Jews*. U.S.A.: 1947.

Guenther, H. *The Racial Element of European History*. London: 1927.

Gurowski, A. *America and Europe*. New York: 1857.

———. *Slavery in History*. 1860.

"The Hamitic Hypothesis." *Journal of African History* (1969).

Hansberry, W. L. *Africa and Africans,* vol. 2. Washington D. C.: 1981.

———. "Ancient Kush, Old Aethipia, and the Balad es Sudan." Reprinted from the *Journal of Human Relations* 8 (1960).

Hasluck, F. W. *Christianity and Islam*, vol. 2. England: Oxford University Press, 1929.

Hawkes, J., and L. Woolley. *Prehistory and the Beginnings of Civilization*, vol. 1. 1963.

Herodotus (484–425 B.C.). *The History of Herodotus, Book 2.*

Hirschfeld, Dr. M. J. *Man and Women.* 1935.

———. *Racism.* 1938.

Herskovits, M. J. *Encyclopaedia Britannica*, vol. XVI. London: 1960.

Hiernaux, J. *The People of Africa.* New York: 1975.

Higgins, G. *Anacalypsis*, vol. 1. New York: 1927.

Historical Miscellanies, vol 1. London: 1823.

History of Nations, vol. 18. 1906.

Hitti, P. K. *History of the Arabs.* 1937.

Holt, H. and Co. *Story of Nations.* New York: 1952.

Horton and Leslie. *The Sociology of Social Problems.* 1974.

Hurlbut, D. D. *Hurlbut's Story of the Bible.* U.S.A.: 1969.

Huxley, and A. C. Haddon. *We Europeans.* 1935.

Hyall, H. M. *The Church of Ethiopia.* London: 1928.

Ilin, M. *Men and Mountains.* 1935.

Jackson, H. C. *Ethiopia and the Origin of Civilization.* New York: 1939.

Jacob, B. *The First Book of the Bible.* New York: 1974.

James, G. G. M. *Stolen Legacy.* 1976.

Jenkins, C. *The Black Hebrews.* U.S.A.: 1969.

Johnson, E. A. *A School History of the Negro in America.*

Johnson, H. H. *Colonization of Africa.* 1905.

———. *The Uganda Protectorate*, vol. 2. London: 1902.

Jones, A. H. M. *The Herods of Judea.* London: 1938.

Josephus, F. *Jewish Antiquities,* vol. 4. London: 1961.

King, C. W. *Antique Gems and Rings.* London: 1872.

Kirwan, D. P. *The Decline and Fall of Meroe "Cush."* 1960.

Koehler, Baumagartner. *The Hebrew Lexicon: Lexicon in Veteris Testamenti Libros.*

Koehler, P. *Hebrew Man.* 1956.

Lamb, H. *Cyrus the Great.* New York: 1960.

La Revue Hebdomadaire (Nov. 1927).

Latourette, K. S. *A History of the Expansion of Christianity.* London: 1939.

Lenormant. *Ancient History of the East,* vols. 2 and 3. Paris: Levy, 1890.

Lewis, J. H. *Biology 61, Biology of the Negro.* 1922.

Lincoln Library, vol. 1. Columbus, Ohio: Frontier Press, 1971.

Linton, R. *The Study of Man.* New York: 1936.

Lockyer, H. L. *All the Men of the Bible.* US.A.: 1977.

The Lost Books of the Bible, and the Forgotten Books of Eden. U.S.A.: 1926 & 27.

Ludwig, E. *Talks with Mussolini.* London: 1932.

Lucas, A. *Ancient Egyptian Materials and Industries.* London: 1926.

Massey, G. *A Book of the Beginnings.* London: 1881.

———. *Ancient Egypt.* London: 1907.

Maxwell, A. S. *The Bible Story* , vol. 3. U.S.A.: 1954.

McCabe, J. *American History.* Jan. 1929.

Mac Iver, R. *Ancient Races of Thebaid.* London: 1906.

Mead, F. S. *Who's Who in the Bible.* U.S.A.: 1934.

Memoires, vol. 5. Chap. 12 and 26. 1885.

Mercer, S. A. B. *The Ethiopic Text of the Book of Ecclesiastes.* London: 1931.

The Message Magazine. "Culture and History of the Black Experience." Nashville: Southern Publishing Association, 1974.

The Metals in Antiquity. Huxley Memorial Lecture. 1912.

Montet, P. *Eternal Egypt.* London: 1964.

Morgan. *History of Barbary and Algiers.* 1728.

Morie, L J. *Histoire de L'ethiope,* vol. 11. Chap. 5. Paris: 1904.

———. *The History of Herodotus.* London: 1875.

Mythology of all Races, vol. 12.

The National Jewish Monthly (May 1981).

The Negritos de la Chine. Hanoi: 1928.

Negro History Bulletin 41 (May/June 1978).

The Negro in Greek and Roman Civilization. London: 1929.

Norden, H. *Among the Black Jews in Africa's Last Empire.*

Origen. *Commentarius in Canticum Canticorum:* 2.360-362, 8113-115.

Osei, G. K. *The Forgotten Great Africans: 3000 B.C. to 1959 A.D.* London: 1965.

Palgrave, G. *Essays on the Eastern Questions.* London: 1872.

Parrinder, G. *Africa's Three Religions.* London: 1969.

Perdrizet, P. *Bronzes Grecs de l'Egypte*. Paris: 1911.

Petrie, F. *The Making of Ancient Egypt*. London: 1939.

Picard, C., and G. Charles. *Daily Life in Carthage*. 1961.

Pittard, E. *Les Races et L'histoire*. Paris: 1924.

Pricard, J. C. *National History of Man*. 1845.

Prehistory Japan. Yokohama: 1911.

Procopius. *History of the Wars*.

Quinn, V. *The Picture Map Geography of Africa*. 1964.

Raglans. *The Future of Civilization: The Nationalist Annual*. 1946.

Rainey A. F. *The Land of the Bible*. 1967.

Rapoport, S. *History of Egypt*. 1904.

Ratzel, F. *History of Mankind*. New York: 1926.

Rawlinson. *The Story of Egypt*. London: 1887.

Reclus, E. *The Earth and Its Inhabitants,* vol. 1. 1893.

Reisner, G. *Anglo Egyptian Sudan*.

Ripley, R. *Believe It or Not,* VI copy. 1934.

Rogers, J. A. *100 Amazing Facts about the Negro with Complete Proof*. U.S.A.: 1957.

———. *World's Great Men of Color*, vols. 1 and 2.

———. *Sex and Race,* vols. 1–3. U.S.A.: 1967–72.

Rolland, R. *Intermediare des Chercheurs et des Curieux*, vol. 34. Paris.

Rutter, E. *Holy Cities of Arabia*. London: 1928.

Schure, E. *Les Grands Inities*. 113th edition. Paris: 1931.

Sergi. *The Mediterranean Races*. 1901.

Sertima, I. V. *They Came Before Columbus*. 1976.

Simmons, W. J. *Men of Mark*. 1970.

Slavery in History. 1860.

Slouschz, N. *Travels in North Africa*. Philadelphia: 1927.

Smith, G. *Egyptian Mummies*. London: 1924.

Snowden, F. M. *Blacks in Antiquity*. 1970.

Solanke, L. *United West Africa at the Family of Nations,* vol. 18. 1906.

Spears P. *India*. U.S.A.: 1911.

Schweich Lectures. *Ethiopia and the Bible*. Paris: 1931.

Spearing H. G. *The Childhood of Art*. 1912.

Speller, G. *Universal Races*. London: 1911.

Statius. *The Biology of the Negro*. 1942.

Thackery, St. H., and J. Josephus. "The Life Against Apion.", vol. 1. London: 1961.

Toppin E. A. *A Biographical History in American Science*. 1528.

Turner, J. K. *Schwarzchild*.

Vloten, G. van, Abu Othman Amr ibn Bahr, Al Djahiz. *The Superiority in Glory of the Black Race over the Caucasians*. Leyden: Basrens, 1903.

Volney, G. F. *Voyage en Syrie*. Paris: 1787.

————. *Ruins of Empires*. 1890.

Waitz, T. *Introduction to Anthropology*. 1846.

Warmington. *Carthage*. 1960-69.

Weigall, A. *Personalities of Antiquity*. 1976.

Wells, H. G. *World of William Clissold*, vol. 11. 1926.

Weisgerber. *Les Blancs d'Afrique*. Paris: 1910.

Weulersse, J. *L'Afrique Noire*. Paris: 1934.

Wheeler, R. R. *Golden Legend of Ethiopia*. 1936.

White, E. G. *The Great Controversy*. 1971.

Whiston, Wm. *The Life and Works of Flavius Josephus*. 1981.

Widney, J. P. *Race Life of the Aryans*, vol. 2. 1907.

Wilkinson, J. G. *The Ancient Egyptians*. London: 1878.

Williams, C. *The Destruction of Black Civilizations*. 1931.

Williams, J. A. *Africa: Her History, Land and People*. 1969.

Windsor, R. R. *From Babylon to Timbuktu*. New York: 1973.

Wolpert, S. *A New History of India*. 1977.

Woodruff. *Effects of Tropical Light on White Men*. 1905.

Woodson, C. G. *Mis-Education of the Negro*. 1969.

Suggested Readings

Bibles

Baird and Dillon. *The 1884 Edition of the Family Bible.*

Ballou, J. *The Oahspe Bible.* London: 1882.

The Black Heritage Bible. Nashville: 1976.

Bible Dictionaries

Aid to Bible Understanding. 1971.

Douglas, J. D. *The New Bible Dictionary.*

The Family Bible Dictionary. Avenel Books, 1963.

Grant and Rawley. *Dictionary of the Bible.* 1963.

Harper's Bible Dictionary. 1961.

International Bible Dictionary. 1969.

McKinzie, J. L. *Dictionary of the Bible.*

Peloubet's Bible Dictionary. 1973.

Schaff Herzog Encyclopedia, vol. 9. 1966.

Schaff, P. S. *Dictionary of the Bible.* London: 1865.

Smith, W. *Concise Dictionary of the Bible.* London: 1865.

Taylor, C. *Calmet's Dictionary of the Holy Bible.* London: 1832.

Encyclopedias

Balfour, E., *Negro Races in Cyclopedia of India.* Vol. 2. London, 1885.

Baccardo, *Neava Encic. Ital.* (see Negri).

Chambers Encyclopedia, vol. 8. 1966.

Encyclopedia Biblica, vol. 1. 1972.

Encyclopedia Judiaca, vol. 16. 1972.

Schaff Herzog Encyclopedia, vol. 9. 1966.

The New Catholic Encyclopedia.

The World Book Encyclopedia. 1970.

Newspapers and Magazines

"Africa . . . Continent of the Future." *Ebony Magazine* (Aug. 1976).

"African Past to the Civil War." *Pictoral History of Black America* 1 (1971).

"Black Jews in Ethiopia." *Scribner's Magazine* (May 1981).

 "Dr. Brock Speaks of a Negro Race in Ancient China." *New York Times* (26 Nov. 1933).

"Egypt." *Reader's Digest* (Nov. 1982).

"Egypt's Former President, Anwar Sadat." *Jet Magazine* (2 March 1978, 28 March 1983).

"Ethiopian Kings." *National Geographic Magazine* (June 1931).

Negro History Bulletin 41 (1978).

"West African Jews." *Scribner's Magazine* (April–June 1929).

Index

NEGRO CANAAN
BEFORE THE JEWISH CONQUEST

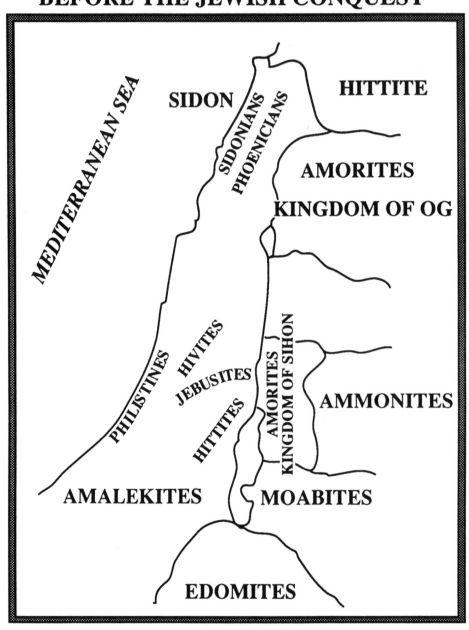

MEDITERRANEAN SEA

SIDON

HITTITE

SIDONIANS
PHOENICIANS

AMORITES

KINGDOM OF OG

PHILISTINES

HIVITES

JEBUSITES

HITTITES

AMORITES
KINGDOM OF SIHON

AMMONITES

AMALEKITES

MOABITES

EDOMITES

HAM'S DISPERSAL

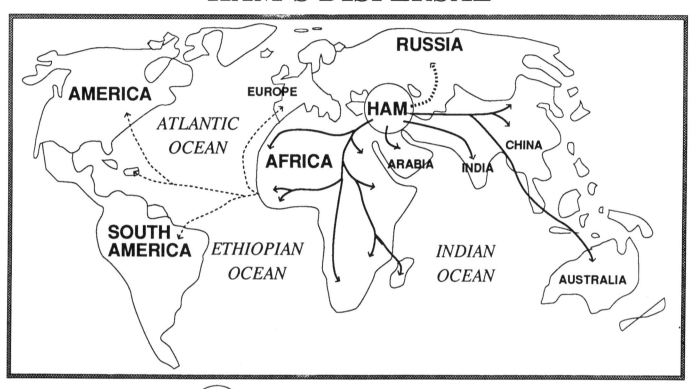

Settlement of the Ark (HAM)

Temporary Settlement ....

Permanent Settlement _____

Later Settlement --------------

DESCENDANTS OF NOAH

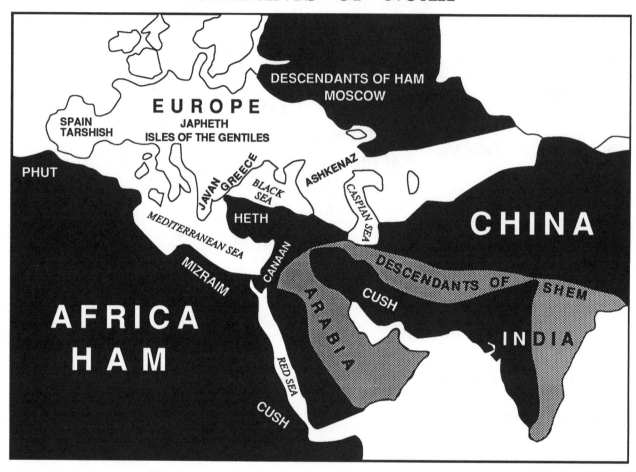

"These are the three sons of Noah;
and of them was the whole earth overspread."

—Gen. 9:19

BLACK MAN'S ROUTE FROM THE ARK . . .

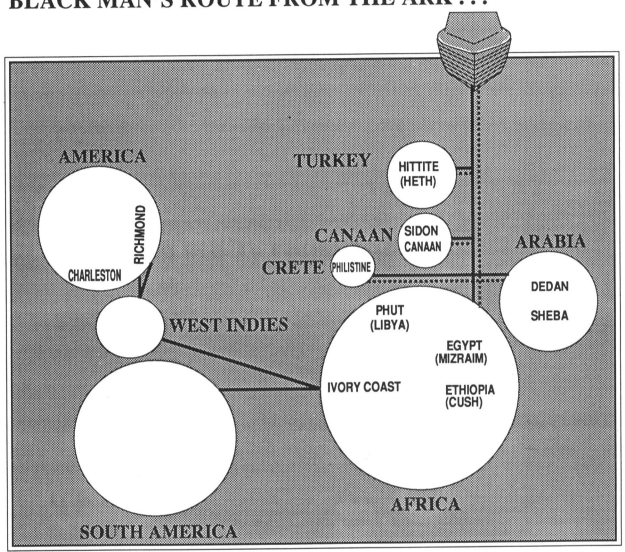

Slave Route ———

Ham's Offspring ....